Negotiating
Negotiating Difference

CULTURAL CASE STUDIES FOR COMPOSITION

Editor's Notes

Negotiating

Negotiating Difference

CULTURAL CASE STUDIES FOR COMPOSITION

Editor's Notes

Prepared by
PATRICIA BIZZELL
College of the Holy Cross

BRUCE HERZBERG
Bentley College

BEDFORD BOOKS OF ST. MARTIN'S PRESS ⚮ BOSTON

Copyright © 1996 by BEDFORD BOOKS *of* St. Martin's Press
All rights reserved.
Manufactured in the United States of America.

0   9   8   7   6

f   e   d   c   b   a

For information, write: St. Martin's Press, Inc.
175 Fifth Avenue, New York, NY 10010
Editorial Offices: Bedford Books *of* St. Martin's Press
75 Arlington Street, Boston, MA 02116

ISBN: 0–312–11706–X

Preface

Negotiating Difference is multicultural for a reason. We're not trying to "expose" our students to the experiences of different cultural groups only to spark their interest or evoke their tolerance. Rather, we believe that the United States has been a multicultural society since even before it was a separate nation. Therefore, life in the United States has always involved negotiating across cultural boundaries. Performing this act well requires knowledge of the rhetorical strategies and cultural archives of diverse American groups. *Negotiating Difference* aims to provide this knowledge.

We are guided in our thinking here by comparative literature scholar Mary Louise Pratt's concept of cultural "contact zones," social spaces in which groups with unequal power "meet, clash, and grapple" with each other for the right to interpret their common experience. As Pat has argued, the contact zone concept generates provocative, creative new structures for organizing work in English studies (see Bizzell). Readings from a variety of genres can be grouped around the contact zone moment for which they were written — the method we have followed in organizing the units in *Negotiating Difference*.

Although we know of no other multicultural reader that takes this approach, we think that it will not be entirely new to you, particularly if you are a new teaching assistant and have been pursuing graduate literary study that is congenial to the contact zone concept. As reflected in the units of this book, the definition of "literature" is already broadening to include all kinds of texts, and one current approach to literary study is already deepening to situate texts in their historical and cultural contexts. Before *Negotiating Difference*, if you wanted to employ these innovative ideas, you may have had to struggle with finding the appropriate texts and assembling course packs. *Negotiating Difference* collects materials that make the new approaches to teaching literature and composition much easier.

Of course, it's not only a matter of finding diverse kinds of texts and providing historical and cultural information about them. You must also adapt the method of analysis to this new, rich material. This is one reason for the new interest in cultural studies in composition. It seems to promise an approach that allows for the analysis of rhetorical strategies in ideologically charged settings. We hope that the apparatus we have provided in *Negotiating Difference* will facilitate this kind of analysis. (Later in this manual, we'll give you specific suggestions for how to pursue this analysis.)

You'll see that students will be asked to write a wide variety of texts, from summaries and argumentative analyses to personal experience narratives and creative dialogues. Thus we have integrated one of the traditional goals of writing courses — to develop students' facility with a variety of texts — into our contact zones and cultural studies approach. Especially noteworthy are the Research Kits attached to each unit, which help students explore unit topics and analogous themes in more depth through library work and research in the community.

Throughout *Negotiating Difference*, we have tried to emphasize the importance of in-class negotiations and collaborations among students. We want students to feel that they own their writing course — that it is dealing with issues of importance to them and that they have some power to direct the course of study (for example, in the sample syllabi we provide opportunities for students to bring in their own reading materials). The biggest influence on our teaching philosophy has been Brazilian literacy educator Paulo Freire as well as such powerful American exponents of his thought as bell hooks. (See the brief bibliography at the end of this introduction for leads to their work.) Through the reflective and creative work that *Negotiating Difference* encourages students to do, we hope to generate what Freire calls "critical consciousness," rather than mere critical thinking.

Negotiating Difference is a challenging book. We want it to be. We know that students may find the readings difficult to comprehend and the analytic and critical perspective difficult to take. We have provided apparatus to ease their transition into this work — historical introductions and headnotes, footnotes, and reading questions that point to key passages in the texts. But finally, we firmly believe that students rise to the occasion if challenged to do their best work. We believe that if college students are addressed as adult citizens of a multicultural democracy, they will respond with serious attention to the rhetorical studies that will help fit them for their academic and civic tasks. This is why we have dedicated this book, above all, to our students.

THE STRUCTURE OF THIS INSTRUCTOR'S MANUAL

We hope you find this manual helpful as you prepare to teach *Negotiating Difference*. In this introduction you will find information that applies to all six units of the book. Under the heading "General Suggestions for Teaching *Negotiating Difference*" are discussions of the structure and rationale of the book:

- How the units are structured
- Using the historical introductions
- Handling difficult readings and controversial topics
- Assigning the writing questions
- Working with assignment sequences
- Using the research kits

Next, under the heading "Other Suggestions for Teaching" are descriptions of three pedagogical techniques that we believe will be useful in teaching any of the units:

- Class journals
- Working in groups
- Portfolio grading

Other specific suggestions for teaching are embedded in a final section of this general introduction, "Developing as a Teacher," and the remaining chapters of the manual.

Each unit in *Negotiating Difference* has a corresponding chapter in this manual. In each of these chapters we give an overview of the unit's key themes and issues, discuss each selection, suggest ways to work through the writing questions after each selection, comment on each assignment sequence and its writing projects, and review the projects recommended in the Research Kit.

Two or three model syllabi are suggested for each unit. For every unit, we offer one model syllabus that uses the entire unit as the semester's work, drawing on two of the unit's assignment sequences. Other syllabi model these variations:

Two-unit syllabi:

Units One plus Six (see p. 53)
Units Two plus Five (see p. 184)

Syllabi for a course ending with a research paper:

Unit Four (p. 152)
Unit Six (p. 216)

Syllabi for a course that adds imaginative literature to unit readings:

Unit One (p. 50)
Unit Two (p. 81)
Unit Three (p. 115)

We have tried to make these models flexible enough so that you can easily combine other units as your interests dictate or assign a research paper with any of the units.

Contents

UNIT TWO

*The Debate over Slavery and the Declaration
of Independence* **56**

UNIT THREE

*Defining "Woman's Sphere" in Nineteenth-Century
American Society*   **86**

UNIT SIX

Policy and Protest over the Vietnam War 187

Negotiating
Negotiating Difference

CULTURAL CASE STUDIES FOR COMPOSITION

Editor's Notes

Introduction

Each unit in *Negotiating Difference* represents a moment in American history when different groups were contending for the power to interpret the meaning of their encounter. Each unit presents an exciting selection of the textual record of those negotiations. In addition to touching on controversies that are still very much with us and still very engaging to students today, these texts illustrate a wealth of persuasive and useful rhetorical techniques. We have found them to be tremendously rewarding to share with students.

The groups in conflict here have, of course, contended not only with words but with guns and money and other weapons. But the rhetorical battles in these conflicts, the attempts to interpret, negotiate, argue, and persuade, have been no less forceful and decisive. With the students in our writing classes, we want to study how argument works and how discourse makes meaning. Studying the texts in these units, analyzing and imitating their rhetorical strategies, and developing strategies to deal with controversies of the present moment all help our composition students grow as critical users of language. Not only are students engaged by these unit themes, but they also become more interested in contemporary rhetoric and more eager to contribute their own materials that illustrate its forms.

How the Units Are Structured

Both the book as a whole and the readings in each unit are organized chronologically (though occasionally a thematic grouping of readings takes precedence over strict chronology). We hope to emphasize in this way that history is not a fossilized record of events but a way of discovering how the human world came to be the way it is today. Delivering a long, connected history lesson is not the book's goal. We do not imagine that any composition class, even one that lasts two semesters, will read through the whole book from start to finish. A single unit may be enough for a semester's work, though there are many ways to use more than a single unit in a semester. Even then, the units need not be covered in chronological order. For example, a semester's work could begin with Unit Five, on the Japanese American internment during World War II, and then continue with Unit Two, to see how similar issues of civil rights for African Americans were treated in the debates over slavery in the early nineteenth century.

We emphasize chronological order where students should notice intertextuality — the references within one text to an earlier text — one phenomenon we want to highlight through the concept of "negotiating difference." In "What to the Slave Is the Fourth of July?," for example, Frederick Douglass could not have referred to the Declaration of Independence if it had not been written *before* he gave his speech (a point that goes without saying for some but by no means all students). Similarly, students cannot fully appreciate Douglass's rhetorical strategies if they have not read the Declaration before reading Douglass.

Another way to make this point is to refer to the traditional emphasis in classical rhetorical training on developing an acquaintance with a rich, shared cultural archive as an aid to comprehending and composing effective persuasion. In general, the more students know about the extraordinarily diverse and abundant American cultural archive, the more they will be able to appreciate the rhetorical strategies not only of the authors under study here but also of modern writers, including the diverse student authors in their own classes. The same knowledge will enrich their own rhetorical resources. We hope that students can gain such knowledge through reading in *Negotiating Difference*.

Several units' readings include a selection of public or legal documents pertaining to the unit theme, such as treaties, petitions, proclamations, contracts, and deeds. We have included these documents because we want to set up interesting interplays between their typically formal or legal language and more discursive accounts of the events they seek to regulate or control, which can be found in the other unit readings. The documents often lay out with dramatic brevity the complex knot of issues posed in the unit.

The rest of the unit readings are intended to present a complicated view of the positions people took on the issues raised in the unit and to prevent any easy dichotomizing of positions. A pro/con approach can stifle rhetorical complexity and creativity as well as creating needless tensions in the classroom. Such an approach also tends to focus classroom activity on the writers' ideas and on whether those ideas are correct or valuable in the readers' eyes. Rather, we want students to focus on how these writers deal with complicated rhetorical situations, presenting themselves to diverse audiences and attempting to persuade them, often from politically vulnerable positions.

The key characteristic that all the readings have in common is what might be called their "public" quality. In emphasizing the concept of "negotiating difference," we have chosen readings that the authors intended to bring forward in public debates over the issues. Another way to put this is to say, as we did earlier, that these texts have all been brought to the contact zone of the period under study. Thus, for example, Native American authors included in Unit One are represented not by tape recordings of oral literature in Native American languages but by texts written in English for an audience intended to include many non–Native Americans.

Every reading is accompanied by a headnote that links it and its author to the historical context outlined in the unit introduction. Every reading is also accompanied by questions for reading critically and writing analytically. The reading questions direct students' attention to what the text is doing, its various rhetorical strategies, stylistic features, and argumentative turns. The writing questions ask students to begin to evaluate these strategies, to compare them with the strategies of other texts in the unit, perhaps to imitate them, and finally to come to some critical understanding of the negotiations they represent.

In selecting the readings, our emphasis on the criterion of willingness to enter into dialogue has allowed us to include a generically diverse range of texts, including histories, elegies, transcribed speeches, polemical essays, memoirs, congressional testimony, oral histories, and more. We want students to acknowledge the rhetorical diversity with which Americans have conducted their cultural and political negotiations.

Some genres may seem to be underrepresented in *Negotiating Difference*. There is relatively little fiction and almost no poetry here. Certainly, these kinds of texts can be analyzed rhetorically, for they do make arguments that bear on the cultural and political issues of their authors' day. But we find that it is easier to introduce students to the concept of "negotiating difference" through texts that are contending more overtly for the reader's allegiance as versions of history. Thus, when we had to make hard choices about what to include, we tended to omit imaginative literature. For three of the units, however, we provide sample syllabi for an "enriched" course in which fiction and poetry are added to the unit readings.

We have also omitted visual genres, although we think that paintings, posters, advertisements, and so on can be analyzed rhetorically. Again, when faced with hard choices about what to include, we decided to concentrate on written texts as being most appropriate for a composition course. Assignments in each Research Kit, however, suggest projects whereby students can assemble visual resources for classroom study.

GENERAL SUGGESTIONS FOR TEACHING NEGOTIATING DIFFERENCE

Using the Historical Introductions

Each unit begins with a brief historical introduction. Most students will welcome the information these introductions provide, as they usually do not bring to first-year composition the basic historical orientation needed to find their way through these challenging texts. Students need to know such very basic facts as, for example, the sequence and duration of the Puritan settlement of New England, the date of the signing of the Declaration of Independence, and the reasons for the Civil War. The introductions, which provide not only basic information but also a sense of the political and cultural context of the conflicts that form the unit themes, can be read by students on their own, before course work in the unit begins.

The introductions can give, at best, only a skeletal view of the history of some very complex periods. Our aim is to provide students with a basic chronological orientation prior to their encounter with the readings, which will amplify and complicate the account given in the introduction. We do have some concern about whether the introductions might tend to reify the historical record, to give students unwarranted confidence in the "truth" of a single master narrative. However, we believe that the diversity of perspectives represented in the readings will guard against any one version of history being taken for gospel. Our main goal in assembling the selections has been to ensure that they do not present a unitary view of the period. Indeed, we have taken care to prevent their dividing neatly into dichotomies. Rather, we have included readings that represent a multiplicity of views and voices. Finally, the Research Kit concluding each unit outlines several historical topics suggested by the unit and invites students to explore those topics in more depth.

We believe that both traditionally marginalized voices and the views of those exercising oppressive hegemonic power are represented in this volume to a degree that is highly unusual in anthologies. Thus the readings dramatize the *problem of interpreting* what was going on — and they do so especially when they are directly in dialogue with each other, arguing over the same event, citing, corroborating, or refuting each other, as they so often do.

Ultimately we would like students to understand how what people take to be "history" is the outcome of processes of negotiation and contention such as those represented in our selections, an outcome that always involves foregrounding some versions of the story and occulting others. But we believe that the best pedagogy for inducing this understanding of the making of history is, first, to give students a fairly basic time line to hold on to and then to progressively complicate their understanding as they work through the unit's diverse readings.

Handling Difficult Readings and Controversial Topics

We know that the readings in *Negotiating Difference* have much to offer students in the way of sophisticated rhetorical strategies and high-interest treatments of important American issues. The readings well repay close study. Yet we also know that, at least initially, students may find many of the readings challenging. Many selections are long and use long sentences and long paragraphs, which students find difficult to get through. The language may be elaborate or archaic, from the students' perspective. There may be references to historical events, ideas, people, places, and texts with which students are unfamiliar.

One way we have attempted to respond to these difficulties is to provide various kinds of supports within the book itself: the historical introductions, headnotes, footnotes, and reading questions, all of which are designed to aid comprehension. Neither you nor your students should have to engage in any further research to develop at least a working understanding of the readings in this book.

We also have found that the difficulty of the readings is somewhat mitigated by students' high interest in the issues. The first four units, where the texts may present the most problems of unfamiliarity, seem to benefit particularly from students' avid interest in discovering that issues they thought were confined to contemporary concern — such as feminism — have in fact been addressed for some time in American discourse. In our experience, students allied with social groups who have been marginalized by race, class, or gender are particularly excited to find that people like themselves have been engaged in rhetorical struggle against oppression for some time, and with some success. African American students, for example, are often deeply stirred to discover the range of effective eloquence employed by African Americans against slavery before the Civil War. Many of these students are initially not aware that there were powerful African American intellectuals in the antebellum period.

What students perceive (correctly, we believe) as the moral seriousness of the issues engaged in *Negotiating Difference* makes them willing to put up with the difficulty of some readings. Not only that, but the difficulty can seem to them to be an appropriate mark of the respect that these serious issues deserve, and it can draw forth serious work from them. We have found that providing students with supposedly more "accessible," contemporary, popular treatments of social issues — which make few initial demands on students' patience and knowledge — tends to evoke thin, opinionated pieces characterized most obviously by an unjustified rush to judgment. Demanding reading, in contrast, stimulates students to do their best work. Even with the aids we have provided, students will not understand everything about the readings. *We* don't understand everything about the readings. People learn more, though, we believe, when challenged with riches.

The seriousness of the issues engaged in these readings, however, while perhaps having the advantage of mitigating the difficulty they present, may at the same time give rise to another kind of problem — bringing explosively controversial issues into the classroom. It is a time-honored practice in composition teaching to bring controversy into the classroom, for reasons very similar to those in the argument we have just made — namely, that such high-interest issues will stimulate students to do their best work. And it is a time-worn truism that discussions of such issues often degenerate into unpleasant confrontations in which the teacher, attempting perhaps only to smooth down the situation, comes off as an enforcer of one or another ideological view.

We think such destructive controversies tend to occur when the course emphasizes students' writing on contemporary issues alone, out of their own personal resources alone, in a pro/con format. We have tried to avoid all three of these conditions in *Negotiating Difference*. First, contemporary issues, because students are likely to be engaged in them through personal experience, are likely to be the most inflammatory. Although we are constantly making connections to contemporary issues in our writing assignments, we have deliberately set all six units in what is the "distant past" to students of traditional college age. This distancing tends to defuse or desensitize the controversies somewhat.

Also, we do not ask students to develop arguments based solely on their own personal resources. Such an approach leads to unsatisfactory writing because it encourages the airing of the sort of settled views with which most people get through life. On a daily basis, most of us do not closely examine our opinions on controversial issues; it is not intellectually efficient to do so. Rather, we think in a sort of shorthand — for example, "Abortion is wrong because my cousin had an abortion and now she really regrets it." It is perfectly reasonable to base daily action on such shorthand beliefs because no one can examine all the moral angles every time a response is called for. Moreover, such shorthand beliefs often carry a charged emotional valence because they are based on some sort of powerful personal experience, as in the example we have given.

Both the shorthand quality and the charged quality of such beliefs make them poor material for writing. Students are inclined to state them with little elaboration, beyond perhaps telling the story of the personal experience that anchors them, and then to become offended if readers do not immediately accept the emotional authority of that experience. This is not an effective form of communication or negotiation with those who do not already share the experience or the belief.

We think it is pedagogically more effective to expose students to the intertextuality of American discourse. The readings in *Negotiating Difference* show them that American rhetoricians have always felt the need to attend to the texts of others to make their own cases. Our questions point out how one writer in the unit engages the work of another writer in the unit; our writing assignments ask students to insert themselves into these discussions and to frame their own views with reference to the readings. Such contention with alternative interpretations of experience enriches the expression of students' own views, allowing them to break out of the "shorthand" mold and perhaps ultimately increasing their chances of presenting their opinions in a way that can be persuasive to those who do not already agree.

This kind of engagement produces good writing, we believe, when the issues engaged are not presented in such a way as to encourage pro/con or "good guys"/"bad guys" debate. Setting units in the past helps avoid such dichotomizing because often the issues under debate in the unit have already been decided legally. For example, slavery has already been abolished. Women now have the right to vote, to hold property, to be guardians of their children, to be protected from marital rape, and so on. The United States government has formally apologized for the Japanese internment. Thus the right or wrong of the situation can be disposed of at the outset: Virtually no students would want to argue that slavery or the subjugation of women is defensible, for example.

Moreover, it should be clear that the focus of each unit is not to determine the right or wrong of the situation: for example, was the internment possibly justified? This is where many pro/con-structured anthologies go astray. Rather, the focus is on the study, analysis, and evaluation of the various arguments and rhetorical strategies that various writers employed in attempts to put forward their diverse views of the situation. This focus has the advantage of not seeming to glorify the writers we would now say are "right" — we can find Elizabeth Cady Stanton fumbling rhetorically, for example, in a speech defending women's right to vote — while also not denigrating the writers we would now say are "wrong" — for example, we can appreciate the way avowed white racist Albert Bledsoe makes an argument about the relative rights of the community versus the individual.

It is absolutely crucial that students not feel that the teacher is attempting to indoctrinate them in any particular view of the issues under discussion. That is why this book's apparatus encourages the kind of analysis just mentioned in the Stanton and Bledsoe examples. Every kind of argument must be taken seriously, its strengths and weaknesses noted. Students should be given choices of the kinds of texts and arguments they want to work on. It is a mistake, for example, to assume that African American students will not want to pay any attention to the work of white racists. Moreover, students should see that their own arguments, from whatever moral angle, will also be taken seriously; this means that all positions are allowed but that all must also be subjected to scrutiny. All arguments may be brought to the classroom "contact zone," but they must be offered in a spirit of negotiating difference.

To manage such discussions, teachers will have to think carefully about how they understand their authority. Beyond maintaining the very basics of classroom civility, such as preventing fistfights and enforcing turn-taking, what are teachers allowed to do? We see this as a very complex question. It cannot be simply dismissed with the traditional advice to remain morally neutral or purely objective and just present the "facts" of the material under study. Few now believe that it is indeed possible for a teacher to be neutral or objective, even if he or she claims to be.

Our view is that teachers should evolve their own classroom ethos in light of two principles. One, teachers should be permitted to promote the values of the community in which (and presumably, for which) they teach. This could mean the "community" of the United States of America, which in turn could mean that teachers should be allowed to promote values that are a part of American civic virtue, such as religious toleration and free speech. Two, it is necessary, in order to maintain the right to promote community values, to maintain community dialogue on values. In the classroom, this means ensuring that the pedagogical process is interactive and that students have many opportunities to select materials, present arguments, and persuade.

Negotiating between these two principles protects the teacher both from attempting to maintain the impossible position of moral neutrality and from the charge that he or she is simply propagandizing for idiosyncratic views. We recognize, however, that this negotiating is a very difficult and necessarily ongoing process. Here we can do no more than sketch a few terms that we hope will be helpful to you as you continue to consider these issues in discussion with your colleagues.

Assigning the Writing Questions

Every writing question is discussed individually in this manual in the unit chapters. The writing process itself is described in "Portfolio Grading" (p. 17). Here we wish to describe our general motivation for the questions we have asked students to write about.

Writing questions occur in two places in each unit — after each selection (under the heading "Writing Analytically") and in the assignment sequences at the end of each unit. This apparatus is designed to give you maximum flexibility in using the book. You may assign individual selections in isolation, using the writing questions that accompany them. We hope, however, that you will link the selections into one or more assignment sequences (as we argue on p. 13). You can use the sequences we've provided, or you can design your own sequences by using the writing questions after the selections. If you opt to use our sequences, you will probably not need to assign the "Writing Analytically" questions (some are duplicated in the sequences).

In addition to these two kinds of writing questions, the book includes "Reading Critically" questions that can be used to generate journal writing, an important preliminary to the more formal writing assignments (see "Class Journals," p. 12). Writing in class journals allows students to enter the discourse of the controversy and of the period in a more informal style. It also lets them begin to take a critical view of the arguments being presented.

One of the best ways for students to make their way into academic discourse is to write summaries of the kinds of texts that are found in *Negotiating Difference.* Writing a good summary is no easy task: Students who find it challenging need to do a lot of it. Writing a summary forces students to be completely clear about the points being presented or argued, the reasons or evidence used, and the conclusions drawn. Faced with unfamiliar ideas and close argument, students can easily lose the thread. There is little to be gained by embarking on an analytical or comparative essay if the writer isn't clear on the positions to be analyzed or compared. Many of the writing questions in *Negotiating Difference* ask for summaries, but we have not given a summary assignment for every reading. If you find that your students often miss the point of a text, make the writing of summaries a regular starting point. First drafts will turn up areas of confusion, which you can then discuss in class. Successful final versions will give students a sense of mastery and help dispel the forbidding obscurity of hard texts.

If you assign a substantial summary following a selection, it probably isn't advisable to assign an analytical question on the same piece as well. However, a series of summaries creates a perfect opportunity to follow up with an assignment that will allow students to synthesize their knowledge of the summarized readings. Choose three or four readings that focus on an issue and ask students to write an essay in which they bring all the related arguments together in a way that reveals the dimensions of the issue. Better, simply find an assignment in one of the assignment sequences, which attempt to do this very thing (see "Working with Assignment Sequences," p. 10).

The writing questions — both those that follow the selections and those in the assignment sequences — have a variety of aims. The central goal, though, is to make students aware of the ways that positions are presented and arguments pursued in civic controversy. The questions use few rhetorical terms, although they often encourage rhetorical analysis. They may, for example, ask students to consider the responses that an author might be seeking from his or her audience through self-portrayal, the positioning of other groups, the use of certain images, or other argumentative techniques. Such questions ask not chiefly for the student's own response but for an imaginative understanding of the audiences of the time. Some of these questions ask students to write in the voice of a person from the period, a further attempt to get students to engage more immediately with the arguments as live issues and to see the dimensions of persuasive writing. Dialogue assignments, which appear in many of the assignment sequences, call on students to understand voice, point of view, and refutation. Finally, some assignments specify a fictitious audience or a nonacademic genre, such as writing a newspaper editorial about a speaker in a controversy. These assignments can sharpen a student's sense of audience and engagement with civic discourse.

A further goal of the writing assignments is to help students analyze a writer's point of view. Some questions ask specifically for this type of analysis. It is difficult for students to burrow into a writer's assumptions or political agenda. Yet they must do so if they are to cast themselves and others into roles, articulate and control the various meanings of experience, and see how "contact zone" arguments attempt to shape the American landscape.

Questions about the success of persuasion and about the student's own responses or conclusions are usually framed in a comparison among several divergent views. Some such questions follow individual selections, but most are in the assignment sequences. There is some danger of a simplistic response to comparison and contrast questions, and in our remarks in this manual on the specific writing questions, we suggest ways to keep students' essays from eliding analysis in the rush to judgment. We don't want to keep students from judging, but rather to make their judgments part of the larger dialogue. They should see their opinions not as the end of the discussion but as an entry into it.

The assignment sequences frequently begin with a question that calls for personal reflection on the ways that the issue at hand has come into the students' own lives. These questions can be assigned as journal entries or as full-scale essays. They serve to heighten the sense of immediacy of issues that were debated in an earlier period and often allow students to explore their own assumptions before they confront, in the readings, a range of opinions, many of which will undoubtedly oppose their own.

None of the writing assignments in *Negotiating Difference* specifies length, although a few genre-specific assignments may hint at it. While we have been reluctant to put suggestions about length in the writing questions, we believe that it is important to give students a clear indication of what you expect. Length is not an unerring correlate of scope, but it is a useful indicator. We strongly urge you to estimate a length for each assignment you give, taking into account your students' capacities for reading and writing. However, students may eventually be able to negotiate with you about length. In fact, we hope that you will discuss each writing assignment in class to see if the assignment is clear, to get students to imagine what ought to be in the essay, and to help them formulate a strategy or sketch an outline. This exercise can include a group estimate of how long a paper may need to be to accomplish the desired goals.

Similarly, we have indicated an audience in some but by no means all of the assignments. Where it is not specified, we generally have in mind the "academic" audience, a fictitious but useful construct that includes some people who are unfamiliar with the issues at hand (they require clear summaries of texts or positions that are referred to) and some who are very familiar with the issues (they require careful and complete analysis). Like length, audience can be a topic of a prewriting class discussion. Some writers find it helpful to have a clear image of the audience; others don't. This will have to be one of your own negotiations.

Working with Assignment Sequences

We think it is extremely important to link the readings in a course using *Negotiating Difference*. Students will not be able to understand and benefit from the rhetorical richness of the concept of negotiation if they do not get a chance to see how the texts speak to one another. Also, they will learn more about the value of revision and rethinking in the writing process if they have opportunities to develop writing assignments that build on one another. As we've explained, you are certainly free to assemble your own list of readings from among the selections, using the reading questions to introduce them and the writing questions to explore them further and put them in dialogue with one another. We have, however, suggested sequences of assignments that put readings together. The writing assignments in the sequences are intended to supplant, for the most part, the writing assignments following individual selections. In the model syllabi, we indicate ways of combining the assignments in the sequences, and we provide suggestions in the unit sections of this manual for teaching each sequence.

Each sequence is organized around a provocative question suggested by the unit theme. Each reading in the unit is used in at least one sequence, and each sequence includes a substantial number of readings from the unit. The writing assignments in the sequence are designed to build on one another. For example, students may be asked to consider the impact of a unit issue in their own lives before tracing its treatment in a reading selection. Or students may be asked to explain how writers on various sides of an issue define their positions before they are asked to synthesize the readings in their own argumentative essays on that issue.

Using the Research Kits

Many of the skills that writing teachers associate with research are taught throughout *Negotiating Difference* and are not confined to the Research Kits accompanying every unit. Many of the assignments ask students to read difficult and lengthy material critically, to evaluate arguments, to contrast conflicting sources, and to synthesize a range of arguments into a position of their own. Consequently, each unit in *Negotiating Difference* may be used as a source book for a controlled research project.

The pervasiveness of such researchlike activities in *Negotiating Difference* prepares students to turn to their own research projects as suggested by the Research Kits. In the kits, we invite students to go beyond the resources offered within the covers of this book. We want to empower students as independent inquirers who can define and pursue research agendas on their own. Something of this idea, we hope, is implied by calling these sections "kits": We'd like to think of each Research Kit as a box of tools students can use for their own investigative purposes.

The Research Kits give students leads to a variety of information sources. In addition to providing bibliographies that cite the works included in the unit and related primary and secondary texts, the kits also point to resources in the community, such as historical societies, churches, civic groups, and so on. We want students to understand that research includes, but is not limited to, library searching.

Also, we believe that research is a social act (Bizzell and Herzberg, 1987). That is, most successful research is collaborative in some sense — at the very least building on the recorded work of others and often (especially in the social and natural sciences and in the world beyond school) conducted in teams. Thus, many of the research projects suggested in the Research Kits lend themselves to group work, which we sometimes suggest explicitly.

Research projects can be considered an integral part of the concept of *Negotiating Difference* because we want to emphasize the open-endedness of every unit and of the book itself. Of course, it is impossible for a book to include everything. But this defect becomes a virtue in the sense that it leaves a lot of room for students to initiate their own projects and to take unit themes in directions that are important to them. Each Research Kit proposes research topics that direct students not only to in-depth explorations of issues raised in the unit but also to related issues in other venues. For example, in Unit One students might find out more about relations between Native Americans and immigrants in colonial New England, or they might explore such relations in another part of the country.

We have been very much aware, in choosing the topic of each unit, that many groups, regions of the country, historical periods, and decisive conflicts are not represented in *Negotiating Difference*. It would of course be impossible to cover everything. But we sincerely hope that the units in the book show what *can* be done to bring together materials that reveal the dimensions of American contact zones. In the Research Kits we invite students to attempt projects (which would have to be undertaken collaboratively by an entire class) to create their own units on our model, addressing periods and issues of special importance to them. We welcome any local tailoring that teachers and students want to do with the approaches offered in *Negotiating Difference*, and we try to provide some resources for a start on such efforts in the Research Kits. We also invite suggestions for new units to be included in later editions of this book.

Interviewing is a vital research skill for many of the projects we recommend in the Research Kits. The commandments of interviewing are as follows:

- Make a firm appointment to meet or telephone the interviewee.
- Arrive or call on time.
- Dress nicely if meeting the interviewee.
- Write down questions in advance.
- Ask questions — don't argue.
- Take notes *and* (with the interviewee's permission) use a tape recorder.
- Telephone after the interview with follow-up questions if necessary.

And, for the teacher: Don't have excessively high expectations. Students who learn to use the telephone, make their way to an interview, and put original research into a paper are having a valuable experience. The appearance of quotations from a personal interview in a research paper can be electrifying, a leap out of the library and into the world. You can help students formulate their questions and figure out what parts of their interviews will be useful in their papers. Citation form for including interviews in an essay's bibliography can be found in a good handbook.

Citing sources is also an essential part of research. You can give your students a little practice in the art of documentation by asking for citations and references to texts in *Negotiating Difference* that they use in their essays. Our citation for each selection appears on the first page of the selection. Just copying over a citation is a good exercise for students. Ask students why we have them there in the first place. (Note that we have not attempted to include rules and styles of documentation in *Negotiating Difference*, as these are readily available in handbooks.)

OTHER SUGGESTIONS FOR TEACHING

Class Journals

To help develop students' thoughtful responses to the reading and writing assignments in this book, we recommend asking students to keep a class journal. Keeping a journal is a very common, time- tested, and well-respected pedagogical strategy in writing classes, and many teachers will not need any elaboration on it from us (see Fulwiler; Gannet). Nevertheless, we will offer a few remarks here on the particular version of the journal that we like to use in conjunction with the materials in this book.

The key feature of the journal, we emphasize, is that it should record responses to course material. It is not primarily a place to record responses to all of college life, not a diary of daily events. Responses to course material, however, can take many forms. One form is a response to the reading questions in the book. We like to ask students to write responses to these questions in their class journals prior to in-class work on a reading and to bring the journals to class. We can then ask them to respond to questions in class by referring to what they have written. Sometimes you can start a discussion by simply asking several students to read what they have written in response to a reading question and then encouraging other students to comment on the differences and similarities in their responses.

You can also encourage students to respond to the readings in an open-ended way in their journals. They can note down any passages they didn't understand and any difficulties they encountered in responding to the reading questions. They can comment on passages whose views they strongly agreed or disagreed with or whose style of expression they greatly admired or disliked. They can make connections with other readings they've done in the composition course, in other courses, or in contexts other than school. They can incorporate relevant newspaper clippings, ads, photographs, cartoons, and their own original artwork. They can tell about personal experiences or family history that bears on the issues raised in the readings.

You can also use these same kinds of written responses to stimulate class discussions. For example, you might encourage students to look back over their class notes every week or so and comment on what has particularly moved them, puzzled them, and even annoyed them. Also, when a lively discussion is cut off at the end of the class period, we like to recommend that students summarize the discussion in their journals and add whatever they want to say about their own views at the moment the discussion had to stop. Then, if we want to resume the discussion at the beginning of the next class period, we can do so by asking several students to read what they have written about the previous exchange.

You can also use the class journal to help teach the writing process. Our assignment sequences often begin with writing questions that call for personal reflection on the sequence issues; these types of assignments can be written in the class journal. Other assignments require collecting evidence from different texts to support an argument; the class journal can be the place where students collect that evidence. They can also use their journals to write preliminary outlines, thesis paragraphs, or even complete rough drafts. They can then bring all these kinds of writing to class to share with the other students.

How often should the teacher see the class journal? There is no one correct answer to this question. We like to collect the class journals two or three times during the semester. We check through them to see that students are keeping up with their work (as when responses to reading questions have been assigned, for example), and we comment informally on the content, usually just writing a few words in the margins. If students have written anything in the journal that they have decided they don't want us to see (a personal reflection entry that got too personal, for example), they may remove it before turning in the journal.

Sometimes, though, we don't collect the journals until the end of the course. The primary purpose of the journal is to help students develop the writing abilities that will be more formally evaluated in their essays. Thus the class journal can be treated as a kind of "practice area" that is for the students' own use and that the teacher does not have to see until the end of the course. Looking at the journals at the end of the course simply provides some incentive for students to make use of the journal throughout the semester.

Regardless of how often you ask to see the class journal, we do recommend that you evaluate it. Here is how we like to do that. First, we tell students that the physical format of the class journal does not matter, as long as it is in a form that they can turn in. They can use a notebook, a folder of loose pages, a computer file that gets printed out or submitted on diskette or via e-mail, or whatever. Also, we tell students that neatness and correctness do not count in the journal, as long as what they have written is intelligible. We evaluate the journal on the basis of whether it appears to have been used regularly (including whether regular assignments have been kept up to date), whether entries are sufficiently numerous and copious (a judgment call, which can often be determined by reading a batch of journals together), and whether the entries show some serious reflection on the issues (again, of course, a judgment call).

We give a letter grade on the journal at the end of the semester (if we collect the journal several times before then, we make interim evaluative comments but do not grade it until the end). Often, the letter grade also comprises an estimate of the student's quality of class participation, attendance, and overall effort. We like to give this grade fairly serious weight, at least as much as one formal paper (if papers are graded on the portfolio method, as we recommend on p. 17, the weight will be increased). The class journal assignment should be one in which any student who makes a serious effort can do well.

Working in Groups

Students often have the idea that writing must be done alone. They imagine the solitary writer, at midnight, in a tower room, writing by the light of a single candle — isolated in time and space. No doubt this image owes something to debased romantic versions of poetic creativity and something to the competitive educational system's insistence on "individual work" and stigmatization of collaboration as "collusion." Current research, as well as the personal experience of teachers, suggests that this image deviates widely from the actual practice of most writers. Most writers must write within a rich social environment (see Gere; LeFevre). Most writers do not write alone.

As writers and teachers, we strongly endorse the idea that writing is essentially a collaborative activity, and we urge you to use group work with *Negotiating Difference*. Collaborative work fits well with the intertextual and rhetorical emphasis of this book. The selections and apparatus emphasize the ways writers attended to other writers and to broader social contexts in framing their own texts. Also, many assignments ask students to work together. Here we wish just briefly to review some suggestions for group work in using this book.

There is no one correct way to form students into groups. Some educators advise that groups be carefully structured so as to represent in each group the class's diversity of race, gender, learning style preference, writing and reading ability, and so on. The idea here is to distribute the students' resources as equitably as possible among groups. This approach may be impractical, however, in a large class where the teacher may not be able to determine all these variables for every student with accuracy. Other teachers prefer to create groups randomly, perhaps by using alphabetical order, which frees them from the burden of researching students' aptitudes and so on and perhaps making tendentious judgments about them. This leaves the distribution of resources to the luck of the draw but is equitable at least in that everyone presumably has an equal chance to be part of a well-equipped group.

In contrast with either of these methods, we prefer to let students choose their own groups. In thinking about our own experiences of collaborative work, we realize how important it is to have a congenial group to work with. We want to choose our own reader-editors and coresearchers, and we see no reason to deny students this privilege. Students work together better when they like their collaborators. If a self-chosen group turns out to be short on particular resources, the teacher can step in to aid students or to direct them to a source of whatever they are lacking (for example, group members who all have difficulty with standard English could be advised to use the campus peer tutoring facility). For most tasks, we recommend a group size of three to five students.

Students can work in groups either in or outside of class. In class, student groups can work together to arrive at responses to a selection's reading questions. This might be a better approach than having students write responses to the reading questions in their journals (as suggested under "Class Journals," p. 12) if students are having considerable difficulty with a particular selection. Collecting evidence for an argument paper (such as usable quotations) or sharing personal-reflection writing assignments from a sequence are other activities that in-class groups can perform. In these cases, each group should appoint one of its members as recorder to keep track of the group's responses to its tasks; allow class time for each group to report on its work and compare its responses with those of other groups.

Many writing teachers also like to use in-class groups for student work on writing projects. We believe that such work should be carefully directed. For example, if you have asked students to write opening paragraphs that include a clear statement of their thesis, you might then have each student read his or her opening paragraph to an in-class group to find out if other members can detect the thesis. If not, they might be able to offer helpful advice on how to clarify it. For another example, if you have asked students to write an argumentative paper in which opposing arguments must be addressed, in-class groups could work together to generate lists of arguments on various aspects of the issue under discussion or could listen to one another's draft rebuttals of opposing arguments and comment on their thoroughness and persuasiveness.

In general, we give a low priority to using in-class groups for students simply to read drafts to one another or to edit one another's writing for correctness, coherence, or style on the sentence and paragraph level. While we acknowledge that such peer interaction is valuable, we believe it occurs most profitably in a peer tutoring setting or in the informal collaborative work of the library or dorm room. In class, we believe it is better to give more clearly defined tasks whose completion the teacher can monitor.

Another kind of in-class group work is the oral presentation. A number of writing assignments in *Negotiating Difference* ask students to imagine an actual dialogue between two or three authors in a unit or to imagine how they themselves would have responded in a particular situation. These assignments can be turned into group dramatic presentations, with different group members playing the different parts. Writing assignments that set up opposing issues can also be translated into in-class debates. For example, one assignment asks students to decide whether Catharine Beecher, in her *Treatise on Domestic Economy*, is trying to promote feminist ideas under the guise of acceptable homage to domestic ideologies or is instead trying to promote domestic ideologies by giving them some slight color of feminism. Each of two groups could choose one side of this argument and present evidence for its case. Of course, these in-class presentations would entail considerable preparation, which could take place outside of class if the student population is largely residential or in class if students are not able to meet easily at any other time.

In addition to these and other kinds of in-class group work, *Negotiating Difference* provides ideas for several kinds of group work to be done outside of class time. Each unit's Research Kit contains many such ideas. Our suggestions for individual research paper topics could be pursued by teams of two or three students working together; we always encourage (but do not require) students to form such teams when we assign research papers. Also, we provide suggestions for larger research topics that would require the efforts of several groups or perhaps of the entire class; the assignments contain suggestions for how to distribute the tasks among groups. When several groups are working on different parts of the same research project, we recommend building in class time for regular reports from the research teams on their findings.

We believe that teachers can and should evaluate group work. In the case of more informal group projects, such as formulating responses to reading questions or critiquing a specific aspect of the group's papers, a teacher might just make an informal estimate of each student's contribution, perhaps on a pass/fail basis, and incorporate this estimate into an overall assessment of the student's class participation. In the case of research papers written by a team of two or three, our practice is to give each student involved in the project the same grade — whatever grade the entire completed paper merits — while also asking that the writers include an appendix to the paper in which they explain how they divided up the work. In the case of more elaborate research projects, such as those undertaken by several groups or the class as a whole, it might be a good idea to specify each person's task (or each group might parcel out the tasks assigned to it among its members). Each student's contribution could then be graded, as well as the project as a whole, and each student's final grade would be the average of the individual grade and the project grade.

Students often express discomfort with group work. This may be due in part to their internalized image of solitary creativity, which we described earlier, and in part to concern about how their own record will be affected by forced teaming with other students. To address such resistance, we suggest, first, disabusing students of the notion that writing is solitary. Teachers should share examples of collaboration from their own experience and also point out the prevalence of collaborative writing in the academy, public press, and workplace. You can also promote group work on the grounds that it enhances students' own creativity and prepares them for the kinds of writing situations that they will likely encounter after college.

Second, we suggest that you respect rather than simply debunk students' anxiety about how group work will affect their individual records. It is perfectly understandable that students should experience such anxiety in the competitive American educational system. Be as clear as possible about how you will evaluate group work, while also allowing students many opportunities to be graded on work submitted under their own names. If teachers think the current educational system is too competitive, then using some group work can help combat the competitive ethos and give students a chance to think about work in another way. At the same time, we don't think it is fair to require students to buck the competitive system entirely in one course when they have no choice to opt out of it in their overall progress through school.

Portfolio Grading

The writing student's portfolio should contain work from early in the course, drafts, and several finished, polished papers. Portfolio grading bases a student's final evaluation on the finished pieces, rather than grading every piece of writing a student produces and averaging the grades to arrive at the final grade.

We believe that the primary value of portfolio grading is that it emphasizes the importance of the writing process and rewards students who take that process seriously. One of the most important things a writing teacher can convey to students is that writing is indeed a process. Thinking, "sketching" (in the form of journal entries, outlines, conversations, and so on), drafting, editing, and stylistic polishing are all normal stages in the process of producing a good, finished piece of writing; moreover, writers may loop through several of these stages recursively on the way to producing the finished piece.

When we ask students to keep writing portfolios, we highlight the writing process because we are asking them to keep in the portfolio many of the pieces of writing they've produced at different stages of the process along with their finished papers. We emphasize that the preliminary pieces are necessary to the production of the finished piece and that students who have been most diligent in producing preliminary pieces will most likely write the best finished pieces. Thus they can see that attending to the writing process really does pay off.

We think portfolio grading has the added advantage of being a fair way to evaluate writing students. It seems unfair to pull down a final grade with an average that reflects the unpracticed abilities that students may bring into the course. Why penalize them for not knowing what they came into the course to learn? It seems fairer to allow them to be evaluated on the abilities they have achieved later in the course.

To institute portfolio grading, the teacher must make clear at what points in the semester students will be graded. This will not be every week, although we think writing students should be writing something every week. The writing teacher should act as a coach in responding to weekly assignments, commenting copiously but not assigning letter grades (or perhaps indicating quality with a coarser measure, such as "check," "check minus," and "check plus"). As coach, the writing teacher helps students prepare the papers that will eventually be graded by the teacher, who has then shifted his or her role to that of judge.

We recommend asking students to submit two papers to be graded around the middle of the school term and two more at the end; the midterm grades can reward or challenge students, who are often uneasy if they receive no grades at all before the end of the course. Some teachers prefer, however, to hold off all grading until the end of the term, asking students at that time to submit as many papers for grades as the teacher feels are necessary to make an evaluation (two at the minimum). Teachers may prefer this alternative when they want to emphasize the need for students to develop their own standards for good writing; teachers can encourage such independence by withholding frequent evaluations. Whenever papers are submitted to be graded, they should be submitted in the complete portfolio, which should also include all ungraded work to date and the class journal, if one has been assigned. (For a collaborative method of evaluating portfolios, see Belanoff and Elbow.)

In commenting on the graded papers, the teacher may sometimes find it helpful to refer to preliminary pieces that contributed to them. For example, a graded paper might be written in response to an assignment that asks for a comparison of two writers. Earlier assignments might have asked for an analysis of each writer alone. In the graded paper, then, the student may have incorporated revised portions of the earlier individual analyses, and the teacher can comment on the success of these changes and combinations. For another example, a graded paper might emerge out of an idea the student originally expressed in the class journal; the teacher can comment on how the student has developed the idea, on stylistic differences between its treatment in the class journal and in the formal paper, and so on.

The apparatus in *Negotiating Difference* is designed to facilitate portfolio grading. The reading questions for each selection may be written as preliminary, ungraded assignments that can be used in completing the writing questions for that selection, which can be graded; writing questions for a selection often specifically mention reading questions that can be helpful. Also, the assignment sequences accompanying each unit are composed of assignments that become progressively complex and that build on earlier assignments in the sequence. Thus, earlier sequence assignments can be ungraded, with only the final assignments graded. Usually the last two or three assignments in a sequence draw on most of the work that has gone before; students might be given a choice of which of these concluding assignments they want to prepare for grades.

Developing as a Teacher

No matter how many years of experience you have as a teacher, you probably know that teaching, like writing, is an art that can be developed lifelong. Just as you never finish learning to write, you never finish learning to teach. Fortunately, both are collaborative activities, so you can continue to learn and improve with the help of your colleagues, students, and other readers and writers. We hope that this instructor's manual can also prove helpful to your development as a teacher. We often felt almost embarrassed as we were writing it, offering advice to readers who may very well be more accomplished teachers than we are. But we hope that perhaps you can profit from our experience researching and teaching the material in *Negotiating Difference*.

In addition, we have provided a very brief bibliography of teaching resources to which we have referred in this introduction. For a more complete picture of the scholarly resources available to writing teachers, we suggest you look at our *Bedford Bibliography for Teachers of Writing*. The fourth edition incorporates suggestions from a number of expert consultants in various specialized fields within composition studies.

We are very eager to hear from you concerning what you found helpful and productive — or the reverse — in this manual and in *Negotiating Difference* itself. We need your help to make this book as useful as possible. Please don't hesitate to contact us.

BIBLIOGRAPHY

Belanoff, Pat, and Peter Elbow. "Using Portfolios to Increase Collaboration and Community in a Writing Program." *Writing Program Administration* 9 (Spring 1986): 27–40.

Bizzell, Patricia. "'Contact Zones' and English Studies." *College English* 56 (1994): 163–69.

Bizzell, Patricia, and Bruce Herzberg. *The Bedford Bibliography for Teachers of Writing.* 4th ed. Boston: Bedford Books, 1996.

———. "Research as a Social Act." *Clearinghouse* 60 (March 1987): 303–6.

Freire, Paulo, and Donaldo Macedo. *Literacy: Reading the Word and the World.* South Hadley, Mass.: Bergin and Garvey, 1987.

Fulwiler, Toby. "The Personal Connection: Journal Writing across the Curriculum." In *Language Connections: Reading and Writing across the Curriculum,* edited by Toby Fulwiler and Art Young. Urbana: National Council of Teachers of English, 1982.

Gannett, Cinthia. "Academic Journals: Panacea or Problem." In *Gender and the Journal: Diaries and Academic Discourse.* Albany: State University of New York Press, 1992.

Gere, Anne Ruggles. *Writing Groups: History, Theory, and Implications.* Carbondale: Southern Illinois University Press, 1987.

hooks, bell. *Teaching to Transgress: Education as the Practice of Freedom.* New York: Routledge, 1994.

LeFevre, Karen Burke. *Invention as a Social Act.* Carbondale: Southern Illinois University Press, 1987.

Pratt, Mary Louise. "Arts of the Contact Zone." In *Profession 91,* 33–40. New York: Modern Language Association, 1991.

First Contacts between Puritans and Native Americans

THEMES AND ISSUES IN UNIT ONE

The idea for this unit grew out of our discovery of nineteenth-century Native American writer William Apess and his fascinating rebuttal of the dominant English accounts of seventeenth-century New England. Pat has taught a writing-intensive course in early American literature, which presents some of the English texts as commentaries on one another. But she has found that including Apess raises this kind of contest of interpretations to a whole new level. Nineteenth-century American literature courses could also be enriched tremendously by the inclusion of Apess. We call your attention to Barry O'Connell's excellent edition of this important Native American writer's entire work (see the Unit One bibliography).

Is It Racism?

Whether or not the contentions between English and Native American people chronicled in this unit seem controversial in a particular course may depend in part on where and even when the course is taking place. At any given time, Native American relations with other Americans may generate new controversies in some regions and not in others. We think it is best for teachers to acknowledge the harsh realities of the invasion of America by Europeans, while at the same time downplaying discussion of either English or Native American racism. Charges of racism do not speak to the material realities of the conflict, and they obscure the rhetorical subtleties of each writer's attempts to shape readers' interpretations of history into agreement with his or her own.

If you have any Native American students in your course, make no assumptions about how these students will react to Unit One. Certainly, do not call on them to be speakers for the "Native American point of view," unless they volunteer for the job. Do not expect them to be particularly eager to discuss unit material — or particularly embarrassed by it, for that matter. If these students are from tribes originating at some remove from

21

New England, they may not feel any kinship with the Native Americans represented in Unit One. They may know a lot or a little about their own people's history, and they may or may not be willing to share what they know. Common politeness is best: Be alert to the degree to which these students seem to want to be defined in your class by their Native American identity, and follow their lead.

The territory that is now the United States used to be well populated with Native Americans. There can be little question both that they were here first and that the massive influx of people from Europe, Africa, and Asia beginning in the 1600s has had disastrous consequences for the Native Americans. Their numbers and landholdings have been drastically reduced over the centuries, although many tribal groups still retain the status of independent, albeit conquered, nations within the United States.

Some students may wish to argue that the transfer of Native American land to other (mostly white) hands was accomplished legally, by sale or treaty, and that therefore the disastrous consequences of that transfer must be attributed at least partly to the Native Americans themselves: Perhaps they shouldn't have sold so much land, or they shouldn't have resisted white settlement violently and thus provoked punitive treaty provisions.

We think that teachers should point out that whatever the immediate circumstances of any land transfer, the ongoing process of the invasion of America took place in a climate of violence for which the aggressors, that is the invaders, must take primary responsibility. There would have been no disaster for Native Americans if Europeans and others had stayed home. At the same time, it is important to acknowledge that many "invaders" did not come to America willingly. Africans who were transported in the holds of slave ships were most cruelly deprived of choice; but other immigrant groups came sadly, unwillingly, driven by starvation or political oppression in their home countries.

The climate of violence surrounding contacts between Native Americans and immigrants is highlighted in the Unit One readings. The texts included in the "Treaties, Laws, and Deeds" section seem only fragile stays against the warfare chronicled in the English and Native American accounts. These accounts show brutalities committed by both sides. After such butchery as Underhill describes the Puritans inflicting on the Pequots, it is not surprising that the Native Americans in New England eventually rose up, under Metacomet's leadership, against the English. After such butchery as Rowlandson describes witnessing the Native Americans commit against her own family, it is not surprising that she describes the Native Americans as "devils."

Students may be inclined to see the conflict between Native Americans and English people as resulting from racism, since students know that racism is often cited as a source of conflict between white people and people of color today. This view is encouraged by the nineteenth-century Native American writer William Apess, who links the treatment of his people with the white racism evidenced in American slaveholding. Protest against slavery was growing in Apess's day, particularly in his home region of New England, and he contributed to the outcry.

Nevertheless, historians disagree about the extent to which the English directed color prejudice against Native Americans. English prejudices may have been simply xenophobic, directed against any groups who were "different" (for example, some Puritan writers of captivity narratives reserve their most violent invective not for their Native American captors, but for the French Roman Catholics in Canada to whom their captors sold them). Furthermore, it is understandable that both English and Native American writers would depict negatively those people who had severely hurt them and their people. Real material conflicts over land and culture separated these peoples. We suggest keeping students' attention focused on how each writer attempts to manage readers' experience by presenting some groups positively and others negatively. In order to do this, it is not necessary to get into a discussion of who is racist, how racist, and so forth.

Narrative

The six English accounts in this unit are all narratives of seventeenth-century history, told by eyewitnesses. Students can be asked to analyze features of narrative in these pieces — for example, how setting and character are described, how "plot" is established through the sequence and emphasis given to events, how the narrator establishes his or her credibility and attempts to manage readers' experience of the text, and more. This kind of analysis of narrative can also be turned profitably to narratives the students write themselves, perhaps, in response to some of the writing questions and sequence assignments.

One of the most important and difficult concepts to get across to students in the study of narrative is that of "selection." Students tend to think that an author simply writes down the story that presents itself, as if the story existed independently in the natural world and all the writer had to do was record it. Students even tend to think this way about stories that they know are fictional; how much more do they have this attitude about stories that purport to be "true" history, like the accounts included here?

Students have to understand that in reality, the story that readers get is shaped by specific choices the writer has made, some deliberate or conscious, some unconscious. For example, Bradford may be said to be consciously choosing which incidents in the early history of Plymouth are worthy of report in his chronicle (for example, he omits his wife's apparent suicide). He may also be said to be unconsciously reflecting English xenophobia in his representation of Native Americans, even though he has no conscious desire to present them in a bad light.

In making students aware of the writer's selection process, you will find it helpful to be able to compare two or more versions of the same event, as the readings in this unit make possible. One way to do this is to point out how different versions are slanted or biased according to the writer's political and social allegiances. This point can be easily illustrated, for example, by comparing what Increase Mather and John Easton have to say about the death of John Sassamon. Students grasp this kind of comparison fairly quickly. They like the cynicism it allows them to adopt about historical sources.

A more subtle point is to get students to reflect on what is *left out* of a particular account. This awareness is especially important for this unit because what is often left out is information on Native American experiences and viewpoints that are of great interest to twentieth-century readers. Sometimes this idea of selection-by-omission can be conveyed by comparing sources: for example, Mather says nothing about the prewar parley between the English and the Native Americans reported in Easton.

Also, the teacher can point out what might be called oddities or discrepancies in what a single text reports. For example, when Mary Rowlandson meets Metacomet for the first time, he invites her into his wetu and offers her tobacco. This should be a very dramatic scene: Rowlandson, the terrified English captive, meets the most important war leader of the hostile Native Americans, someone she has cause to fear and loathe, and his initial response is to offer what to him is a signal courtesy, perhaps trying to assure her that he means her no harm. But Rowlandson comments on none of these dynamics; rather, she turns to a diatribe on the evils of tobacco and her own struggle with the addiction. She neglects to tell us anything about Metacomet as a person or her reaction to him.

This kind of discussion about the construction of narrative helps students to see why we speak in the unit title of "contending" accounts. Students will begin to see that to write a story is to make claims on readers' allegiances, to try to get readers to see the world in particular ways that will have consequences in future behavior. For example, if readers believe the dominant English accounts of this early history, then they'll view the Native Americans in New England as primitive, culturally uninteresting, violent, and dangerous. Clearly, such a view would make it easier for people to consent to the extermination or removal of the Native Americans.

Working with Sources

Since the selections in this unit provide conflicting versions of particular historical events, taken together they can provide a useful experience for students of what it means to research a topic. No matter what the topic, sources usually diverge, as they do here. As noted in the preceding discussion of narrative, many of the readings in this unit contradict or vary from one another, both by providing contrasting accounts of the same incidents and by including or emphasizing different incidents.

The English accounts, however, by and large do not contradict each other explicitly. Mather does announce that his history will correct the "errors" of accounts like Easton's. Easton and Gardener are highly critical of the ways their fellow colonists deal with the Native Americans, but they do not name any particular villains. Gardener, for example, does not specifically decry Bradford's account of policy or Underhill's treatment of the Pequot fighters.

For direct contradiction, we must turn to the Native American accounts, especially to William Apess. All the Native American accounts are intended to counter English views. The Medfield bridge post paper and Waban's speech specifically mention English behavior and question it from a Native American viewpoint, although without citing any textual sources. Apess goes further and attacks many of the English historians by name, including Bradford, Mather, and Rowlandson.

Indeed, as we suggested at the outset, this entire unit may be seen as organized around Apess's brilliant response to the dominant English texts — which students need to read in order to appreciate what he is doing. Apess is particularly striking because his attacks on the dominant historians by name make it very clear to students that they cannot take these accounts at face value. It is a subtle and difficult point, for example, to get students to see what Bradford is omitting when they are looking at Bradford alone. It is an easier point to make when they can read Apess's vehement account of what Bradford left out.

In our experience, students generally have one of two responses to the issues of working with sources that this unit raises. One response is to look for the "true" story: For instance, if students have imbibed popular prejudices against Puritans, they may seize on Apess as the one telling the truth and accept his debunking of English sources without question.

Another response is to decide that there can be no true story: Apess is just as prejudiced as the English sources, say these students, but on the other side. With all these conflicting accounts, they say, there's no way for today's students to figure out what happened in New England, so they might as well quit trying. This is more of the comfortable adolescent cynicism to which we alluded in discussing narrative.

Our goal is to get students to see the problematic nature of all work from sources. They must accept that there will be no way to get a single true story that's not open to question. This, of course, means leaving behind immature notions of what history writing is all about and accepting the critical view of it that is more prevalent in the discipline today.

At the same time, students should not be allowed to opt out of shaping a story, of arriving at an informed opinion. Given the fact that they are not going to find one authoritative account, they must take responsibility themselves for the shape they impose on the material they collect from different sources. They will have to make decisions about whose version to trust, and to what extent. Students will have to realize that their own values play a large part in how they make these decisions — that they are not made "objectively." As responsible readers, they must consider a wide range of sources, but the ultimate shape of the stories they construct will be value-laden.

Notes on the Unit Readings

Each selection in the unit is accompanied by its own headnote, reading questions, and writing questions, so it can be assigned independently of the other readings or combined with others as you see fit. We have also grouped each reading with several other selections in at least one of the four assignment sequences offered at the end of the unit (the sequences are discussed on p. 41). We urge you to assemble your course reading and writing into one or more sequences, of either our design or your own.

In the following notes, we provide commentary on each of the unit's selections as well as guidelines for approaching and evaluating the writing questions.

Dominant English Accounts

William Bradford, from *History of Plymouth Plantation* (p. 19)

This is the longest and most difficult reading in Unit One, yet it is also the most necessary to include in any grouping of selections. It establishes the basic sequence of events referred to by other readings, some of which explicitly cite Bradford's version.

Of course, Bradford is also important because his narrative has become one of the formative documents of American history. Students should be encouraged to note how images of American history so familiar as to become trite, such as the *Mayflower* landing or the first meeting with Squanto, appear in Bradford. Students' imaginative entry into this text can also be greatly enhanced if it is possible to visit the full-scale *Mayflower* replica and recreated Plimoth Plantation, with well-informed staff in period costume, located in Plymouth, Massachusetts.

Students will sometimes say that they find Bradford "boring." In our experience, this complaint often screens difficulties students have in comprehending Bradford because of the archaism of his language. In other words, they think his account is boring because they are not able to follow the really quite exciting story he is telling.

We have attempted to address this difficulty with footnotes as well as with reading questions that direct students' attention to some of the major content issues in the text. We also suggest that you use Bradford to point out the real difficulties that "nonstandard" writing can entail. Bradford violates a number of contemporary conventions of spelling and grammar, even in the modernized version of his text that we have excerpted. These violations can be highlighted for study.

For example, one violation that Bradford commits continually and that causes student readers a great deal of trouble is to leave pronoun references unclear. An excellent in-class exercise would be to track down the referents in extended passages of his prose. Another violation can be found in his nonstandard spellings; Bradford might be compared in this regard with Mather and Easton. You can ask students: What is implied about the writer's attitude toward spelling when variant spellings of a word are used within a single paragraph, or sometimes within a single sentence? Students can be invited to debate the importance of adhering to standard conventions in their own writing, in light of the degree of difficulty they have with Bradford.

Writing Analytically

With writing question 1, students will think that what you are looking for is assessment of whether Bradford is racist in any obvious way in his presentation of Native Americans. Because — in our opinion — he is not, this misapprehension can cause students some difficulties. They'll either distort the evidence to exaggerate the negatives in his portrayal of Native Americans, so as to make a case for racism, or else they'll take the opposite side, often with a bit of annoyance or defensiveness, and insist that he is being "fair" — a view they will often qualify as "fair for a person of his time period (who didn't know all about racism and how to avoid it like we do)." Rather than encourage either of these positions, we suggest you direct students toward the view that what's most striking about Bradford's treatment of the Native Americans is that he uses them as *background* for the English story. They are important only so far as they impinge on English experience. Try to guide students in this direction by telling them to look for what Bradford leaves out. For example, he's one of the first Europeans to encounter a new race of people. If such an encounter happened today, what would students want to know about these "new" people? How many of their questions could be answered by a reporter like Bradford? Class discussion of these points would be a good preparation for this assignment.

We want writing question 2 to give students a more vivid sense of the multiple contending forces in the region — to avoid reducing these forces to a simple opposition of English and Native Americans. To dramatize the contending voices, you might adapt this question for group work in several ways. Student groups might prepare a skit in which several English people, one of whom has just returned from Plymouth colony, are talking together in London about the prospects for emigration in light of relations with the Native Americans. One group might make a case for the safety of emigration, and another group might prepare the case for caution or even for staying home. Other groups could represent conversations in America among Uncas and Miantonomo and their councilors. The groups could then present their arguments to the rest of the class in debate fashion, with or without seventeenth-century role playing.

In presenting writing question 3, you should take care to make clear to students that you are not simply expecting a knee-jerk denunciation of violence. Point out to students that the focus of the question is *not* on whether the violence was in fact justified, but rather on whether the rhetorical strategies employed by Bradford and Underhill to justify the violence are effective. Of course, students' own views on the use of violence in wartime, especially against civilians, will come out in their evaluations of the writers' effectiveness — for example, a pacifist is likely to find these writers less persuasive than a militarist would. That's okay. But the focus of students' arguments has to be on rhetoric, not morality. To this end, we would also suggest to students that any comparison they want to make with similar situations in other wars, for example Vietnam, should be limited to their concluding section. (Note that the sample syllabus on p. 53 matches this unit with Unit Six, on the Vietnam War, to facilitate more in-depth comparisons.)

JOHN UNDERHILL, FROM *NEWES FROM AMERICA* (p. 44)

The Underhill selection can be used as the focus of discussion on what constitutes personal physical heroism in war or in other settings and on how this heroism is conveyed in written reports of the events. Students who have been soldiers in combat or who have been physically threatened in other contexts, such as gang violence, may wish to compare their experiences with Underhill's. The focus should be on situations in which a person not only risks being harmed but also is willing to harm another person.

Students might be invited to compare the meaning of the courage demonstrated in wartime with the courage necessary to undertake dangerous sports, such as football. Also, they might be invited to consider the differences and similarities between wartime courage and the courage shown in defense of oneself and friends against crime. In these cases, students might look at a variety of newspaper accounts to compare the ways they portray different kinds of violence and those who participate in violence.

Writing Analytically

Writing question 1 draws attention to what we think is most interesting in this account: Underhill's concern with appearing to be a valiant soldier. In addition to the questions posed in the assignment, students can be invited to discuss these questions: Why is Underhill so concerned about appearing brave? Is this concern understandable or justifiable? Responding to all these questions requires collecting textual evidence, which should be the focus of the paper. But you might also ask students to discuss, and perhaps to consider in the concluding section of their papers, questions such as these: Do you care what people think about your courage? Why or why not? If you want people to think you are brave, how do you go about demonstrating your bravery? Do men and women face different demands and constraints in establishing their bravery?

In writing question 2, Underhill's way of describing the actual violence can be contrasted with briefer, less graphic accounts of the same battle by Bradford, who was not on the scene. Students might be invited to consider whether Bradford's perspective reflects his more "sheltered" position and whether Underhill's perspective is understandable in light of the trauma of the actual combat he experienced.

Writing question 3 also invites students to consider different perspectives on wartime courage, comparing Underhill with Gardener. Although Gardener was also a frontline soldier — indeed, a mercenary — he does not seem to exhibit quite the same anxiety about being thought brave. Students might consider in what other ways he is concerned about his image.

We suggest that teachers take seriously the possibility that students might consider it important to appear brave. The analytical question underlying all three writing questions is whether courage must be expressed by physical violence — that is, are you brave only if you are prepared to hurt someone else?

INCREASE MATHER, FROM *A BRIEF HISTORY OF THE WAR WITH THE INDIANS IN NEW-ENGLAND* (p. 50)

Mather is likely to strike students as the most stereotypically "Puritan" of the authors in this unit; to those who don't know much about Puritans, he sounds the most like what Puritans should sound like. Teachers might want to deter students from simply condemning Mather as pretentious and moralistic. Point out that no matter how reluctant modern readers may be to take him seriously, he was highly respected in his own day, and there might be something to learn from trying to figure out why.

Writing Analytically

Writing question 1, concerning Mather's rhetorical authority, invites students to consider the classical and biblical references with which Mather liberally sprinkles his discourse. Although most students are initially repelled by these references, which they usually do not recognize (we have tried to help with footnotes), some will, upon further study, decide that they think the technique is legitimately impressive.

We recommend that you not try to push one view or the other; rather, let some students condemn the practice of allusion, while others endorse it. We suggest that you encourage students to collect other samples of highly allusive prose, from as wide a variety of sources as possible — small groups could be given different areas to research, with the examples preserved in class journals. Encourage students to examine readings assigned for other classes. They might also explore popular sources; for example, writing for rock music magazines is often highly allusive, but to another archive. Also encourage students to consider the purposes of allusive discourse: To what archive(s) do the references point? Who is included and excluded by such references? Is the exclusion of particular readers a problem? Why or why not?

Writing question 2 highlights the kind of problem we discuss in "Working with Sources" (p. 24). Mather and Easton disagree sharply about the two episodes on which students' papers may focus — so much so that students should have little difficulty amassing the textual evidence necessary to illustrate these differences. Urge students to focus their efforts on *why* they find one account more credible than the other. This is a good way to get the students' own moral assumptions out in the open.

Writing question 3 explores the authority Mather attempts to gain from dictating a moral interpretation of the history he tells. This question has two options: Students may simply collect evidence of Mather's moralizing and compare it with similar moralizing in Bradford or Underhill, or they may go further and use this evidence to argue that historians ought or ought not to moralize as these men do.

Some students will want to utterly condemn moralizing and to call for purely objective reporting of the facts in historical writing. We suggest that, at the very least, you push these students to explain what purely objective historical writing is for — that is, ask them to explain why society should pay to train and support historians to produce this kind of writing. Even better, we feel, would be to push such students to consider how very difficult it would be to write objective history. (See considerations on this issue in "Working with Sources," p. 24.)

Teachers should also be prepared for some students to find Mather's religious interpretation of history appealing. Such students may say that while his perspective is somewhat narrow, limiting divine intervention to the fate of the Puritans alone, it is in fact appropriate to discuss U.S. history in terms of a national moral destiny. We suggest that you encourage these students to consider the question of whose morality gets to determine the interpretation of national history. Is it fair to impose the morality of only one social group on shared national history — for example, to insist that the United States is a "Christian nation"? How could a compromise or consensus on moral interpretation be reached? Encourage students to consider the problem of how one might go about convincingly communicating to others a highly moralistic interpretation: As writers or speakers, how would students prevent their version of history from being as off-putting as Mather's is to many readers?

If you find both pro- and antimoralizing factions within a single class, you might set up opposing students in small groups to organize in-class debates on the issue. Debates might focus additionally on the question of what kind(s) of history should be taught to young Americans. Is it best to teach a common national history in public schools, or do students prefer a model of private, parochial, or ethnically based schools offering different versions of history from the perspective of each school's constituent group? Certainly Mather, full of the Puritans' typical concern with passing on their worldview to the rising generation, was very aware of the educational impact of his text.

MARY ROWLANDSON, FROM *A NARRATIVE OF THE CAPTIVITY AND RESTORATION OF MRS. MARY ROWLANDSON* (p. 67)

Like Mather, Rowlandson often strikes students as a "very Puritan" writer. She meets their expectations of Puritans because of her constant desire to attach moral meaning to her experience, a tendency that is addressed in writing question 3.

Rowlandson may also seem to be the stereotypical colonist in her violently negative portrayal of Native Americans (see writing question 1), whom she consistently depicts as "devils." She expresses surprise when any one of them shows her kind treatment, and satisfaction when any of them suffers particular hardship (as when Weetamoo's baby dies). In Rowlandson, perhaps more than in any other English text in this unit, the question of white racism arises (see "Is It Racism?", on p. 21).

Writing Analytically

In writing question 1, we think that students have to be allowed to make a case that Rowlandson is a racist, if they so desire. We also suggest that teachers point out that Rowlandson's hatred of the Native Americans actually does not need racism as a source: No doubt most people would respond negatively to another people who inflicted the physical violence on them that the Native Americans inflicted on Rowlandson. Some pity for her physical suffering and excruciating loss of family members and friends is appropriate.

Teachers might also point out that Rowlandson's narrative tells the story of her own spiritual progress as much as of her actual captivity. For the spiritual progress story to make sense, the protagonist has to encounter challenging antagonists on the way, just as Christian does in John Bunyan's *Pilgrim's Progress* (1678), a strong literary influence on the captivity narratives and a colonial best-seller. For Rowlandson, the Native Americans become the antagonists, her Apollyons. The logic of the spiritual narrative, not necessarily racism, requires that she demonize them (the fact remains, of course, that she is willing to sacrifice them for this purpose).

Writing question 2 raises the issue, of Rowlandson's gender. Rowlandson is the only woman writer represented in this unit (it is highly unlikely that the Medfield bridge post paper was written by a woman). Some students may expect to find Rowlandson expressing views that are somehow either feminine or feminist. Yet her text does not readily lend itself to either interpretation. Our writing question might help students to see where Rowlandson emphasizes the feminine aspects of her experience — for example, in the loss of her children, whose care was primarily her responsibility. Students might also consider whether Rowlandson's decision to publish at all and her willingness to give her story a moral significance that goes beyond the merely personal constitute daring enlargements of the traditional place allotted to Puritan women. Such enlargements of woman's sphere are of particular interest to feminists today (see Unit Three).

As writing question 3 suggests, it can be useful to compare Rowlandson's moralizing with Mather's. In general, Mather's is directed toward predicting the fate of a "nation," the whole group of Puritan colonizers. In contrast, although Rowlandson clearly sees herself as part of this group, her fate bound up with theirs, she tends to moralize more specifically on what the captivity experience supposedly means in terms of her own salvation. She sees divine intervention involved not only in large affairs of state, such as who makes war upon whom, but also in such small matters as whether or not her feet get wet when she is crossing a river.

Perhaps by asking students to write in their class journals, you might encourage them to consider whether they see Rowlandson's sense of divine involvement in her life as absurd, arrogant, or perhaps justified. At the same time, students might consider whether they have any sense of divine intervention — or larger, more vague spiritual purpose — in their own lives. Don't be alarmed if students testify to having such feelings and perhaps to being more sympathetic to Rowlandson's moralizing than they would be to Mather's. If you want to encourage further reflection on this issue, ask students to consider how one might go about convincingly communicating to others a sense of personal divine purpose. Does Rowlandson do it effectively or does she repel readers? Can it be done effectively, or are some experiences too ineffable to share?

We regret that space did not permit including more captivity narratives in this unit. They are extraordinarily rich documents for demonstrating the shaping of English perceptions of the Native Americans, and the stories they tell are irresistible to students. Teachers looking for a way to expand the literary content of a course based on this unit would do well to consider the sample syllabus on page 50, in which we have added readings from *Puritans among the Indians*, an excellent collection of captivity narratives by women and men and the later eighteenth-century narrative by Mary Jemison (bibliographic information on both is given with the syllabus).

ALTERNATIVE ENGLISH ACCOUNTS

LION GARDENER, FROM "RELATION OF THE PEQUOT WARS" (p. 85)

Students may need some help understanding in what senses Gardener's account is "alternative," as he will probably sound pretty much like a Puritan to them. You will need to emphasize the ways in which he is critical of the Puritan leadership (who are his employers); the reading questions should help with this task. Also, writing question 2 will give students the chance to evaluate his "alternative" status for themselves.

You should also point out that Gardener is not "on the Indians' side" in any contemporary sense. He is no Dances with Wolves. He does not question the English people's right to settle in North America, and he has no qualms about helping them to protect their settlements with military force if need be — indeed, that's his job. Gardener, however, differentiates sharply between Native American allies of the English and Native American enemies. Native American allies, in his view, should be treated more or less as equals of the English. Moreover, he appears to believe that with better diplomacy most, if not all, Native Americans could be turned into allies. That is, he appears to believe that the English have brought Native American hostilities on themselves by their bad management.

From our contemporary perspective, this view may be naive, in that Gardener is underestimating the scope of English ambitions in the region and the aggressiveness with which they are willing to pursue their ambitions. In other words, there are serious material conflicts between English and Native Americans that would probably lead to war no matter how canny the English, including Gardener himself, are in dealing with the Native Americans. Nevertheless, it is at least clear that Gardener does not condemn Native Americans as a group and would have no problem with a negotiated settlement that allowed them to continue to live in their own areas in the region.

Writing Analytically

Writing question 1 should enable students to uncover Gardener's underlying attitudes as they look at the policy recommendations he appears to be making. This assignment should also help underscore the ways in which Gardener dissents from the views of the colonial leaders. If students write both this assignment and the next one, attending to his dissent can help them deal with the optional questions about Gardener's "alternative" status.

By inviting comparisons with Bradford or Underhill, writing question 2 encourages students to examine the ways in which Gardener attempts to make himself and his views of the Pequot War sound credible. Commenting wryly on the impractical or outright disastrous decisions of the less experienced men under whom he must work (such as Bradford, perhaps), he creates a persona for himself that could be characterized as "wily combat veteran." This persona encompasses Gardener's attempt to emphasize, among other things, his own military prowess.

Thus the Gardener excerpt raises some of the same questions concerning personal bravery that we discussed in connection with the Underhill selection. See that discussion (p. 28) for more ideas about how to pull out these issues for a comparison of the two accounts.

JOHN EASTON, "A RELATION OF THE INDIAN WAR" (p. 93)

Of all the English texts included here, Easton's is arguably the most sympathetic to the Native Americans and perhaps the closest to modern liberal views of the conflict. He goes much further than Gardener. In his accounts both of the death of John Sassamon and of the prewar parley with Metacomet and his councilors, Easton strongly implies that the English are the aggressors in the quarrel and that the Native Americans protest, with justice, only after enduring a number of wrongs.

While students should grasp this perspective in Easton readily enough, you may need to underscore that his view aims explicitly to contradict and undermine the view put forward by Puritan leaders such as Increase Mather (especially since Easton's concluding denunciation of the Puritan leadership is rather incoherent). In fact, one might question Easton's sympathy for the Native Americans on the grounds that he is really not as interested in helping them as he is in opposing the Puritan leaders, who have exercised oppressive religious intolerance against his home colony of Rhode Island. You might ask students to prepare in small groups for class debate on which of these is really his top priority, as indicated by the evidence of his textual presentation.

Writing Analytically

The preceding in-class activity would be good preparation for writing question 1, which calls attention to Easton's characterization of Native Americans. Before students write, raising the possibility that Easton's motives are complex might prevent simplistic papers that extol or lambast Easton's "political correctness."

Since Easton goes head to head with Mather on a number of issues, Easton and Mather make excellent texts to lay side by side for consideration of issues of working with sources (see p. 24). Writing questions 2 and 3 call attention to these comparisons. The questions could also be used as the basis for in-class debates.

NATIVE AMERICAN ACCOUNTS

PAPER LEFT ON A BRIDGE POST AT MEDFIELD, MASSACHUSETTS (p. 102)

This might seem like a rather slight text to bear the weight of the important considerations to which we call attention in the accompanying questions. Nevertheless, the text's very brevity invokes the problem of finding Native American textual evidence of the events of this time period — and we suggest that you highlight this problem in discussing this selection.

In our extensive research in the period, this paper is the only text we have come across written by a Native American who was not an English ally.

Even so, we have the problem of relying on Gookin for preserving it, as the headnote points out. The voice is so important, though, that we want to take the risk of including a text whose authorship may be open to question.

Writing Analytically

For the writing question, we ask students to assume that the paper is genuine. In introducing this assignment, you should remind students of how few Native Americans were literate in this time period. Their own Algonkian languages did not have a written form (although a type of picture writing was sometimes used). John Eliot composed a Bible written in Algonkian, using English letters, and English efforts to teach Native Americans to read either English or Algonkian were almost always associated with attempts to convert them to Christianity. Learning to write in either language was less important, except for the favored few — very few — Native Americans being groomed as Christian clergy for their own people. There probably were few, or no, Native Americans in the 1600s who were sufficiently literate to create written records of their own views of the period's events (oral traditions concerning these events have been preserved in New England Native American communities, however). This information should help students to appreciate the political shock value of the Medfield paper.

A follow-up discussion in class after students have written this assignment might profitably focus on the larger question of the value of education as a means to political activism. Encourage students to contribute to this discussion any contemporary examples they mentioned in their response to the writing question. Students might also speak from their own experience.

WABAN, SPEECH AT THE END OF KING PHILIP'S WAR, RECORDED AND WITH A REPLY BY DANIEL GOOKIN (p. 103)

As with the Medfield bridge post paper, we have here a rather slight text upon which we must nevertheless place much importance because written Native American records of the events of the 1600s are so scanty. On Native American literacy in this period, see our comments concerning the bridge post paper (p. 34). Some credit can be given to Gookin for his willingness, far beyond that of most other English commentators, to record the actual words of Native American participants in the events of the period (or at least to claim to be doing so).

Students may be inclined to suspect that Waban's conversion to Christianity served simply as an attempt to placate or manipulate the English. They might also be tempted to condemn him for abandoning his native religion. While students should be allowed to raise such questions, we think they should also be cautioned against too quickly dismissing the possibility that he is sincere. Students who have experienced religious conversions themselves may want to speak to this point.

Teachers can point out that intercultural contacts throughout human history have resulted in various kinds of conversions. Both Christianity and Islam, for example, have been and still are proselytizing actively worldwide. Western music, film, and fashion have been promoted successfully worldwide for profit, often at the expense of indigenous cultures and sometimes in direct conflict with them — for example, when fashionable Western attire conflicts with what is considered properly modest and chaste for women in a non-Western culture. Students might be asked to speculate in their class journals on whether such changes constitute progress or cultural imperialism.

Writing Analytically

As writing question 1 makes clear, we think it would be best to direct attention in class to the rhetorical issue of whether Waban comes across more as a pointed critic of the English or as a pathetic pleader for the Native Americans. The issues raised in writing question 1 could be parceled out to small groups in preparation for in-class debate. In our experience, students of color are often the most canny analysts of the rhetorical issues in situations like Waban's, and their responses to him are by no means uniformly condemnatory. They appreciate the complexities of his situation. You might be making a mistake, then, if you encouraged wholesale condemnation of Waban in hopes of putting students of color at ease.

Writing question 2 nicely parallels question 1 in that it raises rhetorical issues that European American students may be especially well prepared to address (as students of color are to address question 1). Many European American students come to college vaguely sympathetic to issues of racial justice, only to discover that their well-meaning interest may be taken as patronizing or intrusive by the people they want to help. Talking about Gookin's rhetorical problems can assist them in putting these sometimes uncomfortable learning experiences in perspective.

WILLIAM APESS, FROM *EULOGY ON KING PHILIP* (p. 107)

Apess provides an extremely powerful Native American voice in this unit — indeed, as we note earlier, the whole unit can be said to prepare for and support him. We need him in order to diversify the negotiations more fully, although it must be made clear to students that he is writing more than one hundred years after the main events recounted in the other Unit One texts. Teachers can point out that Apess shares the students' position in the writing course in that he is confronted with the task of piecing together a view of the past from texts that he knows are "partial," in the various senses of that word.

For Apess, added to these usual problems of working with sources is the conviction that the existing record is largely hostile to his own people. But it also appears that he has the oral traditions of his people to draw upon (for instance, this must be the source of the speech he attributes to Metacomet at the start of the war). Apess explicitly takes on the task of correcting the dominant record and arguing for what he knows will be an unpopular, minority view.

Apess is by far the most "modern" of the texts in Unit One, not only in his prose style but also in his perspective. Obviously, he takes a revisionist view of the English histories, pointing out how they fail to do justice to Native Americans. He is, of course, protesting the events themselves, but also the representation of them in these histories. For example, he attacks Mather's attempt to claim religious justification for English violence against Native Americans. It is noteworthy that Apess condemns this strategy as unchristian (he is a Methodist minister).

Moreover, Apess traces what he regards as the distortions in the dominant histories to an overall pattern of white racism. He sees Puritan treatment of the Native Americans as preparing the way for European American society's enslavement of African Americans, which was continuing in his own day. He urges all Americans of color to make common cause against racially motivated oppression. You should point out the sophistication of Apess's rhetorical strategies and theoretical positions.

Student reaction to Apess may vary widely. Some students will embrace him as a champion of justice and an ally in voicing their own distaste for the Puritans. Others will condemn him as another "politically correct" haranguer; these students may argue that they have no way to tell whether to believe Apess or the texts he attacks: "He's just as prejudiced as the other side." Many students will be disturbed by Apess's obvious anger and his willingness to link historical narrative with a polemical purpose: "He's not being objective!"

We suggest that you allow these views to be voiced without endorsing or condemning them. Strive to keep the focus of discussion on Apess's rhetorical strategies, as in writing questions 1 and 2. Students should not be making arguments about whether Apess's view of the history is right; rather, they should be making arguments about how persuasive his view would have been to his contemporary audience — or how persuasive it is to them — basing their response on textual evidence.

Writing Analytically

Writing question 1 calls attention to a rhetorical strategy in which Apess gives his European American audience a glimpse of just how different things look from the perspective of a person of color. Writing question 2 calls attention to a strategy in which Apess demonstrates his awareness of values his white audience holds dear, such as respect for their own legal system — even when these values work against the well-being of his people.

Writing question 3 asks students to confront directly the issue of what to do when sources conflict. (For ideas on how to handle this assignment, see also the discussion of working with sources, p. 24.) Of course, Apess conflicts with the English sources much more dramatically than they do with each other because the moral and political perspective from which he writes is so different. He rejects the validity of the English invasion of America; his highest aspiration is not to be a loyal ally of European Americans; and he voices considerable skepticism that a negotiated settlement that is fair to the Native Americans can be reached. The drastic quality of these conflicts will force students to reveal their own moral and political assumptions.

TREATIES, LAWS, AND DEEDS

These documents are best treated as part of the exploration of a theme addressed in one of the assignment sequences. Special issues relating to each document are noted in the reading and writing questions that accompany it. We briefly discuss the writing questions here.

TREATY OF PEACE AND ALLIANCE BETWEEN MASSASOIT AND THE PLYMOUTH COLONISTS (p. 136)

Writing Analytically

The writing question calls attention to the kind of treaty this is. It cannot really be called a peace treaty because the signers were not at war before it was signed. Perhaps a better title would be "treaty of peaceful coexistence." But the nature of this treaty makes the one major difference between the two versions of it all the more significant: Bradford's version omits the clause promising that the colonists will leave behind their weapons when visiting the Native Americans. Thus Bradford's version emphasizes the threat to the English posed by the Native Americans — who must be cautioned to leave their arms at home — but not vice versa. This imbalance in the official view of their relations was a strong contributing factor to the eventual failure of this treaty to keep the peace.

TREATY OF HARTFORD (p. 137)

Writing Analytically

The writing question calls attention to the imbalance of power implied in this treaty, particularly as it serves English interests.

UNRESTRICTED DEED (p. 139)

Writing Analytically

The writing question calls for a comparison with the restricted deed to consider how relations of peaceful coexistence in a bicultural society might have been worked out.

TREATY OF SUBMISSION (p. 141)

Writing Analytically

Writing question 1 raises the issue of cultural imperialism in relation to Christian conversion efforts. Were the English really concerned about the Native Americans' spiritual well-being, or were they simply trying to make the Native Americans more docile? You should try to forestall the response of easy cynicism here. For further discussion of some of these issues, see our comments on the Waban selection (p. 35).

Writing question 2, by inviting comparison with two other treaties, highlights the issues of power imbalance in treaty-ratified relations. Read chronologically, the three documents suggest a steady erosion of Native American status in the relationships, from equal or even dominant partners to subordinates and slaves.

RULES FOR THE PRAYING INDIAN TOWN OF CONCORD, MASSACHUSETTS (p. 143)

Writing Analytically

Writing question 1 raises issues similar to those raised by writing question 1 for the previous selection. Here we see in detail how the English were attempting to drive the Native Americans away from their own culture and toward a more English lifestyle. But what are their motives?

Writing question 2 turns the issue of motive on its head and suggests that the rules might actually be a clever public relations effort on the part of the Christian Native Americans, supposing that they do want to be Christians but do not want to become entirely Anglicized in lifestyle. This assignment raises fascinating questions about what kinds of information distinctive communities are willing to share about themselves in the larger, homogeneous American public sphere. Such questions are so emotionally loaded for some students that they might best be approached, at least initially, as journal writing assignments. Students might then be asked to volunteer to read journal entries, so as to ease into a class discussion of the issues; but it would be okay, too, to leave the details private in journals.

LAWS PERTAINING TO INDIANS, MASSACHUSETTS BAY COLONY (p. 145)

Writing Analytically

The writing question calls attention to the fact that these laws do not assume total Native American assimilation into an English way of life, certainly not to the degree that the Praying Indian town rules might be said to do. These are what we might call "boundary laws," seeking to define and maintain livable distances between two ways of life that are greatly at odds.

Nevertheless, it would be difficult to argue that these laws treat the two ways of life with parity: The English way is favored.

Contemporary examples could be explosive here, as with the previous selection, and we would caution against forcing students to share them in class. One way to manage a discussion, though, might be to invite students to consider what kind of public education the United States ought to provide for all new citizens. This would be a way of stating the degree to which our society expects immigrants to conform. Must they learn English? stop using their native tongues? dress "like us"? eat "like us"? How much do they need to know about American history and culture, and how much do "we" need to know about theirs? And so forth.

RESTRICTED DEED   (p. 148)

Writing Analytically

The writing question asks students to consider this document as establishing the sort of "boundary laws" discussed in our comments on the previous selection. See that discussion for more ideas on how to handle this question.

ANDREW PITTIMEE AND OTHER NATIVE AMERICAN FIGHTERS FOR THE ENGLISH IN KING PHILIP'S WAR, PETITION   (p. 149)

Writing Analytically

The writing question calls students' attention to the complex rhetorical situation of the petitioners. It is very similar to Waban's, and we suggest you look at our comments on page 35 for help with this assignment. This document could be said to dramatize the situation even more sharply. Pittimee and his fellow petitioners are owed a hearing not because they have suffered passively at English hands, as have Waban and his group, but rather because they have worked actively on behalf of the English cause at great personal risk. Moreover, Pittimee and company have much more explicit requests to make than do Waban and company; it will thus be easier for students to evaluate the likely success of the petition.

ASSIGNMENT SEQUENCES

As noted in the introduction to this manual, we see the assignment sequences as an integral part of the approach we wish to promote in *Negotiating Difference*. The sequences put provocative voices directly in dialogue with each other — both in the readings and then, in discussions of the readings, among the students in your class. Of equal importance, the sequences stress the need to develop material carefully — rereading, rethinking, and revising — in order to produce the richest rhetorical responses in student writing.

You can use the reading questions that accompany each selection to aid students in preparing to write for the sequences. While the writing questions in each sequence tend to build on one another with added complexity as one moves through the sequence, you should also feel free to select among these questions to tailor the sequence to your students' needs and interests (you will see some of this adaptation of sequences going on in the model syllabi that we include beginning on p. 49). In what follows we will briefly discuss each sequence and its writing questions.

Sequence 1. How did Native Americans negotiate with the English colonists in power? (p. 153)

This is the sequence that perhaps most focuses on the "contact zone" aspect of Unit One. Native Americans found themselves increasingly at a power disadvantage in colonial New England, and it became both more necessary and more dangerous to persuade the English to hear their points of view. This sequence is designed to highlight the complex rhetorical arts of this contact zone, forestalling any easy condemnation of Native American speakers as toadies or any easy cynical praise for them as cunning manipulators. To see how the power disadvantage developed, you can pair this sequence with sequence 3, assigning that sequence first. This sequence can also be paired with sequence 2, as in our model syllabus on page 48.

Question 1 reminds students that what they may be inclined to dismiss as toadying might really be a life skill with which they are intimately acquainted. The more sophisticated students, particularly students of color, will probably understand this question very well. You should try to give these students some support in class discussion, to help the whole class perceive the important differences between unequal power relations that stem from personal antagonisms and those that are based on group prejudices.

Question 2 invites students to have some fun with the idea of promoting cultural and moral values via rules. This question might be given as an alternative to question 3, since not all students enjoy the opportunity to write something funny. Or, composing the rules might be done by the whole class together (you write them on the board as they are called out) or in small groups, as preparation for writing question 3.

Question 3 combines issues raised in writing question 1 for Waban and in writing question 2 for the Praying Indian town rules. See our comments on these assignments (pp. 35 and 39) for help with this one. If students have already written either or both of these assignments, they should be encouraged to rework their earlier writing into the response to this assignment if they wish.

Question 4 moves on to a somewhat more challenging assignment, just as the Pittimee rhetorical situation is more challenging than the others (see our remarks on p. 40). Although this assignment is similar to the writing question for Pittimee, it goes beyond that assignment in several respects.

Through the role-playing option, it asks students to consider more seriously and in more detail just what the English response to this petition might have been. Moreover, through the alternative assignment of comparing the petition with Waban's speech (on which students have already been working in this sequence), this assignment invites students to move on from local observations about a particular rhetorical situation to generalizations about a kind of rhetorical situation.

Question 5 shifts to a writer, Apess, whose challenge to English authority is much more open and sustained than any the students have examined so far in this sequence. Apess actually contests the facts in English accounts such as Bradford's. Students are called on here to perform the more analytic task of deciding which historical account is more persuasive, and why. Both this assignment and the next one may recall work students have already done for writing question 3 on Apess (see our remarks on p. 38). We regard such repetitions as positive, because they give students a chance to reconsider and revise their texts.

Question 6 stays with Apess, the most substantial writer in this sequence, for the slightly more abstract issue of contending *interpretations* of facts in his and the English histories. At the end of this question, students are presented with an option that invites them to consider the larger implications of the kinds of struggles for rhetorical dominance that they have been studying in this sequence: namely, who gets the hearts and minds of the schoolchildren of the future. You might give students a choice of writing either question 5 or 6, indicating that you think 6 is slightly harder.

Question 7 puts the issues raised in this sequence in the broadest theoretical framework yet, asking students to generalize on the strategies available to the marginalized rhetorician. Remind them that they may have, in effect, dramatized themselves as marginalized rhetoricians in their responses to question 1 in this sequence. They may wish to incorporate what they wrote for that assignment as one example in the larger paper they are writing for this assignment.

Sequence 2. How did English writers create favorable images of themselves for the historical record? (p. 154)

This is the sequence to choose if you want to focus on the historiographic issues raised in Unit One. It could be nicely combined with sequence 4, which poses for students a practical problem in reading historical sources. We suggest doing sequence 4 first, if you want to pair them. Let students get a sense of the practical problems, and then lead them on to the more theoretical considerations here. Also note that we have paired this sequence with sequence 1 in a model syllabus (p. 48).

Question 1 asks students to examine a time when they wrote a sort of selective history of themselves. In our experience, students have given a lot of thought to the strategies they employ in these obligatory autobiographies (even if we don't always think their strategies are effective). There-

fore, this assignment can get them talking at once about the rhetorical issues raised in this sequence.

Question 2 tries to link the idea of selective autobiography from question 1 with the kind of selective history writing Bradford is doing. Indeed,
you might even point out to students that one striking choice he has made
is *not* to tell the history of Plymouth colony as a background for his own life,
although an autobiography of Bradford, the colony's leader for most of its
existence, would be virtually coterminous with the colony's most important
events. This assignment resembles writing question 1 for Bradford (see our
discussion on p. 31 for further ideas).

Question 3 moves the historiographic analysis along by pointing out that
a historian may shape readers' perceptions by giving open directions, as
well as by silently omitting or emphasizing certain elements. This assignment may seem easier, in a way, than the previous one because it is easier to
find explicit statements in a text than it is to speculate about what statements aren't there. The difficulty comes, however, in that students are willing to accept that a historian must select information to tell us; it's clearly
impossible to tell everything. But they are less willing to accept that the
historian might be allowed to give readers directions for how to understand what is selected. This assignment, then, confronts students'
commonsense notion that all a historian does is report what is "there."

As here, writing question 3 for Mather invites a comparison with Underhill
(see our comments on p. 30). That assignment calls the directions given to
readers "moralizing." If students have already written that assignment, now
would be a good time to ask them to reconsider whether "moralizing" is
really the right term for what these historians are doing. If students have
already written the Bradford and Mather assignments resembling sequence
questions 2 and 3, you might give them a choice of rewriting one or the
other instead of asking that both be reworked here.

Question 4 pauses, as it were, in the progression of levels of analysis to
consolidate the selecting and interpreting or directing issues with a specific
example, Mary Rowlandson's work. This assignment resembles writing question 2 for Rowlandson. There, however, the focus is more on Rowlandson
as a possible crypto- feminist. Here the focus is on the way gender compli-
cates Rowlandson's function as a historian.

Question 5 introduces a new task for the historian beyond mere reporting: refuting accounts that disagree with his or her own. Sometimes, as in
the cases of Underhill and Mather, the competing history is actually mentioned and refuted explicitly. Or, as in the case of Easton, an opposing view
may not be cited in the text, but a certain defensiveness or overqualification
in the tone will suggest that the writer has an opponent in mind. This
assignment sensitizes students to these various strategies of rebuttal by asking them to compare two writers (Easton and Underhill) who approach
the task differently.

Question 6 begins by once again moving the analysis up one level of
abstraction, pointing out moments (in Gardener and Gookin) when the
historian departs so far from a purely reportorial role that he or she com-

ments openly on the power of history writing to shape perceptions and, especially in the case of Gardener, actions. The larger focus of the assignment is not simply to note or analyze this strategy, however, but rather to speculate on the validity of what it suggests — namely, that history writing does have such power. To make the case that it does (but shouldn't?) or doesn't (but should?), encourage students to draw on all that they have written for the sequence and to cannibalize earlier papers to put this final effort in trim running order.

Sequence 3. How did the English colonists attempt to conform the Native Americans to an English way of life? (p. 156)

This sequence concentrates on issues of cultural imperialism that have been raised at various points in the unit. The focus here, really, is on how rhetoric can be used as an instrument of domination — although Apess is included to avoid giving the idea that Native Americans took this kind of pressure without resistance. Another idea is to pair this sequence with sequence 1, assigning sequence 3 first.

The first three sequence questions all repeat assignments that were given as writing questions with the selections (see our comments on pp. 38, 39, and 40). They all ask students to tease out the implications of these terse documents, to imagine what power relations they refer to. Instead of having the entire class write all three assignments, you might parcel them out among small groups, with several groups working on each one if necessary. Groups could report back to the whole class on their findings.

Question 4 asks students to move up one, and maybe two, levels of abstraction. One level: Rather than considering the documents in isolation, students are now encouraged to see them as forming a pattern of a certain kind of interaction between the English and the Native Americans. We are now asking students to generalize about what the English were trying to do to or with the Native Americans on the basis of these texts. Or to go to another level: Students can use this English–Native American interaction (which they will have to identify with the help of textual evidence) as itself an example of a kind of interaction between social groups. Students are then invited to speculate as to whether this kind of interaction is typically American; that is, does it characterize our culture's standard way of dealing with the culturally "different"?

Encourage students to bring in personal experience here: It can be powerful. But you may have to remind them that they must try to analyze their experience in terms of *group membership*. A student (often male) who has developed a debased-Byronic persona may want to claim that he knows how the Native Americans feel because everybody at his high school hassled him for wearing a nose ring. This need not be a bathetic example if you require this student to think about who the nose-ring wearers are and who the groups that hassle them are. Encourage him (or her) to think about what the idea of "youth culture" might mean and why it might be regarded as oppositional by older people.

Question 5 shifts to the issue of resistance to domination. If students have already written writing questions 1 and 2 for Apess (see our discussion on p. 37), they will see that their responses can be used as illustrations of the kinds of rhetorical strategies called for in this larger assignment. Something else that may be new in students' consideration of Apess is the emphasis on his representation of an alternative way of life. He is not only protesting injustice or protesting the destruction of a culture that is now long gone. He also still has something to defend — his Native American culture and its critical perspective on white culture — and students should not be allowed to neglect this aspect of his argument.

Question 6 really builds on question 4. You can have students proceed directly to it, skipping question 5, if you feel that Apess's resistance will be adequately treated somewhere else in your course. This assignment intensifies the focus on the question of what American society does to or with people to make them assimilate. Now students are invited to generalize on this issue — not on the milder model of a dominated people, subject to a conqueror's laws, but on the more painful model of a captive individual, personally terrorized into compliance. Again, students should be encouraged to bring in personal experience but to keep it responsive to the issue of relations among groups. We have found that this assignment is profoundly stirring to students, well worth a little extra time and perhaps some prepared in-class debates on the issues raised.

Sequence 4. *How can readers today piece together a biography of Metacomet or Weetamoo?* (p. 158)

This sequence obviously dramatizes two problems continually raised in this unit: how to select information to write a history and how to select this information if the topic of your research is obscure because of barriers of time, record keeping, and prejudice of record keepers.

Question 1 dramatizes, in very personal terms, the problem of piecing together sources — and students find it to be a lot of fun. Tell them the story of the blind men and the elephant: Each got hold of a different part of the beast and insisted that his characterization was correct: "The elephant is like a rope!" cried the one who grasped his tail. "No! The elephant is like a fan!" insisted another, who held his ear. And so on.

Let students choose to work on either Weetamoo or Metacomet. If they choose Weetamoo, they should write question 3, which helps amass material for a biography, and question 5, which asks them to write the biography itself. If they choose Metacomet (King Philip), they should write questions 2 and 4, which perform the same functions for that project. Students might be encouraged to work on questions 2 and 3 in small groups, pooling their information.

Question 6 asks students to generalize about the experience of history writing that they have just had. They are, of course, invited to use the text they have produced in response to question 4 or 5 as their prime example.

RESEARCH KIT

Please see our remarks on the Research Kits in the introduction to this manual (p. 11).

There are always a few students who become as fascinated by the Puritans as Pat is and who plunge eagerly into the in-depth research ideas suggested in "Ideas from the Unit Readings." In our experience, however, most students are quite happy to leave seventeenth-century New England behind after completing a sequence or two; for them, the "Branching Out" ideas will be more appealing. If you want to keep them on the topic of Unit One, try assignment 7 in "Ideas from the Unit Readings," which asks students to read historical novels set in seventeenth-century New England. This assignment gives them a whole new perspective on the material plus the excitement of discovering that they have some of the expert knowledge needed to follow the stories closely (*Hobomok*, for example, draws heavily on Bradford).

Fortunately, Unit One's general focus is on how Native Americans and immigrant peoples (that is, those from Europe, Africa, and Asia) represented each other. This is applicable to every region of the United States, and the assignments in "Branching Out" encourage students to investigate this issue in their region. These projects have the critical advantage of preventing students from thinking that Native American–immigrant controversies happened only long ago or far away. Also, in many regions Native American written records of these contacts and conflicts will be much more copious than they are in New England, and student researchers will be able to flesh out the Native American perspectives that are only sketched in Unit One.

One of your special concerns in guiding student research in this unit is to make sure that students understand the great diversity of Native American cultures in what is now the United States. The values, customs, and responses to outsiders that tribes in other parts of the country exhibit may be very different from what students have just seen among the seventeenth-century native people of New England. Caution students against generalizing casually about typical Native American attitudes and so on.

At the same time, you must make it clear to students — as is reiterated in the Research Kit itself — that the main focus of their research is never to represent Native American or immigrant cultures and histories in all their complexity. Rather, the focus is always to be on the *contacts* between Native American and immigrant groups and, more specifically, on how these contacts were represented textually by the various participants. Students should also understand that "texts" can be visual materials as well as printed ones — as "Branching Out" assignment 6 makes clear.

Special Research Problems

Some of the topics in "Ideas from the Unit Readings" are sufficiently obscure, especially if your school is located outside New England, that it might be a good idea for you to scout local library resources before sending students on the search. We don't think you should preselect research materials for them. Just make sure that when they do begin searching, they will be able to find some materials.

Another caution: Our opening list of places to search for information includes a pointer to Native American organizations such as tribal councils. We suggest that you do a little advance investigation to find out how such groups in your region would prefer to be approached. If your students are going to be interviewing Native American people in your region, instruct them in advance about proper interview etiquette (see also our advice on interviewing on p. 12). This includes not only coming prepared with questions and requesting permission for any taping or photographing, but also refraining from intrusive comments, such as requests that the interviewee "say something in Indian," or remarks about the interviewee's personal appearance or dress ("Why the funny haircut?"). You should also find out whether "Native American," "American Indian," or some other designation is the preferred terminology in your region (it varies).

Native American students in your class should not be pressured into providing any more information than they are comfortable sharing. You should not make any assumptions about what they know of their people's history or what they might be willing to talk about. Politely ask, before turning other students loose on them, and take no for an answer.

MODEL SYLLABI

The model syllabi are framed on a thirteen-week term, with week 14 being exam week. You can adapt them to your own number of weeks (if different) and number of class meetings per week. The model syllabi sometimes adapt the assignment sequences they use, omitting some questions or substituting others — you should feel free to be similarly flexible in developing your own syllabi. Remember, the sequences are not designed to be lockstep processes.

We assume that you will work in class on the reading questions accompanying the assigned selections as well as on the assigned writing and sequence questions (sometimes we give you suggestions in the syllabi for how to do so). Note that work on these questions can often be performed profitably in class in small groups. (For more information on group work, see p. 14.)

We suggest that students keep a class journal in which they write responses to the reading questions before the questions are discussed in class. (Also remind students to read the headnotes accompanying the selections before they come to class.) In other words, our plan is that each reading assignment ("Read Easton") also constitutes a writing assignment because students should jot responses to the text's reading questions in their journals. (For more information on the class journal, see p. 12.)

You should collect and review these journals at least as often as you collect students' writing portfolios. We suggest that students be graded according to some version of the portfolio method. (For more information, see p. 17.)

Syllabus using two sequences from Unit One

This syllabus combines sequences 1 and 2 to allow students to connect the power of writing history with the power of literacy itself.

Week 1

> Read: Unit One introduction
> Write: Sequence 1, question 1, or sequence 2, question 1

In class, look at both sequence questions together. Sequence 2, question 1 can be seen as a more specific instance of the general kind of situation described in sequence 1, question 1. You might offer students a choice as to which they prefer to write. Writing and sharing of what's written can take place in class.

Week 2

> Read: Bradford
> Write: Sequence 2, question 2
> Collect: Essay from week 1

Week 3

> Read: Underhill
> Collect: Essay from week 2

Week 4

> Read: Mather
> Write: Sequence 2, question 3

Week 5

> Read: Rowlandson
> Write: Revised essays (see next paragraph)
> Collect: Essay from week 4

Try to return the essay from week 4 by the end of this week so that students can consider it for their portfolios (or discuss it in class only, borrowing some time from Rowlandson and repaying the time the following week by spending less time on Easton, which is not as demanding as Rowlandson). In class, spend some time helping students revise, for grades, any two of the essays they've written so far.

Week 6

Read: Easton
Write: Sequence 2, question 5
Collect: portfolios, including class journals and one revised essay from week 5

Week 7

Read: Gardener
Collect: Essay from week 6

Note: The reading assignments for weeks 8 and 9 are relatively light, and no paper is due until week 10. These assignments can be combined into a single week if the class has needed more time on something in an earlier week and is behind at this point.

Week 8

Read: Waban/Gookin; Paper Left on a Bridge Post

Make sure to address the reading questions on Gookin that accompany the Waban selection, as well as those on Waban.

Week 9

Read: Rules for the Praying Indian Town of Concord
Write: Sequence 1, question 4

Week 10

Read: Pittimee
Collect: Essay from week 9

Week 11

Read: Apess
Write: Sequence 1, question 6

Week 12

Read: Apess (continued)
Write: Sequence 1, question 7, or sequence 2, question 6
Collect: Essay from week 11

Discuss sequence 1, question 7, and sequence 2, question 6, relating the power of literacy discussed in the former to the power of history writing discussed in the latter. Let students choose which of these assignments they would prefer to write.

Week 13

Write: Portfolios, including class journals
Collect: Essay from week 12; portfolios (week 13 or 14)

In class, help students prepare their portfolios for final submission. Class time can also be devoted to revising for grades the paper assigned in week 12 and one other sequence 1 paper. This is a good time to give lessons on any grammar or mechanics problems that are common among your students. Collect portfolios at the end of this week or exam week.

"Enriched" Syllabus: One sequence plus additional readings

This syllabus uses sequence 3 and the following texts. Bibliographic information for some of the texts is included here; the information on the others can be found in the Unit One Research Kit bibliography (pp. 162–64).

1. The complete text of Apess, *Eulogy on King Philip,* in *On Our Own Ground.* Teachers might put this book on reserve or, if preparing a course pack, include those portions of the *Eulogy* that are not presented in *Negotiating Difference* (they are brief and readily identifiable by comparing the two texts).

2. An additional Puritan reading that is very lively and much cited in the additional portions of Apess: *A Journal of the Pilgrims at Plymouth: Mourt's Relation.* This collection of journal entries was published by a man named Mourt; the authors are not given, but scholars believe that many of the entries were written by William Bradford. Our syllabus recommends assigning about twenty-five pages of this text, so we suggest that you ask students to buy it. It is available in paperback.

3. Vaughan and Clark, eds., *Puritans among the Indians: Accounts of Captivity and Redemption 1676–1724.* We recommend assigning about half of this collection of captivity narratives (it also includes the complete text of Rowlandson), so we suggest that you ask students to buy it. It is available in paperback.

4. Mary Jemison, who was not a Puritan, was taken captive in the late eighteenth century by the Seneca, an Iroquois Confederacy tribe with a culture significantly different from that of the Native Americans in New England. Also, her narrative was apparently composed orally and transcribed by her publisher, James Seaver, and contemporary scholars question the degree to which Seaver may have influenced the content of her story. Nevertheless, our syllabus suggests including five chapters from her narrative because we think this work provides interesting illustrations of how the captivity narrative genre developed and interesting points of comparison with the reactions of women captives in Vaughn and Alden. Jemison is not included in the Unit One bibliography. Editions include the following:

Jemison, Mary, with James Seaver. *A Narrative of the Life of Mary Jemison.* 1824. Reprinted in *Garland Library of Narratives of North American Indian Captivities,* vol. 41, edited by William Washburn. New York: Garland, 1977.

Seaver, James E. *A Narrative of the Life of Mrs. Mary Jemison.* 1824. Reprint, Norman: University of Oklahoma Press, 1995.

> Material from Jemison should be placed on reserve or included in a course pack.

For variety, this syllabus is not organized around portfolio grading. Instead, you might simply average the paper grades, a grade for the class journal and in-class participation, and the final paper grade counted double (a total of seven grades). The sheer number of papers, however, gives extra practice with the writing process. Also, you might encourage revision by giving students the option of rewriting any or all of the first four papers; the grade recorded for a rewritten paper would be the average of the original grade plus the grade for the revision (if it is higher — some students will try to "rewrite" merely by making a few corrections or responding only to your comments on the first version, but if these amount to no more than cosmetic changes, you should not hesitate to leave the grade unchanged).

Week 1

Read: Unit One introduction
Write: Sequence 3, question 2 and questions 1 and/or 3

Ask students to write and share questions 1 and 3 in class; alternatively, you could assign one or both questions to small groups. Students can then choose which question they would like to write about to hand in. All students will write question 2, which should also be discussed in class.

Week 2

Read: Laws Pertaining to Indians; Waban/Gookin
Collect: Essays from week 1

In addition to asking students to jot down their responses to the reading questions for both selections, have them make notes in their journals on Waban/Gookin writing question 2, and then discuss their answers in class.

Week 3

Write: Sequence 3, question 4

Devote class time this week to working on this challenging writing assignment.

Week 4

> Read: *Mourt's Relation*, the section beginning "Thursday the 22nd of
> March" on the Massasoit/Carver treaty; "Journey to Pokanoket";
> "Voyage Made by Ten . . . "; "Journey to Kingdom of Nemasket";
> and "Relation of Our Voyage to the Massachusets"
> Collect: Essay from week 3

You may want to provide reading questions for *Mourt's Relation* that focus on how these stories present the Native Americans and the possibilities
for peaceful coexistence with them; you can direct attention especially to
the incidents that are also treated in Apess.

Week 5

> Read: Apess (including the parts not printed in *Negotiating Difference*,
> for which you may want to provide reading questions)
> Write: Class journals (make sure they are up to date)

Week 6

> Read: Apess (continued)
> Collect: Class journals

In class, begin to discuss sequence 3, question 5. Parts of this question
might be parceled out among small groups.

Week 7

> Write: Sequence 3, question 5

Week 8

> Read: Rowlandson
> Collect: Essay from week 7

If you choose to assign the entire Rowlandson text from Vaughan and
Clark, rather than the excerpt in *Negotiating Difference*, you may wish to supply some reading questions for the additional parts.

Week 9

> Read: Rowlandson (continued)
> Write: Rowlandson, writing question 2

Weeks 10–12

> Read: Captivity narratives (see the following discussion)
> Collect: Essay from week 9 (collect in week 10)

At this point, the class will take a break from sequence 3 to spend more
time on additional captivity narratives. Assign the narratives of your choice,

and provide reading questions if necessary. We suggest the following, from Vaughan and Clark: Swarton and Mather; Duston and Mather; Williams; and Hanson. From Mary Jemison, we suggest chapters 3–5, 9, and 16.

Hints for discussion: Hanson is female; the narratives of the women Swarton and Duston are "edited" by Cotton Mather; Williams is male. Jemison, in addition to being outside the period, also had enough help from her publisher, Seaver, that some scholars question the extent to which the narrative can be considered her work. This assortment of narratives allows for comparisons between male and female versions (Vaughan and Clark also contain other male narratives). Students might also discuss what is involved in a male editor's assisting — or appropriating — a woman's narrative: How much help is too much? How does the story get slanted by an editor?

You will probably want to devise a writing assignment dealing with the additional captivity narratives, to be collected in week 11 or 12. One possibility: Students might attempt to generalize about the captivity narrative as a genre.

Week 13

Write: Sequence 3, question 6

To conclude this course, we suggest returning to question 6, which invites some pretty broad speculations about the captivity experience and how this experience is represented in various texts. To the texts already cited in the sequence question, add the additional captivity narratives that you have assigned. Students might work in class on this question throughout the week and prepare written responses to it to be due at or after the last class.

Syllabus using sequences from Units One and Six

This syllabus combines sequence 2 from Unit One, on the shaping power of history, with a sequence on a similar theme from Unit Six: sequence 1, "Why were we in Vietnam? Why did we stay?" A few readings have been pared from each sequence to make the load more manageable. In a course that uses much group work, you could perhaps add the deleted selections back in, making them the responsibility of groups that would report on them to the class.

Week 1

Read: Unit One introduction
Write: Unit One, sequence 2, question 1, or Unit Six, sequence 1, question 1

In class, students can write and share, perhaps in small groups, their responses to the questions. Each question focuses on the selection of details in historical reporting and how this selection shapes perception. You might let students choose one or the other question to write about and hand in.

Week 2

> Read: Mather
> Collect: Essay from week 1

Week 3

> Read: Underhill
> Write: Unit One, sequence 2, question 3

Week 4

> Read: Easton
> Write: Unit One, sequence 2, question 5
> Collect: Essay from week 3

Week 5

> Read: Gardener
> Collect: Essay from week 4

Week 6

> Read: Waban/Gookin
> Write: Unit One, sequence 2, question 6

Ask students to make notes in their journals on Waban/Gookin reading questions 4 and 5 and writing question 2, to help prepare for the sequence writing question to be submitted to you.

Week 7

> Write: Revised essay from week 3 or 4; portfolios, including class journals
> Collect: Essay from week 6

In class, help students prepare their portfolios to be submitted next week. Each portfolio must include the class journal and a revision of the essay assigned in week 3 or 4. Also in class this week, to make the transition to the Unit Six sequence, review the work done in week 1.

Week 8

> Read: Unit Six introduction; Dodd
> Collect: Portfolios, including revised essay from week 3 or 4

Week 9

Read: White paper; Stone

Week 10

Read: King
Write: Unit Six, sequence 1, question 3 (modify by omitting Nixon)

Week 11

Read: Nixon
Write: Unit Six, sequence 1, question 5 (modify by omitting Johnson)
Collect: Essay from week 10

Week 12

Read: Potter
Write: Unit Six, sequence 1, question 4
Collect: Essay from week 11

Note that we are reversing the order of questions 4 and 5 to allow students to finish with an assignment that uses more of the sources.

Week 13

Write: Revised essay from week 10 or 11; portfolios, including class
        journals
Collect: Essay from week 12; portfolios (week 13 or 14)

In class, help students prepare their portfolios for final submission. Each portfolio must include, for grading, a revised version of the essay assigned in week 10 or 11. Collect the portfolios at the end of this week or exam week.

UNIT TWO

The Debate over Slavery and the Declaration of Independence

THEMES AND ISSUES IN UNIT TWO

Unit Two is a good choice if you want your course to focus on the teaching of argument. This unit is also a good choice if you have a large number of African American students in your class and want to provide them with rhetorical models from their cultural heritage. We have found that many black students are unfamiliar with the range of literature produced by African Americans before the Civil War, and they find it exciting and empowering to become acquainted with these writers.

The material in Unit Two also works well in a racially mixed class because it allows racist and antiracist arguments to be analyzed in a context at some chronological remove from the present day. There need be no debate about whether slavery was wrong or whether the racist views expressed by its defenders are morally reprehensible. You can simply establish these premises at the outset. Thus students can engage serious issues together without the distracting and potentially divisive pull of contemporary controversies. At the same time, they will find that all of the arguments here — including those that are clearly racist — are rhetorically sophisticated and repay close study.

We have also found that students usually respond with excitement to the unit's historical focus, particularly its sustained engagement with a major national document, the Declaration of Independence, and the ideas of a major national leader, Thomas Jefferson. Students seem to be hungry for the critical encounter with national history that this unit provides. The historical perspective also enhances the moral seriousness of the unit's issues concerning race relations: Students see that these issues are not merely contemporary sound bites but that they have long been fundamental to how we Americans define ourselves and our nation.

This unit grew out of our admiration for Frederick Douglass's speech "What to the Slave Is the Fourth of July?" We liked the idea of interrogating the Declaration of Independence on the subject of race, and we found that Douglass was not the only nineteenth-century African American writer to have done so. Indeed, we learned from *Crafting Equality: America's Anglo-African Word*, by Celeste Michelle Condit and John Louis Lucaites (see Unit Two bibliography), that some scholars consider African American rhetorical efforts, such as those included in this unit, to be a primary force in the establishment of the concept of equality as it is generally understood today.

Condit and Lucaites argue that the Declaration of Independence, although officially revered, was not much invoked in political debate in the first fifty years after it was written. It began to be cited, however, as the debate over slavery heated up, particularly after 1830. Attention then was focused on this document and its foundational importance to the United States, particularly by African American intellectuals who wanted to use its phrase "all men are created equal" to argue against slavery.

The focus in Unit Two on African American attackers of slavery is not meant to imply that no white people opposed slavery. Indeed, many did oppose it, as the Unit Two introduction points out. In addition to the important European American abolition leader William Lloyd Garrison, included in Unit Two, others can be found in Unit Three (such as Sarah Grimké and Elizabeth Cady Stanton). But the focus in Unit Two on African American abolitionists is meant to reflect the actual importance of black intellectuals in this fight and, in particular, their leadership in crafting what would be a very powerful antislavery argument invoking the Declaration of Independence. This argument was so powerful, in fact, that it elicited specific rebuttals from white defenders of slavery, a sampling of whose arguments is also included here.

This unit in no way represents all the kinds of debate that took place over slavery in antebellum America, and you should make this clear to students. The focus here is on one kind of argument only, that is, the argument over whether the Declaration of Independence allowed or contradicted slavery.

What Does "All Men Are Created Equal" Mean?

It could be said that the African American antislavery writers focused attention on a problem of interpretation: That is, if we Americans all say we believe in the words "all men are created equal," what are we really saying? What does this phrase actually mean?

You might ask students to consider this problem in two ways. One way is to try to get at what the phrase meant at the time of the signing of the Declaration of Independence, to try to get at its "original" meaning or the meaning "intended" by the Declaration's signers. Another way to address the question is to ask what the phrase can reasonably be interpreted to mean, never mind what the signers may have intended. This approach focuses on the way meaning is constructed by means of argument and for use in argument.

To talk about interpretation as a problem of getting at the original or intended meaning, invite students to consider a variety of kinds of evidence presented in Unit Two. First, there is evidence from the Revolutionary era itself. The Benjamin Banneker letter, Jonathan Jackson manumission paper, Prince Hall petition, Rhode Island resolution, and Bloomfield manumission speech all testify in one way or another to the fact that there were people at the time of the Revolution who clearly regarded black people as included in the new nation formed by the Revolution and in the ideals expressed in the Declaration. This evidence could be used to argue that the persistence of slavery after the Revolutionary era actually contradicts the ideals of the Revolution, particularly as expressed in the Declaration.

In *Notes on Virginia,* Jefferson condemns slavery as an institution that corrupts slave owners. Nevertheless, this condemnation is qualified by his observations in the same text on people of African descent; he suggests that they are inferior to whites and should be sent away from white society once slavery is abolished. The *Notes,* then, though opposing slavery, might be taken primarily as evidence *against* genuine antiracist feeling at the time of the Revolution. Another piece of evidence is the Virginia petition invoking Declaration ideals in order to preserve slavery.

The Declaration itself provides a mixed example. In his draft, Jefferson's inclusion of a paragraph condemning slavery as imposed on the colonies by the British crown suggests that he initially understood the Declaration as including black people and contradicting slavery. But other delegates to the Continental Congress insisted that this paragraph be removed, suggesting that these inclusive sentiments were not universal, and Jefferson signed the altered document, suggesting that perhaps his own sentiments were not strongly held. Encourage students to consider what bearing (if any) Jefferson's views in *Notes* should have on interpretation of the Declaration and the changes made in the draft text.

We are well aware that these documents constitute only a smattering of the primary-source evidence that could be amassed on this topic. They are certainly too few to allow any firm conclusions about the temper of Revolutionary times — and, consequently, students probably cannot come up with a definitive answer as to whether the Declaration was originally intended to include African Americans. But students will have the experience of trying to construct such an argument and reflecting on its difficulties.

We want students to realize that although the number of pieces of evidence given here is clearly inadequate to draw firm conclusions, it might be hard to say how much evidence would be enough. In other words, they will see that trying to arrive at this kind of interpretation via contemporary evidence is always problematic. That does not mean it cannot be done; it just means that at some point there must be an inductive leap, a decision that a particular amount of evidence, although admittedly not all the evidence, is "enough." You might also invite the class to discuss what constitutes "enough" evidence in different situations — for example, personal decisions, history research papers, and so on.

We also want students to see how one tends to push the interpretation of admittedly inconclusive evidence in the direction one wants to go for other reasons. That is, in the absence of (unattainable) totally "objective" criteria for interpreting the evidence, different motives will influence interpretation. If for some reason one wanted to maintain Jefferson's reputation as a great American, for example, one might wish to emphasize his condemnation of slavery in *Notes on Virginia*, to downplay its racism, and to claim that an inclusive interpretation of the Declaration had widespread power in Revolutionary times. One might then depict the persistence of slavery after the Revolutionary era as a falling off from the Revolutionary ideals that Jefferson tried to promote and that were strong at the time of our nation's founding.

In addition to examining Revolutionary-era evidence, students could also look at arguments in the later readings that attempt to say what was intended originally in the Declaration. For example, both George Fitzhugh and Albert Bledsoe claim that the Declaration was meant to be inclusive, but they deny any idealistic motives for this inclusiveness: Fitzhugh says that the inclusiveness simply indicates that Jefferson was so foolish as to allow himself to be led astray by the destructive ideas of the French Revolution, while Bledsoe suggests that it's a cynical attempt to drum up support for the American Revolution among the white social underclass — to let them think they'll be included in the privileges of the new order. David Christy, in contrast, says that the Declaration was meant to include only white men of property; and such Revolutionary opposition to slavery as there was he puts down to economic rather than ethical motives.

The original-intent argument can be found in attackers of slavery too. For example, Charles Langston presents his father's heroic participation in the Revolutionary War as evidence that African Americans were certainly included, and felt themselves to be included, in the ideals of the Declaration.

An interesting variation on this argument is presented by both David Walker and Frederick Douglass. They talk as if they can assume that the Declaration is inclusive, that its inclusive meaning is so clear as to be above debate — as if there were an inherited tradition that all were privy to, although this was certainly not the case in their day. Walker, for example, feels that simply to quote the Declaration at length is enough to indict his white contemporaries; he doesn't feel he needs to make a separate argument that the general terms of its ideals apply to slavery. Douglass silently appropriates the Declaration for his own position by declaring the abolitionists (white and black) to be the true heirs of the Revolutionary leaders.

Having had the experience of wrestling with some Revolutionary-era sources themselves, students will be in a good position to analyze the effectiveness of these interpretations and to point out what is problematic about them. It will be important for you to make sure they see that all invocations of historical intention here are problematic. Don't let students think that the antislavery people, because they hold the view about slavery that we believe to be morally correct today, must also be correct in their interpretation of the historical evidence. On the contrary, the slavery attackers face exactly the same difficulties in making this kind of original-intent argument as the slavery defenders do — and as students themselves do when they try to make their own arguments from the documents.

How Does Argument Make Meaning?

By exploring how to interpret a document by referring to contemporaneous sources, students will already have begun to see that every interpretation must be supported by argument. One can never simply point to original intention and think that the matter ends there. But the readings in this unit present a very wide variety of arguments concerning slavery and the Declaration, not only arguments having to do with the original intention of the document.

As already noted, if you want to teach argument, Unit Two is an excellent choice. By and large, the focus in these selections is on expository argument. Most of them rely mainly on logical appeals and are fairly moderate in their language, with a minimum of personal attack on opponents (in contrast, for example, to some of the arguments on "woman's sphere" in Unit Three).

The pieces certainly exhibit appeals to emotion and to the authority of the speaker/writer, as well as appeals to logic, which students should be invited to evaluate (the reading questions accompanying each selection call attention to these strategies). For example, masterful at appeals to both pathos and ethos is Frederick Douglass, with his brief but affecting evocations of the sufferings of slaves and his opening pretense of nervousness before a white audience.

Among the logical appeals, particularly interesting are the arguments that move between general principles (of human equality or the necessity for social order, for example) and specific applications of these principles (to slavery). Seeing how a number of writers make this movement should be helpful to beginning college students, who often have trouble with precisely this kind of argument but who must deal with it frequently in introductory courses that focus on fundamental disciplinary theories.

You must make sure that the class treats the arguments of all these writers seriously, not dismissing the proslavery arguments because we now believe that slavery was wrong. The point of this unit is not to prove that slavery was wrong. Rather, what we want to do is to see how different people argued over this vexing, controversial issue. For example, you should encourage students to see merit in such arguments as Bledsoe's general principle that society has the right to constrain the freedom of its individual members for its own greater good, even though here this principle is applied in defense of slavery.

NOTES ON THE UNIT READINGS

Each selection in the unit is accompanied by its own headnote, reading questions, and writing questions, so it can be assigned independently of the other readings or combined with others as you see fit. We have also grouped each reading with several other selections in at least one of the three assignment sequences offered at the end of the unit (the sequences are discussed on p. 73). We urge you to assemble your course reading and writing into one or more sequences, of either our design or your own.

In the following notes, we provide commentary on each of the unit's selections as well as guidelines for approaching and evaluating the writing questions.

JEFFERSON'S VIEWS ON SLAVERY

THOMAS JEFFERSON, DRAFT OF THE DECLARATION OF INDEPENDENCE (p. 174)

Whatever else you assign in Unit Two, of course you must assign this text, as it is the basis for all the other arguments and very few students are familiar with it. The version we have printed here, from Jefferson's autobiography, has the advantage of showing how Jefferson's draft of the document was reworked by his colleagues in the Continental Congress. This version illustrates not only the changes made in the document's content (most notably, the excision of a paragraph condemning slavery) but also the writing process itself. We want to acquaint students with processes of drafting and revising, and this important national document provides a compelling example. Most students will have assumed that Jefferson alone composed the Declaration, and at a single sitting.

Students may need a little help deciphering the way changes in the draft are represented typographically here. Jefferson's draft — before the Continental Congress made its changes — is printed in the main column, under the heading, "Draft Document." Within this draft, wording proposed by Jefferson that the congress decided to take out is printed in italics and enclosed in brackets. In the outside column is wording added by the congress, under the heading, "Text Added." In the last two paragraphs, congress made so many small changes in addition to excising the portion bracketed in italics that the entire new text is printed in the right-hand column.

Writing Analytically

Writing question 1 invites students to imagine the debate that might have taken place as the decision was made to omit the Declaration paragraph condemning slavery. In their papers, they will be playing the role of an eighteenth-century person. To help them get "in character," you should call their attention to the arguments they outlined in response to the first two reading questions. Presumably, these are arguments that students will need to address from the perspectives of the various personae they are assuming.

Writing question 2 sets next to the Declaration an argument by a proslavery writer, Albert Bledsoe, that echoes Declaration language and that does not mention slavery. It is not clear that the views Bledsoe expresses here contradict the Declaration (although when you read the whole passage in context, it's clear that Bledsoe thinks they do). If the Declaration calls for people to choose their own form of government, why could they not choose a "limited monarchy," to use one of Bledsoe's examples, if they decided that this form would be best for them? Of course, Bledsoe does not say who is to decide which government is best for people. There are plenty of complexities here, and you should make clear that you expect a wide range of answers in students' papers. By no means should it be assumed that Jefferson would condemn Bledsoe just because Bledsoe was proslavery.

Also, the general principles that Bledsoe expresses will actually appeal to some students. You should encourage them to express their approval of his ideas and not be put off by the fact that he was a slavery defender. This exercise helps students to see the difference between abstract principles and concrete applications, since they may approve of Bledsoe's principles but deplore his application. Similarly, they may decide that Bledsoe and Jefferson differ principally in the application of their principles.

THOMAS JEFFERSON, FROM *NOTES ON VIRGINIA* (p. 180)

This text is only slightly less crucial to the rest of Unit Two than the Declaration itself. It was widely known and cited by participants in the debate over slavery, often taken as an index of Jefferson's "true" views on slavery and race (see, for example, Benjamin Banneker and David Walker). You really need to assign this reading if you want to engage the problems of historical interpretation discussed under "What Does 'All Men Are Created Equal' Mean?" (p. 57).

When students discover (by reading the previous selection) that Jefferson wanted to put a paragraph condemning slavery into the Declaration of Independence, they will be delighted to hail him as a supporter of contemporary liberal racial views. Then when they read these passages from *Notes on Virginia*, they will discover that his views were much more complex — and problematic.

Writing Analytically

Among other difficulties is Jefferson's scientific tone here, especially in the passage from query 14, to which the rhetorical focus of writing question 1 calls attention. Some students will feel that he discusses people of African descent almost as if they were some sort of subhuman animal. These students will probably prefer the tone of moral reflection and anguish that creeps into query 18. Other students, though, will see no problem with a tone of scientific investigation into human subjects and will deplore the expostulations in query 18 as departing from the appropriate objectivity. Encourage debates between these different viewpoints.

Writing question 2 presents students with a problem in historical biography, asking them to synthesize Jefferson's views on slavery from both the Declaration and the *Notes.* You will need to discuss with students what to do when these sources fail to overlap and even contradict one another.

Writing questions 3 and 4 ask students to analyze opposing arguments. Question 3 is the easier of the two, since Walker's rebuttal of Jefferson's position in the *Notes* is easy to follow. The analysis may be complicated somewhat, however, by your urging students to consider whether Walker's open expression of his anger at Jefferson reduces his credibility. Question 4 is harder, since it is not clear that the Jefferson of the *Notes* would disagree with Fitzhugh here, even though Fitzhugh quotes Jefferson's own words from the Declaration to epitomize the position he rejects. In effect, students will have to deal with the problem posed in writing question 2 before they can answer this question; thus, assigning these two questions in sequence would be a good idea.

THE ANTISLAVERY BATTLE

BENJAMIN BANNEKER, LETTER TO THOMAS JEFFERSON (p. 189)

Written in response to Jefferson's negative assessment of black mental powers as expressed in *Notes on Virginia* and exhorting him in Declaration-accented language to act on behalf of black civil rights, this letter makes a very profitable assignment in tandem with the two Jefferson texts. Students are usually excited to discover that there was a free African American in Revolutionary times who challenged Jefferson in this way.

Banneker's style is especially convoluted and difficult for students. Fortunately, however, the letter is relatively short, and students are usually more willing to be patient with Banneker than they might be with another dense stylist because they admire his project. You may have to help them sort out the shapes of the sentences, identifying subjects, main verbs, and so on.

Writing Analytically

Banneker's style can also be described as one of his rhetorical strategies — that is, he may be using a convoluted, indirect way of developing his ideas in order to present them to Jefferson gently, without offending him. Writing question 1 calls attention to Banneker's difficult rhetorical situation in addressing the famous Jefferson, and style might be one of the considerations students address in responding to it. We have found that while some students admire Banneker's skill in presenting his controversial position, others feel he is excessively indirect and humble. You should encourage students to consider both views.

Writing question 2 gives students some practical experience in dealing with the rhetorical difficulties of writing a letter like Banneker's. If students don't like any of the personae offered in the assignment, you might suggest that they consider playing the part of someone from another disenfranchised group, such as women or indentured servants. This assignment is particularly helpful for students who feel Banneker should have been more aggressive with Jefferson. Writing their own letters will either give them a better appreciation of Banneker's difficulties or allow them to vent their own aggressive feelings.

Writing question 3 again raises the issue of the effectiveness of Banneker's rhetorical strategies. David Walker's style is the antithesis of Banneker's. Walker criticizes Jefferson harshly in his *Appeal* and vents his anger openly (of course, at the time Walker published his diatribe, Jefferson had been dead for several years). In imagining how Banneker might comment on Walker's style, we would expect students to have him gently criticizing Walker for being over aggressive. In contrast, they'd probably depict Walker as attacking Banneker angrily for handling Jefferson with kid gloves. Students might enjoy turning this assignment into a staged debate between a student playing Banneker and one playing Walker. To give more students a chance to speak, you might stage the debates within small groups.

DAVID WALKER, FROM *WALKER'S APPEAL* (p. 193)

Students' interest in Walker is usually heightened by the mysterious manner of his death, suggesting political martyrdom. They are also intrigued by the fact that the primary audience of his *Appeal* was African American. In most American schools, the primary audience of most reading materials is not racially specified and therefore is presumed to be white. Consequently, it is edifying for all students — and empowering for African Americans and other students of color — to find something assigned that is addressed without embarrassment to a black audience.

Writing Analytically

As writing question 1 points out, Walker was well aware that white people also would read his *Appeal*. They are, in effect, the audience "overhearing" the *Appeal* or sitting in the back rows of Walker's theater. Since Walker is thus addressing at least two audiences, his rhetorical purposes and strategies are complex. The first writing question attempts to get students to appreciate this complexity. You might ask half the class to write on Walker and his black audience and half to write on Walker and his white audience; students may wish to choose one or the other option based on their own racial identity, but you should not insist on that kind of match. Then have the students compare notes in class discussion or in small groups to put together a more complete picture of Walker's strategies.

A very timely issue raised by Walker is whether violence is justified in the resistance of racism (and, in his day, slavery). Walker threatens violence at several points in his argument, and white reaction to the *Appeal* suggests that these threats were taken seriously. Writing question 2 invites exploration of this issue by way of juxtaposing Walker with European American abolitionist William Lloyd Garrison, who was deeply committed to nonviolent resistance only. We would expect students to depict each man as condemning the other's approach to resistance, probably in pretty fiery language! Students might enjoy turning this assignment into a staged debate between a student playing Garrison and one playing Walker. To give more students a chance to speak, you might stage the debates within small groups. You might also invite students to diversify these debates by presenting the views on resistance expressed by contemporary leaders, such as Jesse Jackson or Louis Farrakhan.

Writing question 3 implicitly acknowledges that Walker could be said to be unfair in his criticism of Jefferson because he does not mention the condemnation of slavery that Jefferson expresses in query 18. You should make this acknowledgment explicit if no student points it out. You should also mention that Walker probably could not have known about the paragraph on slavery excised from the draft of the Declaration of Independence because Jefferson's autobiography, in which the paragraph is printed, was not published until 1829, the same year in which the *Appeal* came out. Nevertheless, even though Jefferson does condemn slavery in query 18, he seems to be concerned primarily with its evil effects on slave *owners* and with the threat of divine vengeance it brings on the white race. Thus there is still room for Walker to attack Jefferson here. We would expect students to develop a variety of positions in their responses to this assignment.

MARIA STEWART, AN ADDRESS DELIVERED AT THE AFRICAN MASONIC HALL (p. 200)

Maria Stewart is a bit of an awkward fit in Unit Two because she is the only writer who does not mention Jefferson or the Declaration. It's certainly worth including her, however, because she was one of the first women of any race to address mixed audiences on social reform issues, and students are usually quite excited to discover her. She also makes an interesting match with her friend David Walker, whose style shares some affinities with her own. Like Walker, her primary audience is African American (see our comments on Walker, p. 64, for why this is a provocative focus).

Writing Analytically

Stewart does use Declaration-accented language, as writing question 1 points out, and we hope that by writing this assignment, students will see the connection between her work and the rest of the unit. Stewart urges her African American audience to take various steps toward independence, which can be compared with the steps toward independence the colonists vow to take in the Declaration.

Writing question 2 raises the issue of the influence of Stewart's gender on her rhetorical strategies. To convey a sense of just how controversial it was in her day for a woman to address mixed audiences, read the Unit Three introduction and summarize the relevant parts for the class. Ask students to consider not only the few specific references Stewart makes to her gender but also the ways her gender inflects other remarks she makes, such as her frequent exhortations to black men. In class discussion, you might encourage students to compare Stewart's public persona with the personae of contemporary women political leaders.

Writing question 3 offers students the opportunity to collect a complete account of Stewart's rhetorical strategies, including points they may have included in responses to the first two writing questions. We have no problem with allowing students to use portions of earlier papers in later ones, if relevant. One way to approach the writing on Stewart might be to offer students a choice of the first two assignments and then have everyone write this one. A major issue in this paper will be the effectiveness of an aggressive approach to an audience. Stewart, while firm, is not as aggressive as Walker; some students will prefer the more aggressive approach, however. You should accept considerable variation here.

FREDERICK DOUGLASS, "WHAT TO THE SLAVE IS THE FOURTH OF JULY?" (p. 208)

Frederick Douglass, of course, is a major intellectual figure in nineteenth-century America, and many students know who he is. Most, however, are unacquainted with the powerful address included here, which has come to be quite well known among scholars of American literature. Since, as we explain on p. 56, it is one of the foundational pieces of this unit, we strongly suggest that you assign it, even though it's quite long and therefore perceived by students as difficult (the language is not, in fact, particularly challenging). To orient students to Douglass's complex argument, you may want to spend some class time going through the essay paragraph by paragraph, asking students to write a brief summary or gloss of each. In the process, you can collect responses to the reading questions.

Writing Analytically

Because of the length and difficulty of this speech, writing questions 1 and 2 do not ask students to deal with it in its entirety, but rather to focus on two passages that illustrate two particular rhetorical strategies. You could develop similar writing questions from the reading questions, and if your students are having particular difficulty with this selection, you may want to confine their writing to such limited issues. Yet justice could be done to the speech as a whole by assigning different questions (our two and/or others you develop) to different groups of students, who could then report back to the whole class.

Writing question 3 is much more difficult than the first two, asking not only for a more comprehensive inventory of Douglass's strategies but also for a comparison of them with Langston's, which, of course, must also be inventoried to write the assignment. Students may perceive Langston as the more aggressive arguer, in part because his situation was more perilous at the time his speech was given (he was on trial for violating the Fugitive Slave Law). We think that Douglass and Langston are actually fairly close in their approaches to their rhetorical problems, however, and we would encourage students to see the similarities and maybe even to generalize from these two masterful examples about how a hostile audience can be persuaded.

CHARLES LANGSTON, ADDRESS TO THE COURT (p. 232)

Students usually find the situation in which Langston delivered this speech so exciting that they are quite interested in what he has to say; but he touches on so many topics, and his language is so elevated in spots, that it might be a good idea to go through the speech with your students and have them summarize or gloss every paragraph, as we suggest for Douglass (this work could also be done in small groups). You can collect responses to the reading questions in the process.

Writing Analytically

Writing question 1 accommodates the difficulties students may have with this piece by inviting them to focus on only one passage. Langston's opening is interesting, though, because his apparent diffidence actually translates into a veiled attack on his primary audience, the European American judge and jury. He impugns their fairness, at the least, if not additionally implying that they are racist, by predicting that his speech will have little effect. You may find that some of your students are ready to explain this point, and a lively discussion can ensue on how one should address a potentially unfair or biased audience from a vulnerable position such as Langston's. Also, as the writing question points out, this strategy is similar to the apparent diffidence with which Douglass begins his address, and you might encourage students to generalize on the basis of these two examples about how to gain the initial attention, or even goodwill, of a potentially hostile audience.

Writing question 2 requires a more thorough analysis of Langston's speech. Like some other questions attached to the African American selections in this section of Unit Two, this one points out the complexity of the audience question for these writers. Usually the writers are in the position of addressing one audience, whether white or black, while acknowledging that the other audience is, in effect, listening in. In our experience, students often find this duality intriguing, and they admire the skill with which these writers deal with it. African Americans and other students of color are often particularly sophisticated in analyzing this kind of rhetorical situation, because they are personally familiar with it. You might stimulate some discussion of dual-audience situations that students have experienced, such as speaking to a teacher in class while remaining aware of how the other students may be responding to the exchange.

Writing question 3 also requires a thorough inventory of Langston's strategies and of Walker's or Stewart's as well. Students will probably rank Walker as the most aggressive and Stewart as the least aggressive of the three, but you should certainly accept variant readings if they are well supported. We intend for alternative 2 to focus attention on these writers' political activism. Students of color may gravitate to this alternative because it will allow them to talk about how these writers aim to motivate people of color to stand up for their rights. You should urge any student who chooses this alternative to be specific about what audience(s) the invited speaker will address and what effects his or her words might be expected to have. You may need to have a class discussion about what happens on a diverse campus when a speaker addresses only one campus group, but his or her remarks might seem exclusionary or downright hurtful to other groups.

THE PROSLAVERY DEFENSE

GEORGE FITZHUGH, FROM *SOCIOLOGY FOR THE SOUTH, OR THE FAILURE OF FREE SOCIETY* (p. 239)

Fitzhugh will seem very strange and unfamiliar to students, especially if he is the first proslavery writer you have assigned. You will probably need to clarify for students at the outset that, yes indeed, this American writer is attacking well-known American leaders and ideals, including Jefferson and the Declaration of Independence. It might also be a good idea to point out that Fitzhugh was no academic sociologist such as students may encounter in other courses (the headnote attempts to explain the appearance of the word *sociology* in the title of this work). All in all, Fitzhugh is a very challenging selection.

Writing Analytically

Given Fitzhugh's attack on cherished American ideals and his support for the blatantly evil institution of slavery, students may be alarmed to discover that they find some of his general principles attractive. We think some of his general principles *are* attractive, or at least defensible, and we have highlighted two of these in writing questions 1 and 2, which encourage students to take the ideas seriously, without reference to Fitzhugh's use of them to defend slavery. In our experience, if you really want to have a free play of discussion in your class, you have to show that you are prepared to take all ideas seriously. It would be a big mistake to assign Fitzhugh (or any other reading) just so that you could mock or denounce his obviously incorrect views.

Pointing out the possibility that good principles may be given bad applications also helps students learn to distinguish between general principles and specific applications as categories of thought, one of the overall goals of this unit (see p. 60). Lively discussion should ensue when students who have attacked Fitzhugh's condemnation of radical individualism share their specific examples in defense of individualism — one person's individualism perhaps being another person's oppression. Be prepared, too, for some interesting conflicts to arise within students who are ethically or religiously motivated to approve Fitzhugh's attack on radical individualism but who abhor its source. These kinds of conflicts, in our view, enhance students' ability to deal with the complexities necessary for critical thinking.

The focus of writing question 3 is less abstract, asking students to catalog and compare rhetorical strategies rather than to experiment with abstract ideas. Nevertheless, the task of collecting these strategies from two rather lengthy and complex selections is formidable enough in itself. You might want to ease students into this assignment by first discussing some examples of how contemporary politicians discredit their opponents and, particularly, the sources on which their opponents attempt to draw for moral authority.

DAVID CHRISTY, FROM *COTTON IS KING* (p. 244)

Although clearly racist, David Christy is perhaps the least obviously offensive of the three proslavery writers we have included in Unit Two. Unlike Fitzhugh and Bledsoe, he does not attack Jefferson and the ideals of the Declaration of Independence, at least not directly. Rather, Christy argues that Declaration ideals were never meant to apply to African Americans, and he enlists the aid of the views Jefferson expresses in our excerpt from *Notes on Virginia* to help prove his point. Christy thus provides one of the unit's best examples of the interpretive argument from original intentions, and you should assign him if you want your class to focus on issues discussed in the section on interpretation (p. 57).

Writing Analytically

Christy's relative mildness and his reliance on seemingly value-neutral arguments concerning original intent or economic necessity may be attributed to his seeing his primary audience as European Americans who are undecided about slavery. This is the audience he was most likely to encounter in the border state of Ohio, where he first published *Cotton Is King*. Writing question 1 invites students to consider one of the strategies Christy may be employing to appeal to this audience. To underscore the point of the appeal, ask students to imagine how readers who are strongly proslavery would react to it. You could expand this assignment by asking students to look for other examples of ways Christy is appealing to this on-the-fence audience.

Writing questions 2 and 3 both deal with the original-intention issue. Question 2 looks at Christy's strategies for presenting Jefferson's views and engages students in the question of whether Jefferson's intentions can ever be established conclusively. Question 3 looks at ways other Revolutionary-era documents included in Unit Two might affect Christy's argument. Here the issue is not primarily what Jefferson intended, but rather what the spirit of the times could be said to have been.

Students may correctly point out that they do not have enough evidence to generalize about Jefferson's views or the spirit of Revolutionary times. You can make use of this observation in two ways: One, encourage discussion of how much evidence would be enough, what kind of evidence it would be, and so on. In other words, use this occasion to teach students about the nature of evidence. Two, suggest that they view these writing questions as opportunities to practice arguing from original or primary sources under controlled conditions, without the burden of collecting "adequate" evidence.

ALBERT TAYLOR BLEDSOE, FROM *LIBERTY AND SLAVERY* (p. 250)

Bledsoe is perhaps the most difficult selection in Unit Two: long, dense, abstract, and full of views that students will find counterintuitive. Yet his argument is so interesting that, especially if you want to focus on the issues of argument, you will want to assign this reading. It might be a good idea to go through this piece and ask students to summarize or gloss each paragraph, collecting responses to the reading questions along the way (this work could be done in small groups).

Writing Analytically

In spite of his indefensible views on race, some of Bledsoe's general principles might be considered attractive. We have highlighted two of these in writing question 1, which encourages students to take these ideas seriously, without reference to Bledsoe's use of them to defend slavery. As we noted in connection with Fitzhugh, if you really want to have a free play of discussion in your class, you have to show that you are prepared to take all ideas seriously. It would be a big mistake to assign Bledsoe (or any other reading) just so that you could mock or denounce his obviously incorrect views. Furthermore, pointing out the possibility that good principles may be given bad applications helps students learn to distinguish between general principles and specific applications as categories of thought, one of the overall goals of this unit (see p. 60).

Bledsoe is perhaps the most thorough attacker of opposing views among all the writers in Unit Two. For example, like Fitzhugh, he attacks the Declaration of Independence. Writing question 3, the easiest one offered for Bledsoe, suggests simply comparing the two writers on the ways they conduct these attacks. Writing question 2, however, asks students to look not only at Bledsoe's handling of the Declaration but also at his treatment of other opposing views. This is a valuable assignment because students are often reluctant to treat opposing views in their papers — they seem to think they'll be giving away a damaging secret if they admit that such views exist — and when they do try to deal with them, they often just resort to abuse. We think that there are both good and bad points to Bledsoe's treatment of the opposition, from which students can learn.

PROCLAMATIONS AND PUBLIC STATEMENTS

These documents are best treated as part of the exploration of a theme addressed in one of the Assignment Sequences. Special issues relating to each document are noted in its accompanying reading and writing questions. We will briefly discuss the writing questions here.

JONATHAN JACKSON, MANUMISSION PAPER (p. 260)

Slave owners sometimes allowed their slaves to hire out as paid workers for other people when their work for their owners was completed and to keep part or all of the money thus earned. Slaves were sometimes allowed to use this money to buy themselves or their family members out of slavery (your students may be familiar with a fictional example of this practice in Toni Morrison's novel *Beloved,* in which Halle buys the freedom of his mother, Baby Suggs, in this way). Some such arrangement may explain how Pomp acquired the five shillings that Jackson says he will accept in part payment for Pomp's freedom (this sum could not have been Pomp's full slave-market value).

Writing Analytically

In response to writing question 1, we hope that students will note the contrast between Jackson's expression of support for the "liberty every man ought to enjoy" and his willingness to take money from Pomp in exchange for his freedom. Thus there is room for disagreement about how idealistic this manumission paper really is.

Similarly, we hope that writing question 2 will reveal that both texts offer both idealistic and more materialistic reasons for abandoning slavery (in general or in the single instance of Pomp). Both writing questions require only brief papers and might be used as journal entries instead of full-scale assignments.

PRINCE HALL ET AL., PETITION ON BEHALF OF MASSACHUSETTS SLAVES (p. 261)

The authorship of this petition is usually attributed to Hall because of his prominent place in Boston African American society. Also, he is known to have been literate. Clarify for students that neither Hall nor the other signers of this petition were in fact slaves at the time it was written, although they speak in the voice of slaves. As free African Americans, they are using their liberty and literacy on behalf of those still enslaved.

Writing Analytically

Explaining the contradiction noted in the writing question should take students no more than a paragraph. Evaluating the effectiveness of the argument may require a bit more discussion — logical though it may be, history is full of examples of imperviousness to the Golden Rule — but still, not a discussion at length. The assignment might work best as a journal entry.

RHODE ISLAND RESOLUTION FOR THE FORMATION OF A COLORED REGIMENT (p. 264)

Writing Analytically

On the one hand, this resolution proposes to treat Native American and African American soldiers pretty much like all other soldiers — they will be paid the same wages and so on. On the other hand, the resolution seems to overprotest the military necessity and historical precedent for enlisting "colored" troops, as if its signers were embarrassed for doing so. Also, because the former owners of the black soldiers are to be reimbursed for their value as slaves, the resolution implicitly supports the institution of slavery. It's not so easy to say whether this resolution embodies egalitarian ideals, and students will find something to discuss in the writing assignment — but not, we think, at great length. The assignment might work best as a journal entry.

DR. BLOOMFIELD, FOURTH OF JULY MANUMISSION SPEECH (p. 266)

Writing Analytically

We think that in this speech, antislavery and egalitarian ideals linked to the Declaration are less mixed with more mundane motives than in any other Revolutionary-era document in this section. Nevertheless, some students will feel that there is something patronizing in the fact that Bloomfield exhibits his slaves on stage and quizzes them about their ability to take care of themselves. Writing question 1 allows for this range of reader response.

Writing question 2 provides a miniature version of the issue concerning the interpretation of historical sources that is discussed on page 57 and considered in greater detail in assignment sequence 1 (p. 74). Students might draft this assignment in class as preparation for the lengthier consideration in the sequence.

PETITION SUPPORTING SLAVERY (p. 268)

Writing Analytically

It will not be difficult for students to answer the questions posed in the writing question. You should be prepared, however, for students to want to discuss at some length the extent to which the right to property *should be* the primary ideal on which the United States is based. This assignment might work best as a topic for discussion in small groups or as a journal entry.

WILLIAM LLOYD GARRISON, "DECLARATION OF SENTIMENTS OF THE AMERICAN ANTI-SLAVERY CONVENTION" (p. 270)

Writing Analytically

Garrison's text, the longest in this section, repays close study of his rhetorical techniques. Writing questions 1 and 2 call attention to two sources of moral authority on which he draws: God and the Declaration of Independence. You should encourage students to see that there are two fundamental issues involved in the evaluation of persuasive techniques that attempt to draw on moral authority. One, of course, is the question of whether the references are handled skillfully — whether quotes and allusions are correct and appropriate, too numerous or too few, and so on. The other is the question of whether the audience acknowledges the rhetor's moral authority *as* an authority: Allow students to say so if they themselves feel little or no reverence for God or the Declaration and thus little or no response to these appeals of Garrison's.

ASSIGNMENT SEQUENCES

As noted in the introduction to this manual, we see the assignment sequences as an integral part of the approach we wish to promote in *Negotiating Difference*. The sequences put provocative voices directly in dialogue with each other — both in the readings and then, in discussions of the readings, among the students in your class. Of equal importance, the sequences stress the need to develop material carefully — rereading, rethinking, and revising — in order to produce the richest rhetorical responses in student writing.

You can use the reading questions that accompany each selection to aid students in preparing to write for the sequences. While the writing questions in each sequence tend to build on one another with added complexity as one moves through the sequence, you should also feel free to select among these questions to tailor the sequence to your students' needs and interests (you will see some of this adaptation of sequences going on in the model syllabi that we include beginning on p. 79). In what follows we will briefly discuss each sequence and its writing questions.

Sequence 1. Does the Declaration of Independence contradict slavery? (p. 276)

This is the sequence that concentrates on the question of historical interpretation. It begins with two experiments in uncovering "original" intent, of the Declaration's principal author (question 1) and of people in general in Revolutionary times (question 2). Note that both of these assignments acknowledge that the questions they pose are unanswerable on the basis of the limited information provided in Unit Two. The point is to give students the chance to practice writing this kind of paper from sources. You might, at the same time, encourage discussion of what would be enough evidence to make a convincing case for either of these assignments.

Question 3 turns to two nineteenth-century proslavery writers who take opposite views of the Declaration. Fitzhugh sees the document as opposing slavery, and therefore he condemns it. Christy argues that the document was never intended to apply to African Americans, and therefore he enlists it on his side. In evaluating the writers' persuasiveness, students will inevitably have to confront their own views on which interpretation of the Declaration seems more correct.

Question 4 puts a slightly different twist on the question of the Declaration's relation to slavery: Both Banneker and Douglass, in effect, assume that the Declaration has always contradicted slavery — from the very day of its signing — but that people (presumably even the signers) have not always recognized this truth and hence have contradicted it in their behavior. If you are looking to shorten this sequence, you might offer students a choice of writing either question 3 or 4.

In our experience, students usually have a lot of fun with question 5, at least the part that requires writing the new Declaration paragraph. They usually tend to have a harder time with the discursive part, in which they must explain why they made the changes they did. You might suggest that they set up this part of the paper in the form of a series of notes on their rewritten paragraph. This is also a good assignment for students to work on in small groups.

In their responses to question 6, we've found that few students come up with anything heterodox to say about their own interpretation of "all men are created equal." They almost always give this phrase the standard liberal reading ("all men" means "all people"; "created equal" means "with equal rights" or "opportunities"). The serious argumentative problem here is how they justify this reading in light of the original historical context of the Declaration. Encourage them to pay special attention to this part of their papers.

Sequence 2. *What power should society have over the individual?* (p. 277)

Of the three Unit Two sequences, this is the one that concentrates most on the issues of argument. The questions are abstract, philosophical, and open-ended. This sequence is also challenging because the ideas it examines have strong resonance with contemporary political issues, such as how much the government should do to support social services for education, welfare, health care, elder care, and so on. You may need to point out these connections. Initially, most students will champion the individual, especially since that position is antislavery in the context of Unit Two. But in the context of modern welfare reform, for example, championing the individual could be construed to mean ending welfare payments that promote dependency and government surveillance. Politically liberal students who are quite sure of their opposition to social control as expressed in the institution of slavery may be startled to realize that they support social control in the form of welfare payments. We like to encourage students to probe such complexities.

Question 1 is designed to get students thinking about the power issues involved in individuals' participation in society. We suggest working on this assignment in class, perhaps in small groups.

Question 2 also focuses on these power relations, but as they are represented in a more complex and resonant text. Most likely, students have never looked carefully at the actual language of the Declaration, and they will be inclined to assume that it gives uncomplicated support to unfettered individualism. You will have to encourage students to study the document's language so that they can develop more complexity in their reading here.

Questions 3 and 4 look at the issue of social control or, as it might be called today, government intervention, from opposite sides. Douglass and Langston are speaking against control, on behalf of people who have been controlled too much. Encourage students not to miss these writers' implicit arguments for African American independence — for example, through the examples of intellectual excellence they present in their own persons. Fitzhugh and Bledsoe are speaking in favor of control, concerning people who they believe need to be controlled because they are incapable of controlling themselves. You should help students to distinguish here between the general principle that society should help those who need help and its specific application to the defense of slavery. You should also insist that students distinguish among the various arguments that Fitzhugh and Bledsoe make: Are all the arguments simply racist? Some students may wish to argue that although African Americans should not be enslaved, African Americans in Fitzhugh and Bledsoe's day who emerged from slavery might indeed need some kinds of social assistance — for example, education — that the government might appropriately provide.

These considerations would segue nicely into the modern applications of the writers' general arguments that we offer as alternatives in both questions. It might be quite interesting to ask students to share in class the groups they selected as modern examples and the reasons they gave for these groups' needing more, or less, social intervention. Such in-class sharing would be particularly helpful if, in the interest of shortening this sequence, you assign question 3 to half the class and question 4 to the other half.

Question 5 deals with another issue that arises in discussion of the individual's relation with society, namely what forms of action an individual should take to effect social change. We don't want to give the impression that in the power struggle that defines social relations, the action is all one way, with the larger society simply deciding to control, or to refrain from controlling, individuals. Individuals, too, or groups of individuals may exert some influence over how society relates to them. You might point out that this issue is actually implicit in the rhetorical efforts of Douglass and Langston explored in question 3 — their speeches constitute social protest.

Although question 6 asks students to draw on at least four sequence readings in making their arguments, they might not mention slavery in their papers at all. Instead, they might talk about the relationship between the individual and society purely in abstract terms, or with only a contemporary illustration (perhaps the one they used for sequence question 3 or 4). They can find quotations in the readings that discuss the general issue without mentioning slavery; or, if they wish to use a quotation that does refer specifically to slavery, you can advise them on how to accommodate that reference to a different argument — for example: "Although Douglass's point here pertains to African Americans escaping slavery, it can also be applied to U.S. resident aliens resisting the unreasonable demands of the Immigration Service. . . ."

Throughout the class's work on this sequence, you should make sure that anti-individualist, procommunity arguments get a fair hearing (for example, in discussion of question 4). Play devil's advocate, if necessary. Students may be prone to knee-jerk defenses of the dominant American ideology of individualism, and even if they end up still quite committed to this ideology, the commitment will be better informed if at some point they have also had to acknowledge the claims of the community. Some students may present a procommunity perspective, such as those who wish to advocate for particular social services or who wish to describe the rewards of participating in a warmly united ethnic or religious community, and you should assist them in being heard, if necessary.

Sequence 3. *How can a hostile audience be persuaded?* (p. 278)

The focus of this sequence, more than the other two in Unit Two, is on rhetorical issues of ethos and pathos rather than logos. The questions ask students to look not so much at the content of arguments as at the inflection writers give them by the ways they present themselves and characterize their audiences, the kinds of allusions they draw on, and more. Consequently, unlike the other two sequences, this sequence really has little to do with slavery and its attendant issues of political philosophy.

You will be looking, in effect, at the techniques most likely to give rhetoric a bad name, most likely to look like mere manipulation to students. Your task will be to move them beyond adolescent cynicism about these techniques and toward a more mature view of persuasion as involving the whole person of both rhetor and auditor/reader. This is the view they will have to take in the last assignment in this sequence.

Question 1, which works well as a journal assignment, may elicit accounts of sly or cynical "How I got over" narratives: that's okay. After everyone has a good laugh, you can encourage a little more serious discussion of just how immoral or necessary the techniques they describe really were. Encourage students to analyze why particular techniques did or did not work for them.

Question 2 asks students to take a similar rhetorical perspective on the Declaration, seeing changes in the text as necessary not just to clarify some objective content but rather to modify ideas in response to the views of different constituencies. You might ask students to compile their responses to this question in class, perhaps in small groups.

The first two sequence questions, then, are designed to break the ice and demonstrate to students that the use of persuasive techniques they might initially be inclined to condemn as manipulative can be found pretty commonly both in their own texts and in highly formal and widely respected documents such as the Declaration.

Questions 3, 4, and 5, by asking students to inventory writers' rhetorical strategies, encourage a sort of "toolbox," or repertoire, approach. These questions ask students to analyze the language of the writers closely and to break down their texts into identifiable rhetorical choices. Students should get the idea that there are many ways to approach a persuasive task and that certain approaches can be transferred from one task to another. All of this focus on tinkering with texts may seem very strange to students. They are inclined to think that accomplished writers just sit down and let it flow. We hope this kind of work will reinforce the idea that writing comprises recursive processes — and that students will also see strategies in these writers that they can use.

You may recognize this kind of analysis as traditionally pertaining to rhetoric, in the classification of tropes and figures, for example. We have chosen not to burden students with any elaborate nomenclature so that, to paraphrase Samuel Butler, the rhetorician does not spend all his or her time learning to name the tools. We want to be flexible in what we call a "strategy" — from alliteration to biblical allusion to a consistent pattern of characterizing oneself as a true patriot, to give just a few examples. The central point is to get students to see that a written text is not seamless, that it has parts that could have been assembled in another way or combined differently with other parts.

Questions 3, 4, and 5 might be handled entirely in class, with students making their lists of strategies together, perhaps in small groups. Also, you could ask students to choose one or two of these questions and to write the paper option described in each.

This work should lead up to the final assignment, question 6, which asks students to consider the general question of how to address a complex audience — some hearers or readers who are indifferent or hostile and some who are friendly or anxiously interested — in terms of the specific strategies the students have just been analyzing. For example, Douglass and Langston could be used to illustrate the strategy of beginning diffidently; Walker and Christy could illustrate the strategy of enlisting a nationally recognized source of authority, in this case the Declaration of Independence, on one's side.

An interesting follow-up to this sequence would be to ask students to bring to class examples of contemporary prose that exhibit some of the strategies they have just analyzed.

Research Kit

Please see our remarks on the Research Kits in the introduction to this manual (p.11).

The unifying concept for Unit Two is rather abstract, having to do with interpretations of the Declaration. Many of the topics we are suggesting for student research will not be organized around this concept in the sources the students find. You will have to encourage them to look for mentions not only of specific Declaration ideals but also of issues concerning the relations between individuals and society that students will have encountered elsewhere in Unit Two. This caution applies particularly to assignments 1, 2, 3, 6, and 7 in "Ideas from the Unit Readings."

Students are usually fascinated by Jefferson, and research into "Ideas" assignment 5 would make a good group project. Encourage students to collect many different scholarly opinions about Jefferson's views and to make some effort to adjudicate among them — to talk about which ones are most persuasive and why.

Either "Ideas" assignment 8 or the option given in assignment 6 makes an excellent class project on popular culture. You may have to provide students with additional guidance in tracking down visual materials. Also encourage them to discuss July Fourth celebrations with which they are familiar, perhaps comparing customs across families, ethnicities, and regions if the mix in your class permits.

"Ideas" assignment 9 can be the basis of an "enriched" Unit Two syllabus.

Assignments 1, 2, 3, 4, and 7 in "Branching Out" will help students discover the many uses of Declaration language in civil rights struggles in this country. These assignments might work as the focus of a class project to collect as many such uses of the Declaration as students can find. The class can then compare their rhetorical nuances; sometimes the exact same words quoted from the Declaration seem to mean slightly different things depending on who is doing the quoting! An option here would be to invite students to design their own "unit" (modeled on the units in *Negotiating Difference*), using material drawn from throughout this book and perhaps also incorporating new material they have found, on the theme of "the uses of the Declaration of Independence."

MODEL SYLLABI

The model syllabi are framed on a thirteen-week term, with week fourteen being exam week. You can adapt them to your own number of weeks (if different) and number of class meetings per week. The model syllabi sometimes adapt the assignment sequences they use, omitting some questions or substituting others — you should feel free to be similarly flexible in developing your own syllabi. Remember, the sequences are not designed to be lockstep processes.

We assume that you will work in class on the reading questions accompanying the assigned selections as well as on the assigned writing and sequence questions (sometimes we give you suggestions in the syllabi for how to do so). Note that work on these questions can often be performed profitably in class in small groups. (For more information on group work, see p. 14.)

We suggest that students keep a class journal in which they write responses to the reading questions before the questions are discussed in class. (Also remind students to read the headnotes accompanying the selections before they come to class.) In other words, our plan is that each reading assignment ("Read Stewart") also constitutes a writing assignment because students should jot responses to the text's reading questions in their journals. (For more information on the class journal, see p. 12.)

You should collect and review these journals at least as often as you collect students' writing portfolios. We suggest that students be graded according to some version of the portfolio method. (For more information, see p. 17.)

Syllabus using two sequences from Unit Two

Here we have combined sequences 1 and 3 because appeals to particular interpretations of the Declaration of Independence often are aimed at convincing particular audiences.

Week 1

Read: Unit Two introduction; Declaration of Independence; *Notes on Virginia*
Write: Sequence 1, question 1

On the first day, ask students to free-write in their class journals on what the phrase "all men are created equal" means to them. Ask them to save this writing so they can look at it again at the end of the course.

Week 2

Read: Petition Supporting Slavery; Jackson; Hall; Bloomfield
Write: Sequence 1, question 2
Collect: Essay from week 1

Week 3

Read: Fitzhugh
Collect: Essay from week 2

Week 4

Read: Christy
Write: Sequence 1, question 3

Week 5

Read: Banneker
Collect: Essay from week 4

Week 6

Read: Douglass
Write: Sequence 1, question 4

Week 7

Collect: Essay from week 6

Now turn to sequence 3, discuss question 1, and perhaps ask students to write a response in their class journals.

Week 8

Read: Walker

Week 9

Read: Langston
Write: Sequence 3, question 3

Week 10

Read: Stewart
Write: Sequence 3, question 4
Collect: Essay from week 9

Week 11

Write: Sequence 3, question 5
Collect: Essay from week 10

Review Christy and Fitzhugh in class to prepare for the writing assignment.

Week 12

Write: Student-designed essay (see next paragraph)
Collect: Essay from week 11

In class, discuss sequence 1, question 6, and sequence 3, question 6, together, considering issues such as these: How is a given interpretation of the Declaration aimed at a particular audience? Can multiple audiences be accommodated in this way? Encourage students to devise their own plans for papers responding in various ways to this discussion, which will be due next week. Also tell them to prepare their portfolios for work in class next week.

Week 13

Collect: Student-designed essay; portfolios including class journals
    (week 13 or 14)

Work with students to select two papers from their portfolios to be revised and resubmitted for grades. Some of this work might be done in small groups with peer editing. This is a good time to give lessons on any grammar or mechanics problems that are common among your students. Also tell them to make sure their journals are up to date. Collect portfolios at the end of this week or exam week.

"Enriched" Syllabus: One sequence plus additional readings

We suggest supplementing sequence 1 with the following texts.

Nineteenth-century African American orators:

Hamilton, William. "An Oration Delivered in the African Zion Church, on the Fourth of July, 1827, in Commemoration of the Abolition of Domestic Slavery in This State" [New York]. In *Early Negro Writing, 1760–1837*, edited by Dorothy Porter. Boston: Beacon Press, 1971.

Osborne, Peter. "July 5th Oration, 1832." In *A Documentary History of the Negro People in the United States*, edited by Herbert Aptheker. Vol. 1, *From Colonial Times through the Civil War.* Secaucus: Citadel Press, 1951.

Williams, Reverend Peter. "Fourth of July Oration, 1830." In *Early Negro Writing, 1760–1837,* edited by Dorothy Porter. Boston: Beacon Press, 1971.

We suggest placing these readings on reserve or including them in a course pack.

We also suggest inviting students to provide contemporary examples of pulpit oratory or political writing that echoes Unit Two themes (see week 11).

Finally, we suggest adding at least two chapters from Harriet Beecher Stowe's classic nineteenth-century novel *Uncle Tom's Cabin*: chapter 17, "The Freeman's Defense," and chapter 43, "Results." *Uncle Tom's Cabin* is now readily available in a number of inexpensive paperback editions, which you may order for your class. Depending on how much reading you think your class can handle, you might have them read the entire novel; it is resonant throughout with themes addressed in Unit Two.

Week 1

> Read: Unit Two introduction; Declaration of Independence; *Notes on Virginia*
> Write: Sequence 1, question 1

On the first day, ask students to free-write in their class journals on the question of what the phrase "all men are created equal" means to them.

Week 2

> Read: Petition Supporting Slavery; Jackson; Hall; Bloomfield
> Write: Sequence 1, question 2
> Collect: Essay from week 1

Week 3

> Read: Fitzhugh
> Collect: Essay from week 2

Week 4

> Read: Christy
> Write: Sequence 1, question 3

Week 5

> Read: Banneker
> Collect: Essay from week 4

Week 6

> Read: Douglass
> Write: Sequence 1, question 4

Week 7

> Read: Osborne; Hamilton; Williams (You may wish to provide read-
> ing questions to accompany these selections; if so, students should
> respond to them as usual.)
> Collect: Essay from week 6

We suggest assigning Osborne first. Here are some ideas for writing questions: On what grounds does he argue that the Declaration of Independence includes African Americans? How would his uses of the Declaration
have been likely to affect an African American audience?

Then Hamilton: How does he use the Declaration? What contradictions
does he find in Jefferson's thought and how does he handle them? What is
the effect of the implied threat of violence in his opening? Compare with
Douglass, who addresses a primarily white audience — does the race of the
audience make a difference here? On what grounds does Hamilton attack
European Americans? When you get to Stowe, compare with George Harris's
indictment in "The Freeman's Defense."

Then Williams: How does he use the Declaration in his opening? What
problems face free people of color, according to Williams? What arguments
does he make against "returning" to Africa (most of his audience would
have been born in the United States)? When you get to Stowe, compare
with George Harris's explanation of his decision to emigrate to Africa in
"Results." What arguments does Williams present in favor of acquiring land
for an African American settlement in Canada?

Week 8

> Read: Osborne; Hamilton; Williams (continued)
> Write: African American oratory essay (see the following discussion)

Using these three examples plus Douglass, ask students to write a paper
on the African American antebellum abolition address, attempting to generalize about its characteristics (in effect, a genre study). If you wish to
assign secondary reading as well, consider a selection from Condit and
Lucaites's *Crafting Equality: America's Anglo-African Word* (see the Unit Two
Research Kit bibliography).

If you choose to assign all of *Uncle Tom's Cabin*, you might try to squeeze
work on the African American orators into a single week to gain more time
for the novel (which you could then start in week 9, with the activities we
currently describe for week 9 moved up here to week 8).

Week 9

> Write: Two revised essays from portfolio
> Collect: African American oratory essay

Work with students to select one or two of the first four papers in their
portfolios to revise for a grade. Some of this work might be done in small
groups with peer editing. This is a good time to give lessons on any gram-

mar or mechanics problems that are common among your students. Also tell them to make sure their journals are up to date.

Week 10

> Read: *Uncle Tom's Cabin*, chapters 17 and 43 (you may wish to provide reading questions); contemporary oratory (see the following discussion)
>
> Write: Harris and Hamilton/Williams essay (see the following discussion)
>
> Collect: Portfolios, including two newly revised papers and class journals

If you are not reading the entire novel, you may want to provide the class with a plot summary that identifies the characters who appear in these chapters. Since Stowe's novel was originally published serially, however, each chapter stands fairly well on its own. Direct students' attention to what George Harris says in these chapters about his feelings as an American, his political rights, his reasons for emigrating to Africa, and other points of contact with Unit Two themes. Ask the students why Stowe calls Harris's armed resistance to the slave catchers his "declaration of independence" (no capital letters).

If you are reading the entire novel, you will want to develop other writing questions treating the many contacts with Unit Two themes. Suggestions for foci: Augustine St. Clare's arguments with his brother and Miss Ophelia about the rights and wrongs of slavery; the contrast between George Harris's active resistance to slavery and Tom's martyrdom; Stowe's concluding address to the reader.

To get time in the syllabus to read the entire novel, you may want to compress the work on African American oratory into a single week, as suggested in week 8, or you may wish to begin the novel in week 9 without spending time in class on the preparation of portfolios, grammar lessons, and so on. This model syllabus, however, assumes that you will be reading only chapters 17 and 43.

Work in class on a paper that compares George Harris's attacks on European Americans with those found in William Hamilton or his arguments for emigration to Africa with Reverend Williams's arguments against it (let students choose one of these two topics). If you are reading all of *Uncle Tom's Cabin*, you will want to provide some other choices for paper topics, perhaps relating to the foci just suggested.

Also ask students to collect contemporary examples of pulpit oratory or political writing that repeats Unit Two themes (these need not be by people of color). You might bring in the "Black Declaration of Independence" issued by a group of clergy in 1970, to be found in the Philip Foner collection *We the Other People* (see the Unit Two Research Kit bibliography).

Week 11

Collect: Harris and Hamilton/Williams essay

In class, discuss the contemporary materials students bring in and perhaps also the piece from Foner. You might ask students to work in small groups to devise reading and writing questions for their materials along the lines of those in *Negotiating Difference*. These could be recorded in class journals or shared with the entire class.

Week 12

Write: Sequence 1, question 6

Ask the students to write sequence 1, question 5, in class, perhaps working in small groups, with each group taking one of the writers listed in the question; other groups might wish to write the assignment using one of their contemporary examples. The groups should then share their work with the entire class.

Week 13

Write: Revised essay (see the next paragraph)
Collect: Essay from week 12; portfolios, including class journals (week 13 or 14)

Work with students to select either their paper on African American oratory or the one on *Uncle Tom's Cabin* to revise for a grade. Some of this work might be done in small groups with peer editing. This is a good time to give lessons on any grammar or mechanics problems that are common among your students. Also tell them to make sure their journals are up to date. Collect portfolios at the end of this week or exam week.

UNIT THREE

Defining "Woman's Sphere" in Nineteenth-Century American Society

THEMES AND ISSUES IN UNIT THREE

Unit Three presents a selection of materials from a writing-intensive course on nineteenth-century American women writers that Pat has taught many times. The issues raised here will be very familiar to those who know current criticism of women's literature, and if you want to integrate fiction into your writing course, this is perhaps the best unit to choose (see the model syllabus on p. 115). Unit Three provides some materials in this area that are hard to find or not widely known and that make particularly interesting supplements to fiction reading, if you choose to take your course in this direction.

Feminisms

In Unit Three, feminist issues are often presented in ways that sound quite contemporary. The gender role issues debated in this unit are still very much alive. True, women now have the vote, and no one seriously contends that they should not. But this is only one specific issue among others in the unit, and the overarching issue of the extent to which a woman's life should be dominated by domestic responsibilities is still very much in contention. We think the potential for emotions flaring in class is higher with this unit, perhaps, than for any other in the book.

We strongly caution you against setting out to teach Unit Three with the idea that you will be actively promoting feminism. You shouldn't teach *any* unit in *Negotiating Difference* with the aim of overtly promoting liberal views, but it would be particularly risky to do so here. You will find that some students are well armed with conservative arguments about gender roles and prepared to endorse the positions of Catharine Beecher, Reverend Jonathan Stearns, or even Louisa McCord. Other students will passionately defend contemporary feminist positions. We think it is best to present the course as an investigation into forms of feminist thought. Emphasize the plurality of feminisms presented both in the unit and in contemporary inheritors of these thinkers. Here, too, it is particularly important to keep before students' eyes the main project of *Negotiating Difference,* which is to study how different perspectives represent themselves and their opponents rhetorically.

You can point out the tension in the Unit Three texts between versions of what is now often called cultural feminism and what is called egalitarian feminism. Sounding like cultural feminists, some writers here describe women as essentially different from men, indeed different in traditional ways (more nurturing and so on), but as having something distinctively important to offer to society precisely because of these differences. And of these writers, some (such as Catharine Beecher) say that this distinctive offering must be made within the home while others (such as Anna Julia Cooper) argue that for this very reason women need greater public scope for their activities. In contrast, sounding like egalitarian feminists, some writers (such as Sarah Grimké) argue that there are no important differences between men and women and therefore their moral and social duties should be the same.

You can encourage students to concentrate on the perspectives that most appeal to them. Opportunities will arise for them to bring in contemporary materials that address unit themes. At the same time, you can insist that all perspectives presented in the unit readings be accorded serious treatment and careful attention to their arguments and rhetorical strategies, even if distasteful to particular students.

Argument

As in Unit Two, the focus in Unit Three is primarily on expository argument (see the discussion of argument on p. 60). General principles are applied to specific cases in provocative ways. This is a good unit to choose if you want your course to focus on argument. It is a bit more challenging than Unit Two, however, and might be a better choice with more accomplished students or as a follow-up to Unit Two (many of the rhetorical themes and much of the content are related as well).

In Unit Three, appeals to emotion and attempts to establish the speaker/ writer's authority or to discredit the opposition are intense, even violent (see McCord, for example). The logical appeals — the "straight" arguments — are harder to sort out from among the luxuriant growth of other attempted means of influencing the audience. We will discuss ethical appeals at greater length in the next section.

Unit Three is also challenging because the issues are complicated. Although the focus is on gender roles, race is also frequently brought into the discussion. This is partly because much of the impetus for early-nineteenth-century feminism came from women who initially wanted to work for abolitionism, not women's rights, but were prevented from doing so because of their gender. Race also enters because many of the same arguments were made to keep women and people of color down — for example, all were deemed inferior by nature — or to liberate women and people of color — for example, all were deemed equal in the sight of God.

In studying argument here, you may want to suggest that students focus first on the logical appeals, particularly those arguments that lay out general principles and apply them to the specific case of women's rights. You can then move on to analyzing emotional and ethical appeals.

If you wish to focus particularly on texts that interweave issues of race and gender, look at McCord, Grimké, Cooper, Folsom, the *New York Herald* editorial, Douglass, Truth, and Stanton.

Ethos

Debates over the issue of "woman's sphere" seem to involve issues of ethos to a very high degree. In classical rhetoric, *ethos* is the speaker's depiction of his or her character, as conveyed to the audience by specific personal statements as well as by his or her reputation, diction, dress, gesture, and so on. The "ethical appeal" is the persuasiveness of the speaker's ethos; the more likable, trustworthy, and respectable a speaker appears to be, the better chance he or she has of persuading the audience.

Literary critics talk about the author's (or implied author's) attempts to influence readers (or implied readers), to shape readers' experience of the text, to persuade readers to enter into the world that the work of literature creates. In a sense, these are all concerns of ethos. The difference between the literary critic's perspective and the perspective of classical rhetoric (or modern rhetoric for that matter) is that critics tend to treat the reading experience as self-referential. Critics, in other words, usually don't talk about the literary work trying to make something happen in the material world, other than to create a certain kind of reading experience. In contrast, the classical concept, and the approach we want to emphasize, suggests that attempts to shape readers' or listeners' experience have definite intentions in the material world. The emphasis is on the effectiveness of the persuasion, as demonstrated when the audience acts in the manner that the author desires.

All of the readings in this unit are intended, most definitely, to make something happen in the world. Stearns, Folsom, and the Massachusetts minister who wrote the "Pastoral Letter" are not interested just in grabbing readers' interest with their metaphors of abolitionist women as perambulating prostitutes or trampled vines. They are trying to keep women home, to stop their public activism. And in rebutting the "Pastoral Letter," writers such as Grimké are not interested just in making an argument that readers will appreciate as well structured. Instead, Grimké wants readers to support her with their sympathy, money, and lecture attendance as she continues her abolitionist work in defiance of the ministers' sanctions.

The main idea of *Negotiating Difference* is to look at texts that are trying to do something in the world. So it would be appropriate to look at issues of ethos throughout the book, and indeed our apparatus directs students to do that, though without the terminology of classical rhetorical theory.

But issues of ethos seem especially vexed in this unit. Why? It may be partly because of the complexity of the issues addressed, as noted earlier. These writers sometimes have the tricky job of explaining their allegiance to several causes at once — Douglass, for example, and Stanton, to take a very different example, must show how they balance their commitments to African American rights and women's rights. Very few of the unit's writers are able to speak only as a member of a particular race or gender.

Not only is the writer seldom allowed to speak from one subject position alone, to speak just as a man, let's say, or just as an African American, but the writer is unable at any time to set aside all subject positions, whether of race or gender. Very few of the writers included here can speak as a sort of disembodied, raceless, sexless voice of philosophy, although some make an effort to do so — for example, Beecher and, in a very different way, Emerson. Thus in these pieces the writer's individual identity is involved in his or her self-presentation to a particularly intimate degree.

Moreover, the issues the unit addresses affect by implication every aspect of a person's life. We are talking not just about how these writers relate to the government, but also how they relate to the other people who are closest to them. It's as if every writer in Unit Three can hear his or her parents, spouse, or children saying, "How can you as a woman (or man) say such things?" Through its readings and apparatus, the unit invites students to investigate the sophisticated ways these writers negotiate this tricky issue of ethos.

NOTES ON THE UNIT READINGS

Each selection in the unit is accompanied by its own headnote, reading questions, and writing questions, so it can be assigned independently of the other readings or combined with others as you see fit. We have also grouped each reading with several other selections in at least one of the three assignment sequences offered at the end of the unit (the sequences are discussed on p. 107). We urge you to assemble your course reading and writing into one or more sequences, of either our design or your own.

In the following notes, we provide commentary on each of the unit's selections as well as guidelines for approaching and evaluating the writing questions.

CIRCUMSCRIBING WOMAN'S SPHERE

CATHARINE BEECHER, FROM *A TREATISE ON DOMESTIC ECONOMY* (p. 294)

Beecher is a fascinating character — a major nineteenth-century intellectual and sister of novelist Harriet Beecher Stowe, whose *Uncle Tom's Cabin* you may want to assign in a literature-enriched version of this unit (see p. 115). Beecher's work is also mentioned in the Margaret Fuller selection.

For all these reasons, Beecher is a good choice to assign. Also (like all of the other readings in this section of Unit Three except McCord), the Beecher selection is relatively short and therefore easy to add.

Twentieth-century scholarship on Beecher has emphasized her anticipation of contemporary feminist concerns, particularly her work for high-quality education for women and her creation of an independent career. As you can see by our placement of Beecher in the "Circumscribing" section, however, we are less inclined to accept this view of her as a proto-feminist. We see her as analogous to a native colonial functionary who, educated by the colonizers, uses that training to help keep the other natives down.

Writing Analytically

Rather than promoting either of these views of Beecher, however, we have used writing questions 1 and 2 to dramatize the problem of interpretation. We suggest letting each student choose one of these assignments (although you may have to step in to ensure that both questions find adherents) and then asking them to present their arguments in class in an informal debate. The discussion should be interesting because often students arguing opposite sides of the question will choose the same textual evidence to support their positions.

Writing question 3 highlights the practical consequences of Beecher's views on marriage and may therefore appeal especially to students who are or have been married. Students who see Beecher as fundamentally anti-feminist can have some fun exaggerating their marriage agreement for satiric effect. Those who choose to see Beecher as a kind of feminist will have a more subtle task before them in phrasing their document. Students might enjoy working on this assignment in small groups in class and then sharing the results with everyone.

JONATHAN F. STEARNS, FROM "FEMALE INFLUENCE, AND THE TRUE CHRISTIAN MODE OF ITS EXERCISE" (p. 299)

This selection is important to assign because the concept of "influence" recurs through Unit Three, and Stearns provides a good introduction to it. It is also interesting to compare his version of the vine metaphor with very similar wording in the "Pastoral Letter."

Writing Analytically

One of the interesting features of the "influence" concept is that it could be said to use flattery to get women to comply with the directive that they stay at home. Writing question 1 invites students to discover and analyze this strategy of flattery, as Stearns expresses it in his doctrine of influence and in other ways. You might ask students if they can produce any contemporary examples of attempts to flatter women into accepting subordinate roles.

Writing question 2 calls for students to compare and contrast contemporary materials with Stearns's negative portrayal of women who choose occupations outside the home, particularly activities directed toward social reform. Expect students to find striking similarities and differences. It's easy and fun to enrich this assignment with Folsom, as his piece is quite short and quite outrageous.

ALBERT A. FOLSOM, FROM "ABOLITION WOMEN" (p. 302)

In all fairness, you should remind students that we have not included Folsom's entire sermon — only those passages chosen as most offensive to feminist and abolitionist interests by the profeminist, proabolitionist editor of *The Liberator,* William Lloyd Garrison. Garrison intended that the excerpts be inflammatory. Perhaps Folsom qualifies these remarks elsewhere in his sermon. If we can assume that Garrison is quoting correctly, however (and we believe that is a safe assumption), then this part of what Folsom did say is disturbing enough.

Writing Analytically

In our experience, students usually need the teacher's guidance to see that Folsom is impugning the chastity of the abolition women he attacks and that one of his nightmares is miscegenation. We hope that writing question 1 can help students get into these issues. You should point out that responding to this assignment requires, first, explaining the way Folsom portrays the activist women and, then, inferring the other evils he hints will follow from their activism.

Writing question 2 allows students to analyze all of Folsom's strategies, including the ones discussed in the first writing question. We expect the comparison with Stearns to show Folsom operating mainly negatively, with threats and invective, and Stearns mainly positively, with flattery and gentle correction, although he also has his threatening side (for example, in the "vine" being trampled). Students usually judge Stearns to be the better persuader because he is less extreme. You can use this assignment as an opportunity to discuss how students handle opposing arguments in their own writing (since when they deal with them at all, they have a tendency to overstate their attacks).

MASSACHUSETTS CONGREGATIONALIST CLERGY, FROM "PASTORAL LETTER" (p. 305)

Note that if you intend to assign Grimké, then you must also ask students to read the "Pastoral Letter," since Grimké replies to it explicitly. You might inform students that, as we have recently learned, the author of this letter is the Reverend Nehemiah Adams, who in 1854 published a defense of slavery called *A Southside View of Slavery*.

Writing Analytically

The "Pastoral Letter" raises interesting questions not only about how socially acceptable attitudes get enforced institutionally (through official pronouncements such as this letter) but also about how much influence religious leaders should have on people's daily lives, especially their political decisions. These questions are quite timely, and writing question 1 invites students to connect them to contemporary religious examples of their own choosing. Students who are not religious or who do not wish to use examples from their own religious traditions can find plenty of material in the popular press.

The "Pastoral Letter," a formal public document, repeats some of the arguments found more informally in the sermons by Stearns and Folsom. Writing question 2 encourages students to explore these connections through mining the three texts for information on positive and negative models of womanhood. Because of the high degree of repetition among the three texts, this assignment can also be connected to the issue of the dissemination of hegemonic attitudes.

LOUISA CHEVES MCCORD, FROM "ENFRANCHISEMENT OF WOMEN" (p. 307)

This is a difficult and lengthy text, and you don't need to assign it for students to see representative views on the confinement of women to the domestic sphere, which may be gleaned from other, easier readings in this section. Furthermore, as a proslavery southerner, McCord was virtually ignored by the other writers in this unit, so you don't need to assign her for students to be prepared for other selections. Indeed, McCord has been little noticed by feminist scholarship in this century, and her work is hard to come by.

Nevertheless, for a number of reasons, we urge you to make the effort with McCord. We think her essay well repays close study. She is a brilliant stylist, and she and Stanton are perhaps the two best organized, most aggressive arguers in the unit. One by one, McCord cites feminist arguments and proceeds to demolish them on the basis of her own assumptions concerning human nature, as our reading questions attempt to point out (you'll find that any one of them could be good for an entire class period's lively discussion). This selection is an excellent choice for a course emphasizing argument.

Not only are McCord's arguments clear and well structured, but they are also complex. Like Stanton, McCord interweaves issues of race and gender in provocative ways. Her arguments will help students to see, more completely than any other reading in this unit, how hierarchical thinking can be expressed in defense of both an "aristocracy of sex," as McCord puts it, and an "aristocracy of color." It's important for students to understand, in light of McCord's example, that white women could be racists and could assent to the oppression of African Americans and that women could even be sexist and assent to the oppression of women.

Writing Analytically

Writing question 1 calls attention not only to the complex structure of McCord's arguments but also to the problematic quality of her assumptions. The assignment encourages students to see the crucial distinction between general principles and specific applications by juxtaposing McCord's defensible principle against her questionable applications of it to white women and people of color. (For a discussion of the distinction, see "How Does Argument Make Meaning?" in Unit Two, p. 60.) It is our intention that by writing this assignment, students will discover that they probably cannot evaluate McCord's arguments (whether they agree with some of them or not) on the basis of logic alone; they will have to call on their own values and assumptions and at times, perhaps, simply admit to living in a different moral universe from McCord's.

McCord is also interesting for the kind of emotional appeals she makes to her women readers. As writing question 2 will help students discover, McCord flatters her readers by assuming that they are suffering saints who cope with their painful situation by force of intellect alone. McCord could even be said to lay more stress on the suffering of the wife and mother than do writers like Stanton, who use accounts of female suffering as part of a justification for change. If McCord wants women to stay home, why emphasize the pain that is to be found there? Evidently McCord thinks her readers will respond positively to a picture of a woman who commands attention through the guilt she awakens in those she serves — a kind of passive-aggressive mother-monster that has come to be commonly condemned in contemporary popular psychology but that, of course, is still very much with us.

And at the same time that she holds up this model of the suffering saint, McCord herself constructs an ethos in this essay that is far from passive. (For a discussion of ethos, see p. 88.) Indeed, one of the striking aspects of McCord's persona here is what could be characterized as a relish for violence. Several times she conjures up images of activist women being physically attacked for what she regards as their effrontery, as when the refined white "Miss Marta" receives a black eye and other injuries from illiterate black "Sambo" at a political rally. This example, too, suggests the threat (as

McCord sees it) of miscegenation. Ironically, though, given her basic position, McCord herself clearly has not chosen to suffer in silence. Writing question 3 invites students to explore these questions of ethos. The comparison with Beecher will probably elicit more differences than similarities, enhancing the interpretation of Beecher as a proto-feminist.

NEW YORK HERALD, "THE WOMAN'S RIGHTS CONVENTION: THE LAST ACT OF THE DRAMA" (p. 318)

Some of Folsom's and McCord's themes are present in this brief text, notably the ideas that women's departure from the domestic sphere carries the threat of miscegenation and that physical violence is an appropriate response to finding women out of their sphere.

Writing Analytically

The *Herald* editorial can be said to deal with these race and gender issues in an oversimplified, almost cartoonlike fashion, as might be expected in the popular press, with its appeal to more of a mass audience than Folsom's middle-class New England congregation or the well-educated readers of the scholarly journal in which McCord published. The rhetorical strategies particular to this genre are highlighted in writing question 1, which calls for a comparison of the *Herald* piece with a contemporary example of what we might call "hate journalism." Encourage students to consider what kinds of argument can and cannot be made in this format.

Students will probably need your help to see that the editorial's concluding images of women giving birth in public constitute physical threats that are also explicitly sexual — that is, these images suggest that women who work outside the home will be punished by being forced to bare their private parts in public. Writing question 2 invites students to explore the connections with Folsom and McCord, particularly concerning race issues.

Women activists in the nineteenth century, of course, were well aware that they were attempting to gain a hearing in a public climate strongly influenced by negative representations in the popular press. The Seneca Falls "Declaration of Sentiments and Resolutions" was intended to counteract such bad press and put the women's rights cause in a better light. Writing question 3 asks students to consider how this document combats the ad hominem and ad feminam arguments to be found in the editorial.

CONTESTING WOMAN'S SPHERE

SARAH GRIMKÉ, FROM *LETTERS ON THE EQUALITY OF THE SEXES AND THE CONDITION OF WOMEN* (p. 321)

Sarah Grimké and her sister Angelina Grimké were major figures both in abolitionism and in antebellum women's rights activism. For their activism in these causes, they were denounced by Catharine Beecher and others; the Massachusetts Congregationalist clergy's "Pastoral Letter" was apparently largely provoked by their activities. Because of Sarah Grimké's importance to these mingled strands of thought in the period, the excerpts from her *Letters* are an excellent reading to assign.

Grimké argues powerfully when she explicitly rebuts the "Pastoral Letter." The two pieces go together nicely, especially if you are emphasizing argument in your course. Grimké's arguments, originally published in a Boston newspaper, also provide an interesting example of how the hegemonic power of a document like the "Pastoral Letter" might be resisted.

Writing Analytically

Grimké's arguments, however, are largely reactive rather than proactive. She is a classic example of a woman thrust into feminism by sexist roadblocks thrown in her path as she tries to work for another cause, in her case abolitionism. Her initial motive for writing is simply to clear these roadblocks, not to articulate a new, liberal view of woman's sphere. Nevertheless, she does articulate such a vision in the course of making her arguments, and writing question 1 encourages students to piece it together.

Writing question 2 asks students to bring Grimké and Beecher into dialogue. In the process, they will have to review an especially strong line of argument in Grimké, concerning her opposition to women's subordination to men. Because this assignment will tend to encourage an antifeminist interpretation of Beecher's position, it might be a good idea also to encourage students to look for possible points of agreement between the two writers.

Writing question 3 raises the issue of Grimké's ethos. (For a discussion of this term, see p. 88.) Presumably she was acutely aware of audience reactions since, like most of the other writers in this unit (McCord and Fuller are notable exceptions), she often spoke in front of large groups. Also, of course, as her engagement with the "Pastoral Letter" makes clear, she was aware of the ways in which women activists were negatively characterized by their opponents. What we find particularly interesting about Grimké's response to this rhetorical situation is that, unlike some other women's rights activists (Stanton and Cooper, perhaps), she does not choose to mitigate her feminist views by emphasizing what might be considered traditional feminine traits in herself. Instead, to a greater degree than any other writer in this unit, she takes the spiritual high ground. Responses to this assignment therefore might segue interestingly into a discussion of how people react to social activism that announces itself as religiously motivated. You might encourage some in-class discussion of contemporary examples, such as Operation Rescue activists, who are fond of comparing themselves to the abolitionists.

MARGARET FULLER, "THE WRONGS OF AMERICAN WOMEN, THE DUTY OF AMERICAN WOMEN" (p. 331)

Margaret Fuller is a major nineteenth-century intellectual figure whose contributions to the Transcendentalist movement are only now coming to be fully appreciated. With regret, we decided not to include an excerpt from Fuller's most important work on women's rights, *Woman in the Nineteenth Century*. While acknowledging the essay's importance, we found it just too dense and difficult to excerpt effectively for inclusion in a reader like *Negotiating Difference*. You might want to assign *Woman in the Nineteenth Century* in a literature-enriched syllabus for Unit Three (see p. 115). We have, however, included an essay in which Fuller touches on many of the themes addressed by other writers in the unit — she discusses the work of Beecher explicitly — and thus we have served our book's goal of emphasizing the dialogue among writers.

Writing Analytically

Like Beecher, Fuller is regarded as a feminist or proto-feminist by contemporary scholars. Also like Beecher, although not to the same degree, Fuller's writings can be read as providing evidence that she held some views that would not be considered feminist today. Writing question 1 highlights the problematic interpretation of Fuller's feminism and invites students to develop their own readings. Writing question 2 encourages students to discriminate carefully between the views of Fuller and of Beecher, since a casual reading of Fuller might suggest that they were in total agreement.

Writing question 3 highlights what by contemporary standards would be considered Fuller's feminism through comparing her work with that of a writer (either McCord or Stearns) who is clearly antifeminist. Among the three writing questions offered on Fuller, this is the one that most calls for the analysis and production of argument.

FREDERICK DOUGLASS, EDITORIALS ON WOMEN'S RIGHTS (p. 338)

Frederick Douglass, of course, is an important nineteenth-century intellectual, but one whose work on behalf of women's rights is not widely known among students. They will think of him primarily as an advocate of abolitionism and African American rights. We are pleased to include two of

Douglass's editorials on women's rights because we like to show the intersection of issues, then as now.

Writing Analytically

Writing question 1 is particularly important for getting students to understand how Douglass's complex political loyalties affect his rhetorical strategies. You should keep the class from digressing into a discussion of which oppression is worse, or more worth combating — that of women (of all races) or that of African Americans (of both sexes). Douglass was genuinely committed to both causes, but his primary commitment, particularly before the Civil War, had to be to the abolition of slavery. Class discussion should focus on how he manages to honor his two commitments *without* the kind of single-issue divisiveness that often besets the political rhetoric of representatives of oppressed groups today. At the same time, students must be allowed to be critical of the way Douglass balances his commitments — not all will approve of the choices he makes.

Writing question 2 follows up on the first writing question nicely because it allows students who may feel that Douglass has unfairly slighted women's issues to explore more carefully what he really says about woman's sphere. We think that Douglass shows himself here to be a more egalitarian feminist than many of the women writers in this unit — more egalitarian, perhaps, than Cooper or even Stanton. His position is more like Grimké's. We do not find him making arguments for greater freedom and responsibilities for women (such as women's suffrage) on the grounds of some special, higher nature belonging only to women.

Writing question 3 returns to the issue of Douglass's multiple commitments and invites students to imagine how his loyalty to feminism might have resulted in greater abuse from opponents such as Folsom and McCord than he would have received if he had confined himself to advocating African American rights alone. By stepping forward for feminism and sharing the speaker's platform with white women at Seneca Falls and other women's rights conventions, Douglass seems to embody the threat of miscegenation against which these white racists inveigh. His convictions, as you may have to point out to students, have brought him into the kind of close contact with white women that these writers find suspect.

SOJOURNER TRUTH, RECORDED BY FRANCES D. GAGE, "A'N'T I A WOMAN?" (p. 342)

Students are usually fascinated by Sojourner Truth and impatient with contemporary scholarship that would deny them the pleasure of believing Gage's riveting story about Truth's "A'n't I a Woman?" speech. While we have tried to summarize the controversy about versions of the speech in our headnote, we have also assumed in our reading and writing questions that Gage's version represents Truth's ideas quite well. When we ask questions about what Truth says in her speech, we assume that these questions can be answered with reference to the Gage text.

Writing Analytically

In asking students to analyze Truth's speech for the way she balances her commitments to abolitionism and women's rights, writing question 1 does *not* ask them to worry about whether Gage's version has somehow skewed this balance. Truth is clearly committed to both causes, and our sense is that her commitments are relatively equal, at least in this speech. You should not let the class digress into a discussion of which cause better deserves Truth's allegiance. Rather, keep the focus on the sophisticated ways in which she balances these commitments rhetorically (see also our discussion of a similar issue in Douglass, p. 97).

Truth's position is complexly ironic. White men have justified white women's confinement to the domestic sphere on the grounds that women have a special need for such careful treatment. Truth points out, however, that men have contradicted themselves in that they do not accord all women such treatment. Ironically, she implies, her treatment as a slave woman at the hands of professed sexists has been remarkably "egalitarian" — they have oppressed her just as harshly as they have treated their male slaves. Speaking out of her commitment to abolition, then, Truth is able to use a critique of white men's racism as a club to beat them for their sexism. At the same time, she points out that her oppression as a *woman* slave had some uniquely harsh features — for example, the loss of her children. She speaks out of her commitment to women's rights to heighten the power of her indictment of slavery. It seems to us that her treatment of the two causes is very effectively evenhanded.

Truth's evenhandedness makes for an interesting comparison with Frederick Douglass, as writing question 3 invites, since it is our sense that he more clearly maintains a priority for African American rights in his writing. Students who have answered writing question 1 could then incorporate this response into a paper for writing question 3.

Where we do challenge Gage's representation of Truth's speech in our questions, we focus not on the way she has transcribed Truth's words but rather on the way she has dramatized the surrounding scene of the convention and the part Truth played in it — as in writing question 2. This assignment is perhaps best offered as an option to students who are already able to see what might be offensive about Gage (and who, perhaps, are eager to take her to task). If you assign it to the whole class, you will have to make sure that all the students understand in what ways Gage could be considered patronizing and racist. You can let those students who do see the problem lead the explanation.

Ralph Waldo Emerson, "Woman" (p. 346)

Emerson has many enthusiastic proponents among American teachers. Thus students often come to the study of this essay already introduced to Emerson's "Self-Reliance" and prepared to take a reverent attitude toward the Sage of Concord. "Woman," however, is usually kept out of sight by Emerson enthusiasts, and students may be quite startled not only by what we might call the sentimental cultural feminism of this essay but also by the meandering, not to say maundering, style. You can reassure them that it is not necessary to admire every one of Emerson's works wholeheartedly in order to retain respect for this important intellectual leader. And, after all, here he does advocate women's suffrage.

Also notable in this essay are Emerson's allusions to poets, philosophers, political leaders, and other writers through the ages, made more frequently, perhaps, than in other works of his that students may know. In general, we have been reluctant to burden the reader with footnotes in *Negotiating Difference* unless an explanation is absolutely necessary for comprehension (unlike a scholarly edition, in which every reference must be tracked down). So you will see that in the Emerson essay we have identified only those allusions that we feel will help students appreciate Emerson's point. For other references, the context itself should be sufficient.

Writing Analytically

Writing question 1, by asking students to explain how Emerson defines woman's nature, acknowledges the possibility that he can be read as a cultural feminist. Lest students make too easy an equation with contemporary feminisms, however, we also point out the possibility of a social-class aspect to Emerson's definition (even though he explicitly denies any necessity for "easy circumstances" on p. 349). The kind of refinement he attributes to women, for example, may not be innate but may be the product of education and leisure, as when he depicts women as uniquely suited to regulating social intercourse. We think there could be a very wide range of responses to this assignment.

Writing questions 2 and 3, in effect, triangulate Emerson's feminism. A comparison with Stearns will highlight the degree to which Emerson is a feminist by contemporary standards: He advocates a far wider sphere of action for women than Stearns does. At the same time, we hope that students will notice some similarities in the two clergy's views of female influence. Comparison with the egalitarian feminist Grimké, however, will highlight the degree to which Emerson's views of women's special powers could be considered sentimental or even subtly degrading — a species of the kind of flattery that Grimké denounces.

If you are spending some time on Emerson, it might be productive to assign writing questions 2 and 3 first, giving one to small groups in half the class and the other to the remaining groups; then ask the groups to present their findings in class. After hearing these reports and the ensuing discussion, everyone could write a response to question 1.

ELIZABETH CADY STANTON, "A SLAVE'S APPEAL" (p. 357)

Most students have heard of Stanton and know that she was an early women's rights advocate. But, interestingly enough, they may tend to regard her as a comic figure, as they often regard women who were public advocates for suffrage and other feminist concerns. It seems to be the act of going public, taking to the street and the public rostrum, that brings down the most severe sanctions. See the *New York Herald* editorial for an example of how these mocking images of women activists got started.

Most students do not know that Stanton began her activist career working for abolition, a fact that usually raises her in their estimation. Nor do they expect her address to be as clear, sharp, and aggressively argued as it is. As noted in our discussion of McCord, she and Stanton are perhaps the two most cogent arguers in Unit Three. Both are acutely aware of opposing positions and concerned with demolishing them. Our reading questions on Stanton help to point out some of these arguments; or you could just go through her essay paragraph by paragraph with the class and catalog her argumentative strategies. Stanton's piece, like McCord's, is long and difficult, but we believe that it well repays close study, especially if you want to teach argument.

Notable in this essay are Stanton's frequent allusions to poets, philosophers, political leaders, and other writers through the ages. In general, we have been reluctant to burden the reader with footnotes in *Negotiating Difference* unless an explanation is absolutely necessary for comprehension (unlike a scholarly edition, in which every reference must be tracked down). So you will see that in the Stanton essay we have identified only those allusions that we feel will help students appreciate Stanton's point. For other references, the context itself should be sufficient.

Writing Analytically

Of course, given Stanton's initial commitment to abolitionism, it is ironic that in her effort to advance women's rights Stanton could be perceived as belittling, or even sacrificing, the cause of African American rights — by calling herself a "slave," for example. Writing question 1 calls attention to her multiple allegiances and asks students to evaluate the ways she balances them (see also our discussions of a similar problem in Douglass and in Truth pp. 97 and 98). Writing questions like this one that ask students to probe complex commitments are particularly demanding. You should encourage students not to oversimplify their judgments, for example, by just pegging Stanton as a racist.

Writing question 2 acknowledges Stanton's vigorous response to opposing positions, as already noted, as well as the subtle differences that may exist between her and fellow proponents of women's rights such as Emerson. This question might be divided among small groups, with each group comparing Stanton to a different one of her adversaries or allies (students may choose authors other than the ones named in the assignment) and then reporting back to the class.

Writing question 3 calls students' attention to another kind of rhetorical dialogue in which Stanton was engaged, not only with public advocates of various positions on women's rights but also with the laws themselves that defined women's rights. Here students can see clearly the practical consequences of Stanton's activism.

ANNA JULIA COOPER, "THE HIGHER EDUCATION OF WOMEN" (p. 371)

Cooper's essay, while certainly well argued, does not rely as heavily on logical appeals as do the essays by McCord and Stanton. Rather, Cooper's essay is a treasure trove of various rhetorical strategies. It is particularly interesting to *study* the development of her ethos. Thus, although the essay is long and difficult, we believe that it well repays close analysis.

Writing Analytically

Writing question 1 allows for exploration of the issue of just what kind of feminist Cooper is. It might be most profitable to urge students to pursue the alternative suggested in this assignment, for a comparison with Emerson. Contemporary readers may well see Cooper as a kind of cultural feminist, similar to Emerson. But she goes much further than he does to advocate a wider sphere of activity for women. Her analysis is also infused with race consciousness, thus providing some nicely complex rhetorical considerations for students to discuss.

This race consciousness is the central focus of writing question 2. Cooper can be seen as another example of a women's rights advocate with multiple commitments (see our discussions of a similar issue in Douglass, Truth, and Stanton, pp. 97, 98, and 100). You might remind students that fully half of the essays in the book in which "The Higher Education of Women" first appeared focused on African American rights, not women's rights.

Notable in this essay are Cooper's frequent allusions to poets, philosophers, political leaders, and other writers through the ages. In general, we have been reluctant to burden the reader with footnotes in *Negotiating Difference* unless an explanation is absolutely necessary for comprehension (unlike a scholarly edition, in which every reference must be tracked down). So you will see that in the Cooper essay we have identified only those allusions that we feel will help students appreciate Cooper's point. For other references, the context itself should be sufficient. But because there is an enormous range of allusion in Cooper — much more than in the other two most prominent examples of this technique, Stanton and Emerson — writing question 3 focuses on this rhetorical strategy, which is closely connected with the development of ethos. You might discuss why Cooper, as an African American woman, might feel that she has to go to these lengths to establish herself as a well-educated, credible commentator on public issues. At the same time, we would invite students to admire the way such allusions can ornament and enrich an essay. To follow up on this point, ask students to provide their own contemporary examples of highly allusive prose, preferably examples they admire and whose allusions they understand.

LAWS, CONTRACTS, AND PROCLAMATIONS ON WOMEN'S RIGHTS

SENECA FALLS WOMEN'S RIGHTS CONVENTION, "DECLARATION OF SENTIMENTS AND RESOLUTIONS" (p. 387)

The great historical importance of this document argues for its inclusion in any Unit Three syllabus. Also, the document's use of the Declaration of Independence is fascinating rhetorically and locates it in an important tradition of American political speech.

Writing Analytically

Students are usually intrigued by this document's use of the Declaration of Independence, and writing question 1 asks them to focus on the rhetorical effects of what we might call the women's serious parody of Jefferson's document. Of course, these antebellum women's rights activists were not the only fighters for civil rights to interpret the Declaration in their favor, as you might point out to students (see, for example, the antislavery arguments invoking the Declaration in Unit Two). In responding to this assignment, students may well involve themselves in arguments about what the original signers of the Declaration intended it to mean and whether, if we can determine their intent, we are bound to follow it. (For more discussion of such interpretive issues, see "What Does 'All Men Are Created Equal' Mean?" on p. 57.)

Writing question 2 links the "Declaration of Sentiments" most closely to the themes of Unit Three by asking students to infer the document's position on what "woman's sphere" should be. Our sense is that the document outlines a fundamentally egalitarian feminist view of what women should be and do — even though there are cultural-feminist tendencies in the speech included in Unit Three by one of the authors of the "Declaration," Stanton.

Writing question 3 invites students to imagine the kind of opposition the "Declaration" faced. As the headnote mentions, this opposition spurred many of the original signers to remove their names from the document. Beecher's objections would probably be quite different from Stearns's, as

Beecher clearly advocates a wider sphere of action for women than Stearns does and shows none of his tendency to threaten women into submission. You might point out to students that they could approach this assignment satirically and write speeches that are exaggerated for comic effect.

NEW YORK STATE MARRIED WOMEN'S PROPERTY LAWS (p. 392)

These brief texts give students a sense of how women's civil rights were legally circumscribed in the period we are studying in Unit Three.

Writing Analytically

Writing question 1 basically asks students to synthesize the information gained from the reading questions. It is a good assignment to use for small-group work, with students taking detailed notes on their group's findings for their use in the second writing questions if it is also assigned.

Writing question 2 builds on the first. Students must have a clear idea of what these laws mean in practical terms for women's daily lives — which we hope they will get from the first writing question — before they can imagine how one of the authors listed in the second writing question would respond to them. Students might especially enjoy sharing their responses to this assignment in small groups.

MARRIAGE AGREEMENTS: ROBERT DALE OWEN AND MARY JANE ROBINSON, HENRY B. BLACKWELL AND LUCY STONE (p. 394)

You may need to help students understand the difference between these marriage agreements, which registered social protest and had little legal force, and twentieth-century prenuptial agreements, which usually do not entail protest and are legally binding. Twentieth-century prenuptial agreements aim primarily to allocate property between the marriage partners. Nineteenth-century marriage agreements aimed primarily to register a protest against prevailing social and legal norms governing the marriage relation. A better twentieth-century analogy with these nineteenth-century agreements might be the changes and creative additions some couples make to their wedding ceremonies, often implying some sort of protest — for example, when the bride omits the traditional "obey" from the phrase "love, honor, and obey."

Writing Analytically

Writing question 1 asks students to imagine the practical implications of these agreements. We think the marriages described here are pretty much what many people take to be the modern, egalitarian norm. Students may be surprised to discover that in antebellum America these couples felt it was necessary to "protest" in order to establish their desire to have such a marriage. At the same time, you should be alert to the possibility that some students, from various ethnic and religious backgrounds, may not approve of egalitarian marriages. They can respond to this assignment without having to evaluate the marriages the documents describe.

Writing question 2 picks up the issue we noted concerning differences and similarities between the nineteenth-century agreements and the various ways twentieth-century couples attempt to set the tone for their married life, through prenuptial agreements, creative ceremonies, and so on. You might invite students to include comparisons with ceremonies that do not create legal marriages, such as ceremonies recognizing the commitment of same-sex partners. Once again, we urge you not to assume that everyone in your class favors egalitarian marriage or creative ceremonies.

Writing question 3 works best paired with writing question 1, which could be developed in class through small group work if necessary rather than as a separate, full-fledged paper assignment. Students need to have a clear picture of what kind of relationship the documents aim to create before they can imagine how one of the writers listed in the assignment would react to it.

FROM THE FOURTEENTH AMENDMENT TO THE UNITED STATES CONSTITUTION (p. 397)

This brief text engages students in the problem of interpretation that was later to be tested in the Supreme Court case *Minor v. Happersett* (discussed on p. 105). Given the amendment's opening definition of a citizen, women are citizens; shouldn't they then be granted the full rights of citizens, including the right to vote?

Writing Analytically

Writing question 1 asks students to consider this problem solely on the basis of evidence in the text. Writing question 2 asks students to imagine how ardent women's suffrage advocate Elizabeth Cady Stanton might have responded to the amendment. You might want to remind students that their response here should take into account Stanton's dual allegiance to women's rights and African American rights. It is helpful, but not necessary, for students to write the first assignment, or at least to work on it in small groups, before writing the second assignment.

FIFTEENTH AMENDMENT TO THE UNITED STATES CONSTITUTION (p. 398)

This amendment appears to clarify the lawmakers' intention in the period immediately following the Civil War: to protect African American men's rights, but not the rights of women, whether white or of color.

Writing Analytically

Obviously, this trend in government put special strain on African American men and women, such as the leaders listed in the writing question, who were also committed feminists. This writing question invites students to consider the continuing problems of negotiating a dual allegiance (see also the discussion of this issue for each of the authors listed).

FROM *MINOR V. HAPPERSETT* (p. 399)

Here the interpretive problem posed by the Fourteenth and Fifteenth Amendments is addressed by the U.S. Supreme Court, and the amendments should be read along with this text.

Writing Analytically

Building on information gleaned from the reading questions, writing question 1 asks students to evaluate the justices' rather tortuous reasoning here. Make sure students attend to the logic of the arguments, setting aside as much as possible their own views on what the Court should have decided.

Writing question 2, which can easily be assigned independently of the first writing question, gives students the opportunity to focus specifically on these writers' positions on women's suffrage. Students may not have concentrated closely on this aspect of these writers' views when working on their texts, since there are so many other issues to consider. Their arguments are interesting, and you might encourage some class discussion of how they apply to other categories of United States residents who are currently denied the right to vote, such as citizens younger than twenty-one or resident aliens.

RESOLUTIONS OF THE AMERICAN WOMAN SUFFRAGE ASSOCIATION CONVENTION (p. 401)

It's a good idea to assign this text along with another set of resolutions from a women's rights convention, the Seneca Falls "Declaration of Sentiments and Resolutions." The earlier Seneca Falls text appears to be perfectly egalitarian, but it does not mention race or the particular needs of working-class women. These omissions could be construed as neglect of certain constituencies. Ironically, by being more forthright about the different categories of issues involved in the women's rights movement, the later text lays itself more open to charges of racism. It does acknowledge the needs of working-class women; however, to advance the cause of suffrage for white native-born women, it exploits white fears of people of color and native-born fears of immigrants. The emphasis in the resolutions on attaining school suffrage as a preparatory step to wider suffrage for women can also be construed as assenting to the identification of women with children's concerns — an identification promoted by ideologies limiting women to the domestic sphere.

Writing Analytically

All three writing questions ask students to consider these mixed allegiances. Writing question 1 poses the problem most comprehensively, while the latter two focus on race. You should encourage students to consider the issues noted in the previous paragraph when responding to writing question 1. Writing question 2 initially treats the resolutions as a case of dual allegiance similar to Stanton's. We would expect students to see that even if Stanton appears to prioritize women's rights over African American rights in her speech, she still does not exploit white racist fears quite as shamelessly as this document does. As writing question 3 points out, Cooper, with her forthright critique of racism within the women's movement, seems the ideal critic of what is wrong with these resolutions. Clever students, however, will make sure to represent Cooper's cultural feminism in their versions of her analysis, perhaps by having her approve of the school suffrage starting point.

NINETEENTH AMENDMENT TO THE UNITED STATES CONSTITUTION (p. 403)

Writing Analytically

If you have assigned the Fourteenth and Fifteenth Amendments and *Minor v. Happersett*, you will also want to assign the Nineteenth Amendment, not only so that students can see some kind of legal closure to the issue of women's suffrage, but also so that they can get involved in the writing question, which poses a series of questions about who is legally entitled to vote and how social barriers may be erected even against those who have that right. You might point out to students that during the Vietnam War, there was much social protest over the fact that eighteen-year-old men could be drafted but could not vote. Depending on where you live, the rights of recently naturalized citizens or noncitizen resident aliens may also be hot topics of discussion. You might assign small groups in the class to work on the different alternatives given in this assignment and to prepare their results for in-class presentation and debate.

ASSIGNMENT SEQUENCES

As noted in the introduction to this manual, we see the assignment sequences as an integral part of the approach we wish to promote in *Negotiating Difference*. The sequences put provocative voices directly in dialogue with each other — both in the readings and then, in discussions of the readings, among the students in your class. Of equal importance, the sequences stress the need to develop material carefully — rereading, rethinking, and revising — in order to produce the richest rhetorical responses in student writing.

You can use the reading questions that accompany each selection to aid students in preparing to write for the sequences. While the writing questions in each sequence tend to build on one another with added complexity as one moves through the sequence, you should also feel free to select among these questions to tailor the sequence to your students' needs and interests (you will see some of this adaptation of sequences going on in the model syllabi that we include beginning on p. 112). In what follows we will briefly discuss each sequence and its writing questions.

Sequence 1. What is woman's proper sphere of activity? (p. 405)

Although it includes McCord and Emerson, two lengthy and difficult texts, this sequence is probably the easiest of the three offered in this unit, because the question it explores is closest to the stated concerns of the texts under discussion (less inferential work or juggling of complexities is required of students here than in the other two sequences).

The whole notion of defining woman's sphere is likely to seem inappropriate to many students, and they may resist question 1 because they will not want to put forward any model that presumes conformity on the part of other people. You should urge them to take a stand on their own values, as expressed in the character the assignment asks them to create. Point out that autobiographical sources include women they have known, not only themselves (if they are female). To establish at the outset where everyone in the class is on the issues, you might ask students to share these papers in small groups or to "introduce" the women in their stories to the class.

Now that they've drawn their own portraits of good women, question 2 asks students to look at the portraits that two supporters of domestic ideologies present. We highlight the ways Stearns and McCord deal with suffering because we think they use it in interesting ways to attempt to glamorize their favored images of womanhood — and also because their emphasis on it could be said to imply that those who adhere to their images of womanhood are in for a lot of anguish.

Note that students can respond to this assignment without taking a position on whether the Stearns and McCord "good woman" is attractive to them. If you think that views on women's roles are particularly charged in your class, you can deny students the assignment's option to evaluate Stearns and McCord. If you make students wait until the last sequence question before they begin to articulate their own views, you will emphasize that the object of study is not ideologies describing women but rather the ways such ideologies are handled rhetorically.

Question 3 further expands students' understanding of just what the proponents of domestic ideologies want women to be and do. Expect students to produce the commonplace that raising a child is a tremendous contribution to the world. You can push them to connect this commonplace to notions of "civilizing" and "influence": What socially beneficial actions would a child have to perform in order to justify the mother's investment? Also, leave open the question of the degree to which Emerson's views on female influence jibe with those of Stearns and the "Pastoral Letter." There is room for honest disagreement, although certainly Emerson seems to take a cultural-feminist view of the matter, at the very least.

Question 4 clearly builds on the two previous assignments. For one thing, students can use parts of their earlier papers in their response to this assignment. They can also set up their response in two numbered parts, one the synthesized portrait of the "True Woman" drawn from the four sources named and the other Grimké's imagined critique of this portrait. The second part of the assignment asks them to move beyond description to analysis, albeit in the persona of Grimké. Students who favor the views of domestic ideologies on women should still be urged to try on Grimké's point of view.

Question 5 is also more challenging than earlier questions because the descriptive task it poses is more complex. Whereas the proponents of domestic ideologies had a fairly clear-cut idea of the model of behavior they wanted to promote (sometimes called the "True Woman"), opponents of this confining model did not have similar agreement on what women should be and do, even if they agreed on certain measures that needed to be taken to assure women's civil rights (such as giving them the vote). Grimké is the most egalitarian of the three; Fuller, while going pretty far in advocating egalitarian activities for women, still seems to conceive of women's psychology in ways that might be identified as cultural-feminist or even True Woman-like; Emerson seems to have the least imaginative alternative activities for women (although he advocates suffrage) and the most cultural-feminist or True Woman-like descriptions. Clever students might realize that they should consider the possibility that echoes of domestic ideologies in the writings of these women's rights advocates may be a rhetorical strategy for gaining more acceptance from conservative audiences. Point out this possibility if no one in the class mentions it.

Whatever their own views, at this stage in the sequence students will have thoroughly explored both a "True Woman" model and more egalitarian treatments. It is now time to turn them loose, in question 6, to make their own arguments about how women should behave. The model they develop could be an idealized portrait of woman incorporated into their paper, or it could be a set of behaviors that the reader infers from the paper's various arguments. At this point, we would expect students to be dissatisfied with the stories they wrote in response to the first sequence question. In-class discussion, perhaps in small groups, might focus on a critical rereading of these stories; the alternative assignment in question 6 allows for a complete reconception of them, this time accompanied by an explanation of what's being dramatized.

Sequence 2. *What are the responsibilities of women as American citizens?* (p. 406)

This is perhaps the best sequence to choose if you are emphasizing argument in your course. Its questions are rather abstract. The readings, which are lengthy and consider many aspects of the issues, include strong arguers McCord, Grimké, and Stanton. You will see that the first two sequence questions are basically warm-up exercises to get students thinking more creatively about the abstract issue of citizenship. Students are then asked to move immediately into rather demanding writing assignments involving multiple readings. It will be especially important in this sequence, then, to use the reading questions following each selection to prepare students for the sequence writing assignments.

You should anticipate the possibility that some students will use this sequence to ardently defend the contributions to American society of full-time homemakers. Just ask that they support their views with good arguments, not sentimental evocations of mom and apple pie.

Question 1 is intended to broaden students' notions of what citizenship entails. They may be inclined to think of it only in terms of legal obligations such as paying taxes or legal privileges such as voting. If students work together to make their lists as complete as possible, they will see that people pursuing their own interests may also be contributing to the common good. We hope they will see society as more of a communal enterprise.

Question 2 highlights the differences between how women's citizenship is understood today and how it was treated in antebellum times. All three texts considered here request many civil rights that students will already have listed in their responses to question 1 as responsibilities of women. You could ask one small group to work on the "Declaration of Sentiments," another on Stanton, and another on Douglass, while the rest of the groups are working on question 1. Then allow time for the different groups to compare notes. In effect, these two sequence questions compare nineteenth-century and twentieth-century definitions of woman as citizen.

Question 3, as we've noted, assumes that students have already done some preliminary work sorting through the arguments in Beecher and McCord. They are now asked to continue what, in effect, becomes an extended project of extrapolating a definition of the domestic woman as citizen from these two readings and *Minor v. Happersett*. In helping students develop their responses to this question, you should remind them to focus on the citizenship issue and not on other fascinating but distracting arguments on women in these sources (particularly McCord).

Question 4 poses exactly the same question — What is a woman citizen? — while drawing on three sources that argue for a wider, more modern definition. Once again, some preliminary work on these three rather difficult and lengthy readings is assumed. And, once again, you should remind students to focus their reading on the citizenship issue and not be distracted by the other fascinating arguments the sources contain.

If you feel that your students will be sufficiently challenged by dealing with the lengthy readings in questions 3 and 4, you can tell them not to pursue the evaluative option offered in each question. Simply describing what is going on in the readings may be plenty for them to do.

By the time you get to question 5, however, you should be pushing students to step into the evaluative mode. The question as stated, even without the specified option, will seem evaluative to many students, as they will not see the sources' arguments as anything other than purely altruistic or purely selfish (depending on their ideological orientations). Keep before students' eyes the dialectical relationship inherent in the concept of citizenship — the tension between the needs of the individual and the needs of the community. Encourage advanced students to write the option attached to this question, and make sure they feel free to express their own preference for whether individual or communal needs should have priority.

Question 6 allows the students finally to make their own views on women as citizens the central focus of a paper. Encourage them not only to draw on the sources, as the assignment suggests, but also to draw on their own earlier papers for this sequence. This paper should be in the form of an argumentative essay. You may want to rule out the alternative attached to this assignment if you want to maintain a heavy emphasis on argument in your course. At any rate, the alternative might work well as an in-class collaborative project after students have written question 6.

Sequence 3. How are women's rights and African Americans' rights connected? (p. 407)

This sequence is perhaps the most rhetorically focused of the three offered for Unit Three, in that juggling dual treatment of women's rights and African American rights creates interesting problems in persuasion for the source authors. The reading load is moderate, more like sequence 1 than sequence 2.

Question 1 gives students the opportunity to make personal connections with the sequence theme of multiple or conflicting commitments. Encourage students to pay special attention in their narratives to how they made their cases persuasive to the audience to whom they had to appeal, especially how they attempted to distinguish their cause from the claims of competing groups.

Question 2 immediately poses the problem of juggling commitments. Stanton and Cooper, as the students will know from their work on these readings, are committed to African American rights, but they also support women's rights and will not want to abandon this allegiance. Stanton, indeed, may give the latter cause priority. Point out to students that as political activists, Stanton and Cooper will want to retain the attention and favor of the largest possible audience; students should take that desire into account in writing their papers.

Question 3 is more analytic than the previous two more imaginative or "creative" assignments. It asks students to abstract the elements of the negative portrait from the sources and in some instances to draw inferences about what these elements might be. For example, students will often have to infer that the association of white women's rights activists with African Americans and abolitionism is meant to discredit the white women. The option given with this assignment might be fun to do in class; have students share their contemporary examples after they've written their response to question 3.

Question 4, also analytic, asks students to focus on how two African American writers balance their dual commitments. We would expect that in comparing Douglass and Truth, students will find that he prioritizes African American rights over women's rights, albeit subtly, while she deals with these commitments more evenhandedly. That difference, of course, does not necessarily mean that Truth is the better arguer.

Question 5 asks basically the same question as 4 about a different set of texts. Here we would expect students to find that Cooper deals with the commitments more evenhandedly, while Stanton and the resolutions prioritize women's rights over African American rights. The latter two sources could even be said to betray African American rights to promote women's rights; there is room for honest disagreement about this evaluation of Stanton and the resolutions.

Question 6 takes a slightly different slant, putting writers who disagree with each other about both women's rights and African American rights into dialogue. You should encourage students to note particularly how each writer attempts to make his or her views attractive. Students should also take into account the fact that McCord evidently addresses a different audience from that of Douglass or Stanton (although it might be possible to argue that while Douglass would have no interest in attracting any members of McCord's audience, Stanton might hope to move a few of them her way).

Question 7 asks students to draw on all their work for the sequence and the knowledge it has allowed them to accumulate on the rhetorical difficulties and rewards of merging the two causes. You should remind students that their arguments must address the rhetorical strategies that would be available to either a merged project or separate efforts for women and for African Americans.

RESEARCH KIT

Please see our remarks on the Research Kits in the introduction of this manual (p. 11).

Unit Three provides an especially rich ground for research development. There are many fascinating aspects of the period's battle over "woman's sphere" that simply could not be included because of space limitations. For example, we have not been able to consider the influence of social class on the conflict; but see assignment 2 under "Ideas from the Unit Readings." The unit does not include what we would now call feminist humor; but see "Ideas" assignment 3. We've merely touched on the important role of Protestant Christianity in women's activism; but see "Ideas" assignment 4. And to this topic should be added temperance activism, an important women's issue in the nineteenth century and a crucible for training women's rights activists that was arguably as important as abolitionism; see "Branching Out" assignment 8.

Furthermore, of course, there are many important premodern women's rights activists and thinkers on women's issues whom we could not treat fully, or even represent at all, in Unit Three. Fortunately, one of the easiest kinds of research for students to do is to attempt to find out about a person: See "Ideas" assignments 1 and 5 and "Branching Out" assignments 1 and 2.

The relationship between women's rights and African American rights is both historically and philosophically important, as Unit Three has suggested. Students who are committed feminists might be particularly urged to explore this area (see, for example, "Ideas" assignment 4 and "Branching Out" assignment 3). The issues involved will help these students become even more sophisticated in their thinking.

Also, as we suggest in one of the model syllabi (p. 115), Unit Three lends itself particularly to being taught in a format enriched with nineteenth-century American fiction by women. There has been a tremendous upsurge of literary criticism and literary history in this area in the last twenty years, most of which is not represented in the Unit Three bibliography, where we chose to concentrate on nonfiction sources that might be less familiar to teachers of English. You could devise wonderful research projects to explore this recent scholarship, particularly in the scholarly journals, which students often do not know how to search. You could encourage students to select interpretive problems that intrigue them from the additional books in the enriched syllabus and then to do a final research project in which they attempt to discover some recent critical sources on their chosen problems.

MODEL SYLLABI

The model syllabi are framed on a thirteen-week term, with week 14 being exam week. You can adapt them to your own number of weeks (if different) and number of class meetings per week. The model syllabi sometimes adapt the assignment sequences they use, omitting some questions or substituting others — you should feel free to be similarly flexible in developing your own syllabi. Remember, the sequences are not designed to be lockstep processes.

We assume that you will work in class on the reading questions accompanying the assigned selections as well as on the assigned writing and sequence questions (sometimes we give you suggestions in the syllabi for how to do so). Note that work on these questions can often be performed profitably in class in small groups. (For more information on group work, see p. 14).

We suggest that students keep a class journal in which they write responses to the reading questions before the questions are discussed in class. (Also remind students to read the headnotes accompanying the selections before they come to class.) In other words, our plan is that each reading assignment ("Read Stanton") also constitutes a writing assignment because students should jot responses to the text's reading questions in their journals. (For more information on the class journal, see p. 12.)

You should collect and review these journals at least as often as you collect students' writing portfolios. We suggest that students be graded according to some version of the portfolio method. (For more information on the portfolio method, see p. 17.)

Syllabus using two sequences from Unit Three

Here we have combined sequences 1 and 2. The first looks at a more general question of what a good woman should be and do; the second, employing some more difficult readings, focuses this question more sharply around the idea of how a woman can or should be a good citizen.

Week 1

Read: Unit Three introduction; Stearns
Write: Sequence 1, question 1, or Sequence 2, question 1

On the first day, ask half the class to write responses to sequence 1, question 1, and half to respond to sequence 2, question 1; then let students compare notes. You might inquire how many of those responding to the sequence 1 question included any ideas relating to citizenship in their models. For the next class, ask the students to read Stearns, and then do the related reading questions in class.

Week 2

Read: McCord
Write: Sequence 1, question 2
Collect: Essay from week 1

Week 3

Read: Emerson; "Pastoral Letter"
Write: Sequence 1, question 3
Collect: Essay from week 2

Week 4

> Read: Grimké
> Write: Sequence 1, question 4
> Collect: Essay from week 3

Week 5

> Read: Beecher; Fuller
> Write: Sequence 1, question 5

Week 6

> Write: Sequence 1, question 6; portfolios, including class journals
> Collect: Essay from week 5

In class, discuss approaches to question 6. Also spend some time helping students prepare their portfolios for collection at the end of the course — for example, putting their class journals in order, perhaps choosing a paper to revise, and so on. This is a good time to give lessons on any grammar or mechanics problems that are common among your students.

Week 7

> Read: "Declaration of Sentiments and Resolutions"; Douglass; *Minor v. Happersett*
> Write: Sequence 2, question 3
> Collect: Essay from week 6; portfolios

Just before they submit their portfolios, students should review what they wrote and heard when they shared the first two writing assignments (week 1) in class at the beginning of the course. Highlight for them the function of the citizenship issue in defining what a woman should be and do. Then discuss the reading questions from the "Declaration of Sentiments," Douglass, and *Minor v. Happersett* with an eye to how they bear on the question of women's citizenship.

Week 8

> Read: Stanton
> Collect: Essay from week 7

Week 9

> Read: Cooper
> Write: Sequence 2, question 4

Week 10

Write: Sequence 2, question 5
Collect: Essay from week 9

Week 11

Collect: Essay from week 10

Ask the students to bring in contemporary examples of models of women's behavior, both good and bad. They should try to choose images that are presented deliberately as models of what women should or should not be. Sources might include political pronouncements on "family values," an advice column on personal relationships from a fashion magazine, a rap song that demands certain types of female behavior, a video of a television show with a popular female protagonist, and so on. Students should be prepared to articulate the general traits of the women in their samples.

Week 12

Write: Sequence 2, question 6

In class, continue student presentations of contemporary models of good and bad women; discuss and compare with the nineteenth-century examples presented in the sequence readings. Also discuss sequence 2, question 6, which might incorporate revised portions of the paper students wrote for sequence 1, question 6.

Week 13

Collect: Essay from week 12; portfolios (weeks 13 or 14)

Before you collect the essays, students may want to share them, perhaps in small groups. In class, help students prepare their portfolios for final submission.

"Enriched" Syllabus: One sequence plus additional literature

This syllabus uses sequence 1 plus Beecher and Cooper; "The Wife," a short sketch from Washington Irving's 1820 *Sketchbook;* Harriet Jacobs's slave narrative *Incidents in the Life of a Slave Girl;* and three novels: *Uncle Tom's Cabin* by Harriet Beecher Stowe; *Ruth Hall* by Fanny Fern; and *Iola Leroy* by Frances E. W. Harper. The Irving piece can be handed out in class; the four additional books are all readily available in paperback editions, and we suggest you simply order them for your class to purchase.

Sequence 1 concentrates on the battle over a general definition of the "good woman" in antebellum America, which resolves into a conflict between those who wished to confine women to the domestic sphere and those who wished to enlarge their sphere of action. The added books show nineteenth-century American women writers struggling to redefine woman's sphere without completely abandoning domestic ideologies. This struggle was complicated for some women by the moral imperatives they felt to act against slavery or to resist white racism inflicted on their own persons.

Week 1

Read: Unit Three introduction; Irving, "The Wife"; Stearns

In the first class, you can ask students to read "The Wife" and then to explain the leading traits of Irving's Mary Leslie. How does she help her husband? If, as Irving's narrator suggests, she constitutes an advertisement for marriage, what are men being promised in a wife through Mary's example? Do students find Mary attractive? (Expect a range of responses here — some will like her loyalty.) To conclude this discussion, you can suggest that Irving's sketch gives us an example of how nineteenth-century American domestic ideologies imaged the ideal woman, sometimes called the "True Woman." Tell students that this course will explore these ideologies and those who resisted them in both fiction and nonfiction. Then ask students to read Stearns for the next class. Round out the week with work in class on the Stearns reading questions, noting resonances with the behavior of Mary Leslie.

Week 2

Read: McCord
Write: Sequence 1, question 2

Week 3

Read: "Pastoral Letter"; Emerson
Write: Sequence 1, question 3
Collect: Essay from week 2

Week 4

Read: Grimké
Write: Sequence 1, question 4
Collect: Essay from week 3

Week 5

Read: Beecher; Fuller
Write: Sequence 1, question 5 (modify by adding Beecher)
Collect: Essay from week 4

In class, discuss adding Beecher to sequence 1, question 5.

Week 6

Read: Cooper
Write: Cooper, writing question 1 or 2
Collect: Essay from week 5

Discuss the Cooper writing questions in class and give students their choice of which one to finish for next week.

Week 7

Read: *Uncle Tom's Cabin,* chapters 9 and 13
Collect: Essay from week 6

Week 8

Read: *Uncle Tom's Cabin* (continued)

Continue discussing the portraits of women in *Uncle Tom's Cabin.* Students should finish reading the novel this week and move on to the much shorter work by Jacobs (see week 9).

Week 9

Read: *Incidents in the Life of a Slave Girl*

In discussing *Incidents,* point out to students that Jacobs must tell an unconventional story — she has children out of wedlock, actively resists slavery, and remains estranged from marriage — to an audience whom she presumes to be largely committed to domestic ideologies. Help students read her narrative with an eye to the strategies she uses to cope with this audience. Look at all the portraits of women in the book, not only the way Linda Brent is depicted. Look at the relations between white and black women. Compare with *Uncle Tom's Cabin.*

Week 10

Write: Student-designed essay on *Uncle Tom's Cabin* or *Incidents* (see the following discussion)

Devote the classes this week to students' development of a paper on a topic of their choice but fitting within the following constraints: They must write about either *Uncle Tom's Cabin* or *Incidents,* and they must use three of the sequence readings in their papers. This would be a good time to teach them MLA citation form as well as to give lessons on any grammar or mechanics problems that are common among them.

Week 11

Read: *Ruth Hall*
Collect: Student-designed essay from week 10

In class, discuss *Ruth Hall.* You might suggest that Ruth's life is quite in keeping with the domestic view of women until her husband dies (although there are a few disturbing foreshadowings of trouble to come). The inadequacy of domestic ideologies is then revealed by the suffering she and her children face, alleviated only when she manages to become a breadwinner in her own right. In effect, Ruth is forced out of the domestic sphere. You might also look at the portraits of men in this book. Fern appears to be struggling not only with new roles for women but also with the new roles men will have to assume if women change.

Week 12

Read: *Iola Leroy*

In class, discuss *Iola Leroy.* You might suggest that, like Ruth Hall, Iola spends an idyllic period living in accord with domestic ideologies, until she is driven out of that traditional sphere by the death of her father. In Iola's case, the failure of domestic ideologies is accented by her discovery, at the same time, that she is African American and that, apparently, "woman's sphere" as conceived in these ideologies cannot include African American women; compare with *Incidents.* Iola discovers racial solidarity and becomes an activist for African American rights. As with Fern in *Ruth Hall,* also consider the roles Harper imagines for men.

Week 13

Write: Student-designed essay on *Ruth Hall* or *Iola Leroy* (see the following discussion)

Devote the classes this week to students' development of a paper on a topic of their choice but fitting within the following constraints: They must write about either *Ruth Hall* or *Iola Leroy,* and they must use three of the sequence readings in their papers. These papers will be due at the end of the term.

UNIT FOUR

Wealth, Work, and Class Conflict in the Industrial Age

THEMES AND ISSUES IN UNIT FOUR

Most of our students are focused on — not to say obsessed with — jobs, careers, and money. Unit Four puts their concern with work in a theoretical, historical, and ideological context. The materials were developed in a first-year writing course primarily for business majors that Bruce has taught. But for business majors or any other students, the crucial issue and greatest stumbling block in understanding the history and meaning of work in the United States has been the notion of social class. The materials in Unit Four raise a set of related issues that can lead students to think more deeply and write with greater force on an issue that at once engages them personally (work) and repels them ideologically (class difference).

The Gospel of Wealth and Its Critics

The attitude toward individual success spelled out and defended in the Gospel of Wealth is so deeply ingrained that Americans take it for granted most of the time. We are always conscious of our own efforts. We know how hard we work. Naturally, we wish to think that our successes are our own, the rewards of our labor or our cleverness. It follows that hard work brings success and that each person is responsible for her or his own lot in life. Students will be tempted to defend this point, to give personal examples, and, as in the other conflicts presented in *Negotiating Difference*, to simplify the issues, choose sides, and debate. As before, we urge you to focus on analyzing the issues as presented in the selections and to avoid, at least at first, a general debate on the truth or merits of individualism and the success ethic.

It is, to be sure, important to acknowledge the significance of the issues raised here for U.S. society today. Today, American-style individualistic capitalism appears to have triumphed over its socialistic rivals as a route to economic well-being. At the same time, though, the distribution of wealth in the United States is grotesquely unequal. Economic class differences are becoming more evident, despite the mass-cultural messages that insist we are all more or less middle class. In examining the Gospel of Wealth in the context of nineteenth-century working conditions, we discover the historical, ideological, and social roots of today's incipient crisis. Like the other units of the book, Unit Four reveals that modern conditions have not sprung up overnight. Then as now, unjust material conditions can be interpreted as the inevitable natural order.

Socialism and Social Class

The critics of the Gospel of Wealth counterbalance individualism with the ethic of communal responsibility. For many nineteenth-century American reformers, the practical, political embodiment of the communal ethic was some form of socialism. Henry George argues against private ownership of land and against the accumulation of large personal fortunes. Edward Bellamy projects a utopia in which all citizens earn the same salary, regardless of the work they do. Henry Demarest Lloyd attacks the immorality of capitalism. William Z. Foster became a leader of the American Communist Party.

Many students instinctively reject socialism, failing to see its many forms and historical avatars — failing, in many cases, to understand it at all. Their visceral rejection of the very term *socialism* is a living sign of the total victory of capitalist ideology. Socialism has been so thoroughly demonized in the United States that the mere word closes off doors in the brain. Unit Four shows how this demonization occurred, providing a striking instance of the way past negotiations affect us today.

Should your students reject the unit's socialist arguments out of hand, it may be possible to discuss the reasons for their automatic reaction in large theoretical terms (that is, the way experience is constructed by the very kinds of discourses represented in *Negotiating Difference*). However, we think it best to reestablish the historical context of the selections and turn to the particulars of the text at hand. What exactly is being criticized, and with what merit? What exactly is being proposed, and to what effect? Students need to learn to tolerate arguments they hate, as we have pointed out in our comments on earlier units, if only to learn about the methods and motives of those who use such arguments. The theoretical debate on social construction can wait until after students have had a chance to work through the arguments and evidence.

Nonetheless, we think it is important to be clear with students that there is a world of difference between racism or sexism as an ideological position and the socialism of George, Bellamy, and Lloyd. We have warned, in earlier units, against the blinding effects of using the terms *racist* or *sexist* as if they had explanatory power. But there is no question that genuinely racist and sexist arguments and actions are objectionable purely on those grounds. Socialism, however, as we find it here, is largely a critique of injustice. The critics of the Gospel of Wealth establish the tension between the consequences of individualism and the goals of fairness and justice. There is much to criticize in, say, the utopian system envisioned by Edward Bellamy, but the principle of communal responsibility should not be obscured by the faults of his rather fantastic proposal. Students may be tempted to say of Bellamy's scheme, "This won't work — look at the Soviet Union — therefore Bellamy is wrong." The analogy, of course, is false, but more to the point, such a response deflects but does not answer Bellamy's critique of capitalism.

It may be worth pointing out to students that the United States is the only one of the industrialized nations that lacks a serious socialist party. Japan, England, France, Germany, Israel, Italy, and many other capitalist countries have powerful socialist parties. Most of those countries have been and some are presently led by socialist governments.

One more word on this subject. The sources of difference represented in most of the other units of *Negotiating Difference* are impossible to hide or ignore: race, ethnicity, gender, national origin. But Americans are by and large unwilling to admit that there is a class structure in society. The ideologies of individualism and meritocracy that support the myth of a classless society are, of course, the focus of Unit Four. If students seem distracted by discussion of social class, it may be worthwhile to ask for some personal writing on the subject. Focused free-writing on the topic of is one way to do it. Or you may wish to assign question 1 in sequence 3 in two stages — a first draft early in the study of Unit Four and a revision later.

Working Conditions

In a number of the reading and writing questions, we ask students to note the point of view and motives of the writers and speakers who describe working conditions. The tone of these descriptions is, in several cases, so natural and ingenuous that it is difficult to identify any motive other than honesty. Our questions are not, however, designed to foster cynicism but to help identify ways of talking about conditions that are not simply neutral or acontextual. Most of the descriptions suggest that the working conditions of the day are far from natural and inevitable (to use Carnegie's words for the system of vastly unequal wealth). Our questions are designed to elicit discussions of the ways that explanations for these conditions are embedded in the descriptions or hinted at by them.

Students may object to the descriptions because they present such extreme cases or because the conditions described, such as child labor, are now illegal or because the descriptions are melodramatic. Our questions about motive may be helpful here, too. These descriptions are not disinterested: They are part of an argument. Remind the class that the Gospel of Wealth was promulgated in the world of work described here. These are the conditions that prompted the critics of the Gospel to write. The descriptions should help students to see that the Gospel's advice to "work hard and be good" has a problematic side.

Working with Sources

In our experience, students generally have one of two responses to the issues of working with sources that this unit raises.

In the first type of response, students may be inclined to fall back into simple advocacy, merely gleaning supporting arguments from the sources. In this unit, such responses may take the form of a defense of individualism (perhaps laden with personal stories of bootstrap success or exhortations to work hard). On the other side, the response may be a total condemnation of capitalism and the brutality of its defenders. Such responses are truth-seeking and presume that only one "side" of an argument can be correct.

The other type of response is relativism. Students responding this way may summarize sources but not evaluate their arguments or weigh them against each other, claiming (often implicitly) that there is no objective way to adjudicate between them — both opinions are equally valid and unprovable. This response may represent cynicism or simply intimidation in the face of historical information.

As we point out in comments on the assignment sequences, we have tried to phrase the questions to preclude such responses. Our goal is to get students to see the problematic nature of all work from sources. They must accept that there will be no way to determine a single true position that's not open to question. This, of course, means leaving behind immature notions of what history writing is all about and accepting a more critical view of what it means to be a student of history and society.

At the same time, students should not be allowed to opt out of shaping a story, of arriving at an informed opinion. Given the fact that they are not going to find one authoritative account, they must take responsibility themselves for the shape they impose on the material they collect from different sources. They will have to make decisions about whose version to trust, and to what extent. Students will have to realize that their own values play a large part in how they make these decisions — that they are not made "objectively." As responsible readers, they must consider a wide range of sources, but the ultimate shape of the stories they construct will be value-laden.

NOTES ON THE UNIT READINGS

Each selection in the unit is accompanied by its own headnote, reading questions, and writing questions, so it can be assigned independently of the other readings or combined with others as you see fit. We have also grouped each reading with several other selections in at least one of the three assignment sequences offered at the end of the unit (the sequences are discussed on p. 143). We urge you to assemble your course reading and writing into one or more sequences, of either our design or your own.

In the following notes, we provide commentary on each of the unit's selections as well as guidelines for approaching and evaluating the writing questions.

THE GOSPEL OF WEALTH

HORATIO ALGER, FROM *RAGGED DICK* (p. 426)

Few of our students have heard of Alger or recognize the stereotyped reference to "Horatio Alger stories" as any story about bootstrap success. Those who do know the reference are surprised to learn that Alger was the author and not the hero of the stories. This last misunderstanding is not so terrible: Alger regarded himself as an example of someone who rose from near-poverty to wealth and status as a result of hard work, generosity, and a measure of good luck.

This selection is a good one to start with: Students will find the reading easy, and it tends to confirm beliefs they already hold. The story of Ragged Dick is charming. If our students miss its absurdity, they are in the company of many readers over the years who have found the story inspirational and have discounted its implausibility. Realism is quite beside the point for these readers: Stories of heroes must show how the hero overcomes vast odds. There is no need to puncture this bubble, though it is important to point out that it was the story's exceptional appeal that made it so important in spreading the Gospel of Wealth.

The first reading question asks for Alger's underlying assumptions about the qualities that make Dick a success. Because the inherent goodness of hard work and kindness go unquestioned, they may also go unnoticed. It will be essential, in addressing the argument of the Gospel of Wealth, to establish that Alger makes certain personal qualities the source of success. Also note that Alger contrasts Dick with other bootblacks and street boys (the full novel makes much more of this than our excerpt) but does not contrast Dick with Frank, the rich boy.

Writing Analytically

Writing question 1 asks for personal reflection rather than analysis, a good way to ease into the semester. Students sometimes block on this question because they don't think it is acceptable to use television and films as a source of stories. A bit of class discussion about Superman and Schwartzenegger will help. Students should also be encouraged to refer to figures like Samson and Hercules, Lincoln, Gandhi, King, and so on. Ask students about the transmission of models as well as the qualities being transmitted. The preparatory discussion of this question is usually very lively. Later in the semester, after the class has worked through the issues raised in Unit Four, consider asking students to write an afterword to the essay they wrote for question 1: Have they changed how they see the heroes they wrote about? What qualities do they now find admirable?

Writing question 2, a much more analytical question, challenges students to see the world of the novel as an ideological construct. This is more than a question of realism, but some students who like the story will react defensively to the question's implication that the story is not realistic, as if that charge, if true, negated all the story's value. In discussing the question and responding to drafts that have a defensive tone, focus on the way the story makes an argument or takes an attitude. Writers invent characters and select events from an infinite number of possibilities: The selection that they actually make constitutes a way of seeing the world. Alger has a very definite point of view. Get blocked students to say what it is, how he conveys it, and what it implies about how poor people should be judged.

ANDREW CARNEGIE, "WEALTH" (p. 450)

Carnegie's essay is critically important in this unit: It appears in all three assignment sequences. This piece had extremely wide currency when it first appeared and was endlessly reprinted and quoted. This essay crystallized a powerful American attitude and, like Alger's stories, contributed to its preservation and promulgation.

Students typically respond to Carnegie quite positively — as they do to Alger. Carnegie is the sine qua non of individual success. He comes across as rational, hardheaded, and ethical. He out-Perots Ross Perot. Don't expect students to see the flaws in his argument or his philosophy.

The reading questions press students to understand Carnegie's argument and not simply to nod in agreement with it (or, for the rare critic, to be offended and dismissive). The ideas that Carnegie raises here are essential for understanding the themes of the entire unit: individualism, the stewardship of wealth, religious approval of wealth, social Darwinism, the inevitability of industrial capitalism, and opposition to charity. It may be worthwhile to assign all of the reading questions as a required journal entry or ask small groups to answer them and present their answers to the class.

Writing Analytically

The first two writing questions do not ask students to challenge Carnegie's views in broad terms. Rather, they point to problems with having vast wealth that Carnegie himself wanted to address. Question 1 focuses on the problem of fairness in a world that rewards individual rapaciousness. It calls for a close analysis and summary of Carnegie's argument, following up on the reading questions. In their papers, students should be encouraged to quote, paraphrase, and summarize — essential practices in academic discourse — before moving to analysis. Remind students (and yourself) that the task is not to analyze fairness and individualism in the abstract but to see how Carnegie manages this task. The question asks for an evaluation of Carnegie's proposed solution. If you assign this question early in the semester, you might want to play down the evaluative aspect of the essay or to accept an opinion in place of an evaluation. Using a sequence question later in the semester, as we recommend, will bring evaluation back into the picture.

Writing question 2 is quite similar to question 1, but it's a bit more focused, asking students to acknowledge the dilemma that Carnegie himself saw and recognizing the possible contradiction in Carnegie's answer.

Writing question 3 asks students to think about the rhetorical force of Carnegie's essay and invites them to criticize it. They will know from the headnote that its influence was great, and they may think it was universally approved. Other readings in the unit demonstrate that it was not. This question asks students to think about why not, either by imagining an unsympathetic audience or by reading one of the critics of the Gospel of Wealth and bringing a divergent view to bear on Carnegie's arguments.

Additional questions inviting criticism of Carnegie as a proponent of the Gospel of Wealth appear in the assignment sequences (see p. 144).

WILLIAM H. COUNCILL, FROM *THE NEGRO LABORER: A WORD TO HIM* (p. 461)

Councill raises the very vexed question of how African Americans were to respond to the Gospel of Wealth. If you assign the Alger or Carnegie selection before Councill — which we strongly recommend — ask students to speculate about how the recently freed slaves would have responded to Carnegie's arguments or the model portrayed by Alger. To begin this exercise, take an "inventory" of knowledge about the immediate postslavery period. The inventory is a critical-thinking exercise in which you simply ask the class to brainstorm about everything they know or even vaguely connect to the topic at hand. Put everything on the chalkboard. It is usually gratifying, to both students and teacher, to see how much collective knowledge there is in the room. In the case at hand, students can at the very least pull information from the unit introduction: African Americans worked as sharecroppers and agricultural laborers and very slowly entered the factories; discrimination ran high, as did unemployment and accompanying dejection; African American laborers were employed as scabs during strikes, a move that exacerbated union racism. Once some historical context is established, students can speculate about our opening question: How does the Gospel of Wealth fall on black ears?

Needless to say, this is a highly charged issue and may spark a heated discussion. In moderating the discussion, keep in mind that it is good for students to see how historical problems relate to current ones but that an understanding of the historical context and the text at hand is vital if we are to develop that relationship usefully. In other words, if things get too hot, go back to the text.

Councill endorses the Gospel of Wealth wholeheartedly. If we were to delete the title of the piece, there would be little to identify this text as being addressed to African Americans. Ask students to find and underline the few references that do identify it. The greatest distinction, however, is in the identity of the author (ethos) and the intended audience (the "inventory" exercise will provide a characterization of this audience). The first three reading questions focus on the way that Councill defends the Gospel of Wealth in general terms. These questions are important for filling out the students' understanding of the economic, religious, and political arguments that supported the Gospel. Councill and Carnegie are, in fact, the unit's best theorists of the Gospel, and their ideas are the ones addressed by the critics, George and Lloyd in particular. The final reading question draws on the "inventory" exercise but asks about Councill's political logic rather than audience.

Writing Analytically

Writing question 1 asks for a straightforward summary and analysis of Councill's theoretical position on the Gospel of Wealth. This is an important question, one that pulls together the reading questions and furthers understanding of the arguments for the Gospel. The direction to "explain the premises" that underlie Councill's arguments is an opportunity to discuss the need to ferret out the assumptions (or, in the Toulmin model, warrants) behind arguments. Councill is a good example to work with. Assumptions about values (what the arguer believes to be "good") can be seen in his religious premises. Once those have been described, students have a base from which to discover Councill's beliefs about political and economic values.

Writing question 2 puts Councill's theory and advice into its rhetorical and political context. Ideally, students will write an essay on question 1 and then expand it in question 2. Doing so will help students see the importance of understanding rhetorical purpose in analyzing an argument. This question pulls together the inventorying and the discussion of audience markers that we suggested earlier. And, of course, it asks for a critical evaluation of Councill's advice. Students should be reminded to use the inventory and cast themselves imaginatively into the situation of the African American audience. We also refer students to N. R. Fielding's testimony before the Senate. Fielding provides an example of a successful, "self-made" African American entrepreneur who nonetheless recognizes the difficulties faced by others of his race. Keep in mind that students will be speculating and drawing on their own experience in answering the last part of the question. Don't be disappointed by sketchy or unsophisticated responses.

Space limitations prevented us from including further selections on the plight of African American workers, but we have included, in the bibliography, references to the works we had hoped to use. If you assign outside research, these references will be a helpful starting point. The Research Kit suggests projects in this area that interested students can pursue as well.

RUSSELL H. CONWELL, FROM "ACRES OF DIAMONDS"
(p. 466)

Conwell's sermon, like the examples of Fourth of July oratory in Unit Two, brings us the flavor of a form of entertainment and education that has disappeared completely from the modern scene. Students will marvel at the fact that throngs of people paid to hear this lecture and bought thousands of copies when it was published. Nowadays, it is difficult to find a copy at all.

Russell H. Conwell and Horatio Alger are representative of the many clergy who literally preached the Gospel of Wealth from pulpit and page. There is a tone of certainty and self-satisfaction in their texts that exceeds even Carnegie's in his essay "Wealth," though students are not likely to notice or identify this tone. They may express impatience with Conwell's style of storytelling, but they will react positively to his message, as they do to Alger's and Carnegie's. Conwell says that there is no inconsistency in a person (a man, he says) having wealth and being a good Christian. Quite the opposite, in fact: A good person ought to pursue wealth and power because a good person will do good with it. Those who don't have material wealth may be considered to be suffering a punishment from God for their bad ways. Conwell does not pause for reflection — not even to remember the friends of Job, who declared him a sinner because he was evidently being punished.

It takes Conwell a while to explain his opening image, that acres of diamonds are to be found in one's backyard, not in far-off places. Toward the end of the sermon, he clarifies the point: Improve your situation where you are rather than chasing dreams of quick success. His examples at the start depend on luck, but at the end he speaks of business acumen, what we would today call finding a market niche. Like Alger, Conwell believes that one makes luck by working hard and being alert. If you have assigned any of the previous selections in this unit, some of the themes of the Gospel of Wealth should be evident and easily identified in discussion.

Writing Analytically

The first part of writing question 1 calls for a summary of Conwell's arguments. The second part, which asks about the refutation implicit in Conwell's positive arguments, assumes that you have discussed some other selections on the Gospel of Wealth in your class. In other words, the question asks students to imagine arguments opposing Conwell's and to discuss the way he answers them. Part of our aim here is to promote the sense that the issues elaborated in the Gospel of Wealth were in the air at the time, that Conwell had certainly heard and assumed his audience had heard the objections of the Gospel's critics and realized that he needed to answer them. By contrast, there is little if any of this sense of refutation in Alger.

Writing question 2 can be assigned as an extension of question 1 or can stand on its own. It asks directly about the validity of Conwell's arguments today. Students who defend Conwell (and many will) should be pressed, as in question 1, to think about whether there is in fact universal approval of these ideas. In other words, what shape does the debate over wealth take today? The alternative form of the question — the editorial reply — may be assigned to students in pairs to answer in point-counterpoint fashion, perhaps orally.

CRITICS OF THE GOSPEL OF WEALTH

EDWARD BELLAMY, FROM *LOOKING BACKWARD*: *2000–1887* (p. 477)

The dates and first-person narration in this selection will cause a surprising amount of confusion that you can try to dispel at the start. Bellamy wrote the novel in 1888 in the form of a memoir by Julian West, written in the year 2000. Julian announces that he was born in 1857. Take five minutes before the selection is scheduled for discussion and read the opening paragraph together in class. Our excerpting has removed all but a hint of the vestigial background plot of the novel. In doing your preview, be sure that students read the headnote and have a sense of the way Bellamy is proceeding.

Bellamy, like Henry George, was appalled by poverty in the midst of wealth, and, like Henry Demarest Lloyd, saw its cause in a social system that rewarded and rationalized selfishness. During the 1880s, the "labor question" came to the fore in a series of strikes and demonstrations that seemed to Bellamy to be the beginning of a great class struggle and led him to write *Looking Backward*. Bellamy's response was to project a true utopia, not the sort of dystopian vision associated with Huxley and Orwell. Every utopia is equivocal, though, and Bellamy's is no exception: The unquestioning acceptance of their society by the people of the year 2000 may seem like a version of the enforced conformity of *1984*.

The question of whether the society projected by Bellamy could or ought to come about is a material issue, but one that can be deferred for a time in your class discussion. The first concern, as always, is that students understand the argument about wealth and society that Bellamy is making by means of his novel. Reading question 1 asks about the wonderful allegory of the coach at the beginning of the excerpt. It is worth reading through this section in class, not only to be sure that all students get it, but also to point out the way allegory works. If you have time, a ten-minute in-class writing assignment can be to make up an allegory that would dramatize a current social problem — or simply update Bellamy's allegory for a modern audience. Reading question 3 should also be answered thoroughly, as it relates to the disturbing argument about charity presented by Carnegie and Conwell (and discussed in the unit introduction as well).

Writing Analytically

Writing question 1 is deceptively simple. Many students will find themselves falling into utopian thinking (the thing I want most to do turns out, what luck, to be phenomenally lucrative) and must be jerked back to the point: What sources of work satisfaction remain if all jobs are equally lucrative? Writing question 2 places question 1 in the context of Bellamy's argument. You might assign question 1 as a journal entry if you want a formal answer to question 2, or simply combine them.

Writing question 3 raises the query about Bellamy's utopia that we deferred earlier. Here, the context is the problem of individualism, and we ask students to consider the rather complex rhetorical strategy of writing a utopian novel. The bare issue of whether Bellamy's world could or ought to come into existence can be a red herring, especially if readers are speculating broadly about social forces in the nineteenth century or the actual socialist experiments of the twentieth. It's better, we believe, to focus on the way in which the question of "possibility" is mediated by considering how values we take for granted, like individual freedom, or characteristics that we take to be human nature, like individualism, may in fact be constructed by social ideologies and the myths and images that support them.

Writing question 4 assumes that students have read Carnegie, whose essay "Wealth" is exactly contemporaneous with *Looking Backward*. Here is another example of two writers responding to the same public concerns in opposite ways. The question of motives here makes it desirable for students to have worked on question 1 or 2, at least as a journal entry.

HENRY DEMAREST LLOYD, FROM *WEALTH AGAINST COMMONWEALTH* (p. 501)

Lloyd was a champion muckraker and proud of it. The term sounds terrible, but muckraking was a noble calling, bringing nasty business and political dealings to public light. (I. F. Stone in Unit Six is a modern example of the proud muckraker.) Lloyd was outraged by the underhanded, mean-spirited, and largely illegal maneuvering of the oil and railroad cartels. Most of his reportage details the very complex business connections, personal agreements, and legal sleights of hand by which the cartels gained market control. In this selection, Lloyd explains the motivation of the business leaders who took these actions. He blames not individual corruption or evil, but the principle of self-interest that lay at the heart of the Gospel of Wealth.

Lloyd's style is allusive and poetic and can therefore be difficult for students. His key points should, however, be quite clear: The principle of self-interest is primitive, not advanced; communal responsibility is the higher principle; laissez-faire would not be tolerated as a principle of law or politics as it is in the economy. These ideas, presented in the opening pages of the selection, set the stage for the elaboration to follow. Students will not comprehend statements like "Highways are used to prevent travel and traffic" unless they understand Lloyd's basic position that self-interest creates poverty for the many as a deliberate strategy for advancing the interests of a few.

Lloyd's view of the "good" as collective, not individual, is not as unproblematic as it may seem. You should lead students to define it as clearly as they can. Stress the context in which Lloyd is making his case: The Gospel of Wealth does *not* claim, as later capitalist apologias have done, that the wealth of the few trickles down to those below (though undeveloped hints of this argument can be found in Carnegie). Rather, the Gospel of Wealth holds that the poor deserve to be poor. This social Darwinist argument is the one that Lloyd is principally attacking.

Lloyd's characterization of the workers who run the industrial economy can be linked to Bellamy's portrait of the workers of the year 2000: Lloyd explains more cogently than Bellamy why a communal economy might be acceptable. Of course, both Lloyd and Bellamy appear to have been wrong. The Gospel of Wealth was and apparently continues to be more enticing to U.S. workers than any prospect of broad economic parity. Lloyd also gives a portrait of the professional moneymaker that can be lined up with Carnegie's images of philanthropic millionaires. Carnegie envisages cultured "stewards of wealth," while Lloyd portrays "barbarians from above . . . without restraints of culture." Both of these pictures can be topics of worthwhile reflection for students.

Writing Analytically

Writing question 1 asks directly for a summary of Lloyd's theory of self-interest. Challenge students to examine carefully the ways that Lloyd connects personal traits with systemic forces. It is easier to talk about "the economy" than about ideology as systemic forces: Students need to find ways to talk about how ideas rather than "human nature" affect behavior.

Writing question 2 points to the religious element of the Gospel of Wealth. Because the word "gospel" is so often used metaphorically these days ("don't take so-and-so's advice for gospel"), students may not see that *Gospel* of Wealth really does have reference to religion, even though we discuss it in the unit introduction and it appears in the texts of Reverend Alger and Reverend Conwell. It is helpful to remind students that the United States was a deeply religious country in the nineteenth century; they should understand how powerful the Christian lineage and pulpit endorsement of the Gospel of Wealth was at the time. Students may be uncomfortable with the appropriation of Christianity for politico-economic purposes — but that's one of Lloyd's concerns as well and precisely the focus of this question. Students who are interested in this topic will find question 2 a good start on a possible research paper. (Also see assignment 1 in "Ideas from the Unit Readings" in the Unit Four Research Kit.)

Writing question 3 asks students to contrast Lloyd and Carnegie, a very good exercise in a critically important form of academic discourse. This question can be the basis for in-class instruction in organization, summary, paraphrase, and use of sources. Students will need to identify the key areas of conflict and the main lines of argument and then outline the paper based on these subtopics (rather than following the order of arguments in the selections themselves). In preparing their outlines, students must decide how to deal with arguments that appear in one source but are not answered in the other (for example, Carnegie's proposals about inheritance). It may be worthwhile to make summarizing and outlining explicit "prewriting" assignments. Consider allowing time for multiple revisions on this one.

HENRY GEORGE, FROM *PROGRESS AND POVERTY* (p. 511)

This is the most challenging piece in the unit, but the potential benefits of working with it are great. As the headnote explains, George was a major figure in the period and his ideas were widely debated. After you work with this selection, we think you will agree with us that George deserves to be revived, not relegated to a footnote in economic history. His positions on the issues raised in this unit are complex and intriguing. Working through the selection will require careful reading and summary and will draw on knowledge of the period gleaned from the unit introduction and other selections. We recommend using George as part of sequence 1, which will make his the last selection you read.

George's ideas are often reduced, unfairly, to the idea of the single tax, referred to in the headnote. His long technical explanation of the single tax is not included in our selection, though the entire selection explains its basis. As with Bellamy's utopia, the question of whether George's proposed solution could possibly work can sidetrack discussion of his analysis of the problem: Why do workers live in poverty in the midst of the greatest material wealth in the history of the world — wealth that the workers in fact produce?

The single-tax proposal is fascinating, to be sure. George's idea is to set taxes on land at 100 percent of its rental value and do away with all other taxes. Owning land becomes pointless unless the owner uses it for a business or home. Speculation in land becomes prohibitively expensive: As the land increases in value (which the speculator hopes for), taxes soar. The speculator must, in effect, keep buying the property over and over again. Owners who use their own land, however, pay the equivalent of rent but get the benefit of paying no taxes on capital improvements, income, or interest. Economists are divided on the question of whether such a tax could by itself produce enough income for the government — but this is the sort of speculation we want to avoid. The important part, for now, is the analysis that led George to come up with the single-tax idea in the first place.

It is worth noting that the single-tax proposal does not eliminate capitalism, though it "socializes" land ownership and modifies the ways in which wealth can be accumulated. In *Progress and Poverty*, George clearly aims to argue for a significant but not overtly revolutionary reform of capitalism.

His is an excellent example of the way a subtle negotiation can be pursued in a vigorous argument.

George's striking opening evocation of the abundance of the industrial era raises the kind of question that standard history texts ignore, the question, in fact, that George himself had to work hard to formulate: Why did the growth of production, the reduction of costs, and the harnessing of vast new forms of power actually make so many people less able to support themselves? While George's answer shares much with the answers given by Bellamy and Lloyd, his own approach is very distinctive.

The sections of technical argument — about wages, rent, and interest, for example — may seem dense to students at first. The concepts are familiar but become confusing when they are carefully defined. Still, it should not take an economist to get them straight. One real benefit of reading these technical sections is that they show how expert discourse can be used in public argument. George is not trying to trick people into believing him because he can talk over their heads. He truly wants to make his audience understand. This is an effort at logos, not ethos. Do not despair, though, if students do not seem to understand the economic ideas. George's other arguments can be appreciated independently of them.

George's most intriguing idea is to eliminate private ownership of land. He begins by explaining the nature of ownership itself — a fine example of an idea that we take for granted but find it difficult to account for. Students will be fascinated by this section, which asks them to follow George back to the primitive bases of the concept of ownership and then confronts them with George's conclusion that no definition of ownership explains how natural resources can be owned. Reading questions 2, 3, and 4 address this issue and should generate a lively discussion in class.

Writing Analytically

Writing question 1 addresses the question of land and resource ownership, playing on current concerns about the environment and drawing, we assume, on classroom discussion of this point. The question calls for an evaluative summary, always a useful way of testing and ensuring comprehension. It also asks students to think about refuting George — that is, coming up with theories of ownership that would include land and resources. A frequent difficulty in such a refutation exercise is that students feel they are being directed to oppose a view they agree with. Here, as with the similar exercises on Carnegie, for example, it is important to remember that an advocate for any point of view is well advised to imagine the opposing view. In other words, students should consider what opposing arguments *could* be advanced and then say where they themselves stand on the issue.

The alternative suggested in question 1 adds George's powerful argument about freedom to the issue of ownership. Rhetorically, George is appealing to the highest of American values and, at the same time, taking the risk that opponents will claim the freedom to own land as quintessentially American.

Writing question 2 raises the difficult issue of individual motivation. Like Lloyd, George argues that the economic system makes greed a positive quality, encouraging our worst impulses. George is very circumspect in arguing this point. Caution students answering this question to stay very close to the text and remember that the issue is how George manages his argument. An alternative to this question, linking George with Bellamy and Lloyd, is question 3 in sequence 1.

Writing question 3 asks for an analysis of George's rhetorical strategy and should appeal to students interested in the technical economic aspects of his argument. Making complex ideas clear is only part of the battle for George. Question 3 directs students to look at the way George draws technical ideas into imaginative life, shows how rational choices are constrained by their misunderstanding, and reorients us to see them from the perspective of higher values. Why, he asks finally, must economic forces drive our notions of charity, fairness, and goodness?

WORKING CONDITIONS

ELIZABETH STUART PHELPS, FROM
THE SILENT PARTNER (p. 530)

The Silent Partner is fairly easy reading, rather melodramatic, but unexpectedly complex in the way it addresses the issues raised in the unit. Superficially, the novel seems to be asking what a good-hearted capitalist can do to lighten the oppression of workers. The superficial answer is to give them access to education, culture, and human kindness. But like other novels that advocate moderate reforms, *The Silent Partner* vividly depicts problems far beyond the reach of the solutions that the novel recommends.

The personal solution taken by Perley Kelso is terribly attractive. That Phelps herself found it difficult to distance herself from Perley is evident in our selection and even clearer in the conclusion of the novel (not included here) in which Perley is virtually canonized for her self-abnegation. On the one hand, Phelps conveys the seriousness of the problem by having Perley (and Sip as well) step out of the comforting conclusion typical of women's novels of the time (see Unit Three on this subject). On the other hand, Perley's solution leaves the system of unequal wealth in place, calling on people to join hands across the gaps and be good to each other.

But once the proposed solution is on the table, we can evaluate it. Perley keeps her wealth but uses it selflessly. She chooses a life of independence, giving up the chance for traditional domestic harmony. The workers welcome the opportunity to hear concerts and learn about literature. There is much that is satisfactory in this arrangement, but Phelps's picture of the lives and working conditions of the factory hands suggests that fundamental conditions have not changed. Certainly, the real capitalists, Maverick Hayle and his father, do not change their attitudes, or the work schedule in the mill, or the wages of the workers.

Phelps's description of work in the mills and life in the mill towns is confirmed by other accounts, such as the Senate testimony included in this unit (see, in particular, the testimony of R. S. Howard). In fact, Phelps used published accounts, including hearing transcripts, as sources. In a prefatory note to the novel, Phelps emphasizes the critical and satirical angle she has taken. While not wishing to slander those good Christian manufacturers who interest themselves in their workers' welfare, she says, "Had Christian ingenuity been generally synonymous with the conduct of manufacturing corporations, I should have found no occasion for the writing of this book." She believes, she says further, that people are generally ignorant of working conditions in the factories. And finally,

> I desire it to be understood that every alarming sign and every painful statement which I have given in these pages concerning the condition of the manufacturing districts could be matched with far less cheerful reading, and with far more pungent perplexities, from the pages of the Reports of the Massachusetts Bureau of Statistics of Labor.

The true theme of the novel, then, emerges as the wealthy characters' inability to comprehend the lives of the workers. The apparatus questions point to this conceptual gap.

Writing Analytically

Writing question 1 asks about the way that Perley comes to bridge this gap. Phelps's treatment of Perley's change is surprisingly subtle. Students who write this essay will be summarizing a number of scenes — a useful exercise for most students, as we have said before. But beyond summary, students should discover that it takes more than *seeing* the workers' lives to effect Perley's change of view. The Gospel of Wealth, remember, says that the poor deserve to be poor — that is the view that must change.

Writing question 2 is a more complex version of question 1. You may wish to assign question 1 as a journal entry preparatory to writing question 2. Question 2 raises a host of analytical questions, including whether Phelps endorses Perley's solution. A useful in-class exercise to prepare for this essay is to have students write an analysis of the question itself: What is it asking for? What do students have to do to answer it? What sort of paper would constitute a good answer? This exercise (a sort often used in writing centers) instigates a discussion of what multiple subquestions — a very common feature of college essay assignments in many disciplines — are for, how to interpret them, how to respond, and so on.

Writing question 3 points students to other selections on working conditions — the focus of sequence 3, which we recommend as a way of setting Phelps in context and developing the issues raised here. The underlying question here is how a fictional narrative works rhetorically, how it argues. As we note in this manual in our comments on other units, students should see that the way a narrative selects the features of the world it portrays constitutes its perspective. Here the issue is complicated by comparing the rhetorical effect of a fictional portrayal with its nonfictional counterpart. Question 5 in sequence 3 elaborates on this question by using other readings from the unit. Consider assigning question 1 from sequence 3 as a journal entry during your discussion of Phelps.

TESTIMONY BEFORE THE SENATE COMMITTEE ON THE RELATIONS BETWEEN CAPITAL AND LABOR (p. 553)

This committee was formed, amid much politicking, to investigate the causes of the labor strife that was tearing the country apart. A widespread general strike called the Great Uprising occurred in 1877 (see the Unit Four introduction, p. 423), and a long series of less violent but nonetheless destructive strikes and work actions followed, leading up to another year of violence in 1886, capped by the Haymarket incident. On May 4, 1886, a homemade bomb was thrown into a squad of policemen who were coming to break up a labor meeting at Haymarket Square in Chicago, killing one policeman. The police opened fire on the crowd and their fire was returned. Many were killed and wounded. Eight labor activists were arrested and convicted, and four of them were executed, despite the fact that none of them could be connected to the bombing.

The reasons for labor violence, which hardly seem obscure to us now, were also perfectly evident in 1883. The purpose of the committee seems to have been to take official notice of the conflict and to get it on record.

The committee did not treat its task perfunctorily but made a genuine effort to hear a range of views, calling leaders of labor and industry, owners of small businesses, workers, civic leaders, women, African Americans, and so on. The committee also traveled around the country to hear testimony in many regions and from many industries. The result is a fascinating variety of voices and perspectives. It was difficult to choose among them. Henry George testified, for example, as did John D. Rockefeller. Among the witnesses in our selections, only Samuel Gompers and John Roach now have any notoriety outside the hearing room (and Roach is pretty obscure at that).

Though the witnesses are for the most part very articulate and thoughtful in giving their views, they still sound like ordinary people. The information they give is detailed and vivid, their views are strong, and the whole makes for fascinating reading. While it is possible to assign just some of the witnesses and still get the flavor of the whole, the reading is easy and compelling, and students should not find it hard to read the complete selection. (The sequences and some of the questions suggest ways to subdivide it.)

Sequence 3 focuses on working conditions and asks students to reflect on the connections between the conditions described in the testimony and the philosophy of the Gospel of Wealth.

Samuel Gompers (p. 553)

This testimony is full of important details about work, working conditions, wages, the purchasing power of money, living conditions of workers and their families, employers' strategies for exploiting labor, child labor, and much more.

In the opening sentences, note that Gompers says, "Strikes are the result of a condition, and are not, as is generally or frequently understood, the cause." In discussion, see if students can articulate the view that Gompers is attempting to correct, namely, that it is strikes that cause strife between labor and capital. Behind this view (which is expressed by other witnesses) is the belief that workers are greedy or that they are manipulated by radical labor leaders.

Gompers's testimony will point out to students that even where there were laws to constrain the exploitation of workers, employers found innumerable ways to bypass the laws.

Toward the end of his testimony, he speaks of the distance between employers and their workers and the resulting dehumanization of work. Sociology was not yet an academic field: Labor advocates like Gompers (and like Friedrich Engels in England) were among the few who examined and reflected on social relations.

John Hill (p. 561)

Hill discusses wage rates, explaining that the growth of industry in the South reduced the unemployment pool and raised wages. His implication is clear enough, but you should bring it out in discussion: Wages are set by each manufacturer based on the current labor supply. There was no standard wage rate in the South, unlike the North, where communication and union activity had created more uniformity. (Hill makes this point explicitly in an earlier passage not included in our selection.)

In discussion, try to get at Hill's assumptions about employers and workers. Start with reading question 3, which asks about child labor. Hill says it caused by parents who don't care about education. This explanation can be refuted from common sense or by reading Phelps or Gompers.

Follow up by discussing Hill's assumptions about what forces determine wages: the supply of labor, the absence of "vagabonds," and the permanence and intelligence of workers. You can examine and criticize each of these assumptions from the workers' point of view (for example, by reading Gompers). The labor supply means the unemployment rate; vagabonds are people searching for work; the permanence of workers is a function of steady employment, not the absence of wanderlust; and intelligence seems to mean the skills attained by steady work. In other words, Hill's inclination is to explain wage rates as a function of the workers' behavior individually or as a group instead of seeing wages as a function of employment practices. As Gompers says, wages are not related to either profit or cost of living. Although the cost of living in the South was probably less than in the North, use Gompers to get a sense of the buying power of the wages Hill mentions.

Timothy D. Stow (p. 564)

Stow's discussion of the *moral* condition of workers is probably the most striking feature of his testimony and needs to be aired in discussion (reading question 1 points to this issue). Ask, too, what makes Stow an authority on "moral" issues.

Stow's description of the reasons for workers' poor health seems perfectly obvious to us, but he does not treat it as obvious to the members of the committee. Difficult as it is for us to determine the general knowledge of the average U.S. citizen at the time, it is nonetheless striking that a witness could make such connections without even a comment like "of course." Some sense of what people generally thought comes out in comments like Gompers's about the cause of labor strife and Hill's here about petty theft not growing out of "pure cussedness."

The problem of drinking is inherently interesting to students, and both Medill and Howard raise the issue in later testimony. Writing question 2 at the end of the selection asks students to explore these witnesses' different perspectives.

Charles F. Wingate (p. 567)

This testimony is somewhat long but reads very quickly. It is a highly circumstantial account of the construction of tenement houses, the light and air to which residents had access, and the toilet facilities available. Very striking, too, is the apparent powerlessness of the government to do anything about the terrible conditions created by tenement housing. It is difficult to explain this powerlessness with precision. On the one hand, the problem was a new one, so no models for city or state control yet existed. On the other hand, the forces opposing any such control were considerable — and city governments are notoriously susceptible to obstruction by wealthy and powerful groups. Read Gompers to see how tenements were supported and to get an idea of who might have opposed regulation. Wingate, too, refers in passing to opposition by tenement investors. He also details the many complaints about tenement conditions, so there is no question about whether the city authorities knew about these conditions (remember that Wingate was a city employee).

Sequence 3, question 4, asks students to relate the testimony by Wingate and Gompers to the philosophy of the Gospel of Wealth.

N. R. Fielding (p. 573)

Fielding's answers are disappointingly curt, but this brief selection is nonetheless informative and intriguing. Fielding, an African American, appears to have taken the advice of William H. Councill: He is a self-made man — diligent, temperate, and modest. Fielding and Councill taken together make an interesting beginning to the study of African American concerns in the period, but the two selections are not adequate bases for any generalization. Indeed, they are distinctly atypical. We trust that students will not think that they are representative but will be surprised to see that at least some African Americans achieved economic stability in the South so soon after the Civil War. In the Unit Four Research Kit, assignment 8 in "Ideas from the Unit Readings" points toward further study in this area.

It would be interesting to know why the senators did not push Fielding for more information about his success: Who, for example, were his customers? Who worked for him? What wages did he pay? What sort of work, exactly, did he do? There is simply nothing in the transcript to explain the shallowness of the questioning.

In discussing the behavior of other African Americans, Fielding reminds us of how recently his people had been slaves: Many, he says, still cannot adjust to the need to provide for themselves. The Civil War had ended only eighteen years before, after all. Fielding is rather tentative in raising the problem of outright discrimination, but once he brings it up, he does not hold back. Still, he has no suggestions for what the government could do about it.

If to Fielding's fatalism we add the kind of obstructionism described by Lloyd and the government paralysis evident in Wingate, it is easier, perhaps, to understand both the militancy of many unions, on the one hand, and the accommodationism of Councill, on the other. When government intervened in the class struggle, it was taken for granted that it would side with capital.

John Roach (p. 575)

Individualism is Roach's religion, and wealth, of course, his gospel. Students who feel that Gompers and Stow are bleeding-heart liberals will be cheered by Roach. Though Roach is a terrible blowhard (he requires no prompting by the senators), he makes an articulate and powerful case against collective bargaining. Early in his statement, Roach comments in passing on what he perceives to be the motivation for joining a union — for social reasons or because of bribery — but utterly rejects collective bargaining.

Roach demonstrates his own method of bargaining quite vividly. Approached by a worker for a raise, he attacks the worker's initial premise, that he needs more money. Doesn't he live better than he would in Europe? Couldn't he live in cheaper lodgings? Next Roach attacks the worker's complaint about high rent, claiming that rent reflects the wages of construction workers. There is more fast talking here than logic — his employee wants higher wages, not lower rent. Somehow, Roach and his shipbuilding company have fallen out of the equation.

At the close of the argument about wages and rent, Roach addresses a real concern of the senators on the committee: the question of tariffs, which was being debated furiously at the time. Manufacturers like Roach benefited from tariff protection. Opponents claimed that tariffs ate into workers' wages. Roach's paean to American opportunity was a standard protariff argument.

His strongest argument for individual bargaining and differential wages, in the second half of his testimony, will require little explanation in class. This is the problem Bellamy tries to solve in *Looking Backward:* How can you pay the same wage to people whose work is of different value? Roach says quite simply that you don't. The real evil of unions for him is that they destroy the motivation for doing your best, or even for doing reasonably well. Why excel if you don't need to?

Writing questions 3 and 4 ask about Roach's philosophy. Sequence 2, question 4, puts Roach in the context of questions about the Gospel of Wealth, comparing him with Carnegie and contrasting him with Bellamy.

Joseph Medill (p. 581)

Medill takes an extreme social Darwinist position, arguing that the poor are lazy drunkards. His is a very pure Gospel of Wealth argument, as students should recognize from previous reading: Temperance, diligence, and thrift make people wealthy. It is instructive to note that Medill wielded a great deal of political influence and ran one of the nation's most powerful newspapers.

In arguing against the reduction of hours, Medill makes a strong and coherent argument. Direct students to the discussion of the eight-hour movement in the Unit Four introduction (p. 421) and to reading question 2. Medill's argument is entirely economic, but the eight-hour movement had several motives, such as time for rest, family activities, reading, and participation in civic affairs. Medill is nonetheless correct in his assertion that the demand was for a full day's pay for fewer hours' work, and the results he foresaw were entirely plausible: Costs could rise and an expanded labor pool could undercut wages anyway. The main argument against Medill was that manufacturing workers could easily generate about the same production in eight hours as in ten because they would not be exhausted and deliberately slowing down.

Writing question 2 asks about Medill's view of workers' drinking habits, and question 4 asks about his underlying assumptions about unions.

Robert S. Howard (p. 584)

Howard discusses three topics: corporate spies, workers' drinking habits, and blacklisting (a tactic for discouraging union membership). In introducing the second topic, he briefly complains about the manufacturers' inclination to give temperance lectures. (Joseph Medill's comments on drinking give a sense of what lay behind those lectures.) Howard's explanation of drinking is quite different from that of both Medill and Stow and very close to that of Phelps — he attributes the need or desire to drink to the harshness of working conditions and workers' resulting exhaustion. This connection is the topic of writing question 2.

Writing Analytically

Writing question 1 can be a valuable controlled exercise in research and using sources. We identify the possible topics to get students past the first step. (Students may not read the question ahead of time, though, so you might be able to do a brainstorming exercise in class and then compare the students' list of topics with the list in the question.) The next step is to reread the selection with an eye to finding passages relevant to the chosen topic. Students might work in pairs to review the testimony. They should mark the passages and then make a list that briefly summarizes each passage and identifies its source and page number. The synthesis can be a simple summary of what each source says, followed by a discussion of points of agreement and disagreement, or, preferably, a point-by-point summary. The question warns about overgeneralizing from a small set of sources. There are two problems here. One is to recognize a reasonable generalization (Gompers, Stow, and Howard describe similarly bad conditions in two different regions of the country, which suggests a general pattern). The other is to indicate the limits (it seems these conditions prevail, at least in the Northeast).

Writing question 2 asks about the drinking problem, about which many students have strong opinions. The test here is to recognize and analyze the different perspectives from which the three witnesses speak. Challenge students to mine the pieces for the witnesses's assumptions about workers, alcohol, economic conditions, and so on.

Writing question 3 asks for an analysis of Roach in the context of other testimony. Does Roach's philosophy hold up for all workers, or does it work only if Roach or someone like him is the boss? Given the growing mechanization of the worker that Gompers speaks of, what chances are there for distinguishing oneself, or of seeing the boss personally, or of overcoming grinding exhaustion to excel? If Roach seems to be arrogant or overbearing, does that mean that employers should not concern themselves with their employees' moral welfare? Wouldn't Stow and Howard applaud such concern? Try to keep students from simplifying the issues or seeking absolute answers.

Writing question 4 directs students to consider the assumptions underlying an argument. It may help blocked students to work through a series of questions. What does Roach (or whoever) believe about human nature in general? What does he regard as good or valuable? On what does he base these beliefs? What other views of human behavior or goodness does he reject?

Writing question 5 asks for a debate on unions. There is certainly not enough information in this selection for a serious consideration of the pros and cons of unions in the nineteenth century. What we do have, though, is the kind of information and range of opinions that would have affected people at the time. Once again, the challenge is to identify arguments and assumptions, to see that arguments may be refuted directly or indirectly, and to analyze a number of sources that contribute to a theme. This essay is good preparation for a research paper on unions (see the Unit Four Research Kit, assignment 6 in "Ideas from the Unit Readings" and assignment 8 in "Branching Out").

WILLIAM Z. FOSTER, FROM *PAGES FROM A WORKER'S LIFE*   (p. 588)

Working-class activism is represented in this unit by Gompers, Howard, Foster, and the Workingmen's Party of Illinois. The last two are the most radical in their positions, but Foster's politics are not much in evidence in this selection. Students interested in researching labor activism will get a start from Research Kit assignments 4 and 6 in "Ideas from the Unit Readings" and assignment 9 in "Branching Out."

Foster was born in 1881, so he started to work at the end of the nineteenth century. His stories show that the conditions that we have been linking with the nineteenth century continued into the twentieth. Government regulation of working conditions — now so often decried by conservatives as stupid and wasteful — did not begin until well into the century and, at that, every rule was resisted by industry. Opponents of regulation argued, as they do today, that rules were costly and unnecessary and an unfair intrusion of government into the private sector. An additional argument at the time was that workers were free agents who knew the risks associated with the work they chose. This argument was upheld by the courts. Thus, in Foster's day, workers had no health insurance, no workers' compensation insurance, no disability insurance, no unemployment insurance, and no right to sue the employer for work-related injury.

If you have read some of the Gospel of Wealth selections, ask students to reflect on the working conditions that prevailed when Carnegie and others recommended building museums and libraries as the proper form of charity.

Foster's adventures reveal quite a range of shady industrial practices. You may wish to ask for an account of them as a journal entry. The worst abuse, of course, is the treatment of workers as subhuman. Foster's tone indicates that this behavior was taken for granted by employers, supervisors, and the workers themselves. "Peonage in Florida" adds the terrors of the Ku Klux Klan, matched only by the terrorism of the state authorities in abetting de facto slavery.

In "The New York Streetcars," Foster talks for the first time about organizing workers. It is worth lingering over this issue in discussion. To begin with, it seems clear from descriptions of working conditions in Foster, Phelps, and the Senate testimony that industry itself would never have voluntarily moved to improve working conditions. Furthermore, unions had been on the scene since midcentury. Yet Foster finds himself in dreadful jobs with not a hint of union activity around him. Students should note that unionization was by no means universal. Why was this so? Reading question 2 asks about industry tactics for blocking unions, but why weren't workers more forceful?

Writing Analytically

You can assign writing question 1 as a journal entry, and it will be a lively topic for class discussion.

Writing question 2 calls for a perspective shift and a review of some Gospel of Wealth ideas. Foster seems to have the cleverness, energy, and initiative to be a Horatio Alger hero. He rises later in life to a high position in the political world — he was a candidate for president three times. Is he in fact a success? How do you have to change the terms of success to fit him? Why does he deliberately eschew traditional forms of success?

Writing question 3 synthesizes the previous questions, though you need not assign them if you want to do this one alone. Foster, citing Marx, points to an idea that we might take for granted — that we see things through the perspective of our social circumstances. This idea seems to coexist harmoniously with the view that our own experience is pretty much universal. It is the combination of these two views that makes it difficult to understand a different perspective. Students should balance references to their own experience with their reading of Foster, particularly the Harry Black story. Add Phelps if you have assigned her selection.

WORKINGMEN'S PARTY OF ILLINOIS, "DECLARATION OF INDEPENDENCE" (p. 597)

Reading question 1 directs students to read the original Declaration, which appears in Unit Two. In discussing this question, ask why the style of the original has been imitated (students might not immediately realize that this is the case). A fairly close reading of this selection is worthwhile. You may also wish to assign short passages to paraphrase in addition to the one in reading question 2.

The Workingmen's Party "Declaration" raises the question of why unionization and reformism were so slow to take hold in the United States (see the discussion of Foster, p. 141). Conservatism is the answer suggested here, following the original Declaration's reasoning: People are reluctant to change "the forms to which they are accustomed" until "a long train of abuses" forces them to do so. While there was a great deal of social-class conflict during this period, as we discuss in the unit introduction, an uprising comparable to the American Revolution did not, of course, take place. Was the train of abuses not long enough? Were the forces too unevenly matched? Was the society envisioned by the revolutionaries insufficiently attractive? A discussion on this point is necessarily speculative but can bring students to a better understanding of the issues.

The most important discussion here concerns the arguments that the "Declaration" makes. Students must draw on previous reading in the unit to understand the "abuses" listed — and called "facts" — in the middle of the "Declaration"; this piece is thus a useful incentive for reviewing the unit. The first challenge is to understand how all of these charges can be called "facts." In other words, start by playing what Peter Elbow (in *Writing without Teachers*) calls the "believing game": How are these arguments true? Next consider the assumptions that underlie the arguments — beginning with the opening statement about equality. What alternative assumptions could be made or were in fact made by proponents of the Gospel of Wealth? Finally, move to the "doubting game": How might these arguments be refuted?

By putting the workers' complaints and criticism of capitalism in an extreme form, the "Declaration" helps crystallize the conflicts between labor and capital. Students can try, as they review the unit readings, to locate the position of each selection on each point of conflict.

Note how carefully the "Declaration" phrases its conclusion: "we shall endeavor to acquire the full power to make our own laws. . . ." Is this a bold or a weak declaration? Ask students to consider the rhetorical situation here: What force did the writers think the "Declaration" would have?

Writing Analytically

The writing question for this selection draws on the review and discussions we recommend here. It is frightening for most Americans to contemplate the possibility that there might have been an anticapitalist revolution in the United States. Yet the dilemma faced by workers was very real and distinctly worse than anything suffered by the colonists who rebelled from England. This question asks students to compare the two declarations and weigh the seriousness of their arguments, to compare their stated premises, and to decide if the workers' declaration is a language game or a true heir to the original document's philosophy, values, and call to action.

ASSIGNMENT SEQUENCES

As noted in the introduction to this manual, we see the assignment sequences as an integral part of the approach we wish to promote in *Negotiating Difference*. The sequences put provocative voices directly in dialogue with each other — both in the readings and then, in discussions of the readings, among the students in your class. Of equal importance, the sequences stress the need to develop material carefully — rereading, rethinking, and revising — in order to produce the richest rhetorical responses in student writing.

You can use the reading questions that accompany each selection to aid students in preparing to write for the sequences. While the writing questions in each sequence tend to build on one another with added complexity as one moves through the sequence, you should also feel free to select among these questions to tailor the sequence to your students' needs and interests (you will see some of this adaptation of sequences going on in the model syllabi that we include beginning on p. 149). In what follows we will briefly discuss each sequence and its writing questions.

Sequence 1. What kind of society is envisioned by the Gospel of Wealth? (p. 601)

This sequence uses all of the selections on the Gospel of Wealth, pro and con. As we note earlier, you should not be surprised if students staunchly defend the ideologies of individualism, social Darwinism, and economic success promulgated by the Gospel's supporters. In our comments on the individual selections, we suggest ways to keep students focused on understanding the arguments; on seeing the ways that arguments, stories, and sermons construct ideology; and on seriously considering the positions and arguments of opponents. The questions in this sequence serve the same purpose.

Question 1 can be assigned early in the semester as a formal paper or a journal entry or both. It asks questions that students typically don't think about, whose answers they take for granted. It introduces the notion of "social group," which will be an inchoate idea for many students. The discussion part of this question is important and can be handled in a number of ways. Students may simply open the discussion, defending their own views or regarding them as so universal that they won't need defending. If students are shy about getting into the discussion, each student can write an anonymous summary of his or her answers, which can be read by someone else. Alternatively, a group of students can collate the answers. The goal is to dispel the idea that all the answers will be the same and to allow students to raise issues, many of which they will find in the unit.

Question 2 asks for a thorough explanation of the Gospel of Wealth, taking as neutral a position on it as possible. This is an excellent exercise in using sources, in generalizing, and in adopting a historian's perspective. If students are determined to make evaluative comments, tell them to confine them to their journals. The idea is not to stifle them or to suggest that it is wrong to evaluate. The point here is to avoid a rush to judgment, which can short-circuit analysis and comprehension. Judgment *is* called for in question 5, which assumes a reasonable grasp of the issues at hand.

Question 3 asks for the same neutral account of the arguments opposing the Gospel of Wealth. Help students see that the critics are not all taking the same position or making the same general assumptions (this is true of the Gospel proponents, too, but to a lesser degree). It will be harder to generalize for this question than for question 2, and you should examine drafts of the essay for unfounded generalizations about the three critics. The challenge for students is to be subtle — to say that all three oppose the Gospel, to be sure, but with different emphases and different ends in view.

Question 4 asks, at last, for evaluation. The answers to questions 2, 3, and 4 should hang together as a single essay. After explaining the positions on both sides, students evaluate them. Question 4 asks students to do this by trying to imagine the world that each side wants to create and then projecting themselves into it. The kicker, of course, is the last stipulation in the question, which translates: Would you prefer to be at the bottom of the ladder in a society with a long ladder or a short one? Many students will choose the former. Their explanations will help get at the important issue of why workers in the nineteenth century did not unionize or join radical parties to a greater extent.

Question 5 can be used to sharpen and focus the response to question 4, or it can be substituted for question 4. Question 5 puts the issues into more starkly economic and ideological terms. It also invites students to use their own knowledge of economics and brings out the continuity between the concerns of the industrial age and those of the present time.

If you wish to add selections to those in this sequence, we recommend some of the descriptions of working conditions — Gompers, Stow, Howard, and Foster — to give a sense of who is at the bottom of the social ladder.

Sequence 2. Is the "self-made man" a myth? (p. 602)

If so, it is a myth with tremendous power. This sequence focuses on individualism, on economic mobility, and on the idea of meritocracy. The questions in this sequence represent a subset of the larger questions about the Gospel of Wealth, and so the readings are substantially the same as those for sequence 1. You may wish to modify the readings in this sequence to include Councill, the African American proponent of self-making, and some of the descriptions of working conditions by Foster (arguably a self-made man himself), Gompers, or Phelps, which reveal the other side of self-making.

Question 1 is a warm-up that can be a formal paper, a journal entry, or both. Students love to tell these stories about themselves or members of their families. Some are quite touching and apparently genuine. Some, too, reveal unwittingly that the "self-made" person actually had enormous help because of prior circumstances or generous community support. Later in the semester, it may be possible to ask students to review these personal essays for signs of myth as opposed to reality, but there is no necessity to do so.

Question 2 asks for an investigation of the idea of self-making using the readings and taking as neutral a position on it as possible. This is an excellent exercise in using sources, in generalizing, and in adopting a historian's perspective. If students are determined to make evaluative comments, tell them to confine them to their journals. The idea is not to stifle them or to suggest that it is wrong to evaluate. Evaluation should follow demonstrated comprehension, but if students are looking forward to the former, they can short-circuit the latter.

Question 3 asks students to analyze the implications of the ideologies associated with the myth of self-making. The unit introduction discusses some of the implications — for example, the way poor people tend to be judged — and there is no reason for students not to refer to it, providing they show how these implications are brought out, positively or negatively, by the readings. In particular, students should be directed to mine Bellamy and Lloyd for their criticisms of individualism and the goal of personal success, as these are less present to mind for most students.

Question 4 is an alternative to question 3, posing the same problem in a slightly different way. The key term here is *meritocracy*, an idea that students tend to take for granted and want to defend to the death. If "self-made" carries the central connotation that one makes it on one's own without outside help or extrinsic advantages, then *meritocracy* carries the connotation that help and advantages are beside the point — one's fate is a function of intrinsic ability and desire. Lloyd questions this position as part of his attack on social Darwinism. Bellamy's criticism is indirect; his utopia is in fact a society in which merit really is individual rather than a function of social circumstances. Even Alger undermines the notion of merit by placing so much emphasis on luck. In short, students should find much here to complicate this "taken-for-granted" issue.

Question 5 challenges students to take quite a sophisticated perspective. The Gospel defenders, chiefly Carnegie (who speaks of the inevitability of inequity in wealth), argue that the inherent inequalities among people, the natural tendency to compete, and the desire to acquire wealth make capitalism the most natural economic structure for society. Lloyd argues that this view of human nature is partly inaccurate and entirely immoral. Turning Carnegie's assumption upside down, Bellamy argues that "human nature" is a function of the structure of society. Other readings from the sequence can be seen taking positions on this issue, too. This question requires abstract thinking and careful reading. It need not include an evaluation of the issue, though few students can resist taking a stand.

Sequence 3. How can we understand social class conflict in the United States? (p. 603)

Americans are terribly uncomfortable with the idea of social class. Regardless of their own class background, students seem to have trouble understanding the concept of social class or admitting that it has validity. This sequence confronts the problem of class in the United States historically, which makes accepting the concept a little easier.

You can assign question 1 on the very first day of class. It will force students to examine what is likely to be their own very understandable confusion about this issue. Class is by no means a simple category, even for those who aren't frightened by it. Social status is not directly related to economic condition: It is affected by family and cultural background, education, work, and location. Until fairly recently, even academic sociologists in the United States could ignore class differences. So don't be upset if students are tentative or confused. Sharing responses to question 1 is important. Do it in class discussion if students seem comfortable about it, or collect the papers and read selections anonymously next class.

Question 2 pairs Carnegie and the Workingmen's Party and asks for a comparison not only of their ideas of equality, but also of the clash between the ideal of equality and the acceptance (even glorification) of inequality. This is a difficult question, but students rather like to deal with these great abstractions. Part of the difficulty is that it is attractive to believe both positions. Carnegie begins with a notion of equal opportunity and uses that to rationalize inequality. The Workingmen's Party decries unequal conditions and calls for laws to restrain inequities. Carnegie speaks essentially about individuals, while the Workingmen's Party speaks of groups. This sort of analysis might be helpful in a preparatory discussion in class. The question itself asks for a response to Carnegie from the point of view of the Workingmen's Party, a useful exercise for getting students to distance themselves from a position that they tend to find attractive and seamless.

The readings called upon in question 3 reveal class differences that show the complex relations between money and other class-determining or class-marking factors: education, language, race, family relations, and so on. This is quite a different approach from question 2, for it does not ask about the reality or justice of inequalities. Where question 2 is philosophical, this one is sociological. It also poses the problems of using a variety of sources that conflict not only in their direct arguments and use of evidence but also in their premises. (For a discussion of this issue, see "Working with sources," p. 122.)

Question 4 now asks for a synthesis of the problems raised in questions 2 and 3 — indeed, a synthesis of all the readings in the sequence. The underlying question pits philosophical claims about equality and inequality against evidence of material social conditions that are maintained deliberately by the wealthy class to preserve inequality. The question sets up a contrast essay, which again means careful management of sources.

Question 5 is another synthetic assignment and can be used in place of question 4 as the major semester essay assignment. This question begins with Perley's effort to bridge class difference by education and "culture" rather than the equalization of wealth. The question of whether this will "work" should seem very difficult at the end of this sequence. (Perley is in fact doing what Carnegie recommends. Is this an endorsement of Carnegie's view of inequality? Well, no, since Perley is constrained in what she can do by the unreconstructed Hayles. Can material conditions for workers as a group be improved by educating only some of their number?) The question as stated concerns class conflict rather than class itself. Some discussion of class itself is necessary here, but direct students back to the dilemma of conflict in the nineteenth century.

RESEARCH KIT

Please see our remarks on Research Kits in the Introduction to this manual (p. 11).

Like all of the units in *Negotiating Difference*, this one raises issues that have powerful ramifications in our own time and in the lives of our students. The unit readings and questions raise a wide variety of problems that beg for further study and will reward research efforts. In addition, there are a number of topics that are touched on only briefly in the selections — the conditions of women and African American workers, the treatment of immigrants, the development of unions, and so on — and can be fruitfully investigated.

The Gospel of Wealth was always part of American ideology, though its implications before the industrial era were rather different. "Ideas from the Unit Readings" assignment 1 points to some of this history and suggests ways for students to dig deeper.

Unions are terribly important in the story told in Unit Four, yet we were not able to include much on their history, development, major figures, and issues. "Ideas" assignments 4 and 6, and "Branching Out" assignment 8 direct students to some ways of dealing with this fascinating and extensive subject.

Assignment 7 in "Ideas" suggests an approach to many problems of labor in the nineteenth and twentieth centuries. There are exciting and moving stories here in the travail of each successive group of immigrants as they faced astonishing, organized discrimination. Students may well be able to find older relatives or members of the community who can describe their own or their ancestors' experiences and add much to their research base. Race is addressed as a separate category in assignment 8, which would make a good group project.

Students' own work experiences, and the experiences of their families, can make the issues in Unit Four particularly engaging. "Branching Out" assignment 1 draws on this experience, and assignment 2 asks students to look into the community for research on work and working life.

Antifeminist backlash has obscured for many students the impediments faced by women not only at present but in the past. As we note in Unit Three, extensive and exciting new scholarship in the history of women's lives and work can be tapped for research papers (see "Branching Out" assignment 3).

Students will observe that working conditions today are considerably better than in the period covered by Unit Four. Three assignments focus on the way that the government intervened — and in many cases refused to intervene — in the treatment of workers (see "Branching Out" assignments 4, 5, and 6).

Writing about movies is not as easy as watching movies: Students who do "Branching Out" assignments 3, 7, or 8, will need to develop a vocabulary for discussing events portrayed and the style in which they are portrayed.

Assignment 8 is a very difficult project, even for a group. Students who wish to select this project should have some familiarity with the topics already and should be able to demonstrate a very clear focus at the beginning.

Assignment 9, asking students to investigate radical political parties, poses interesting and important questions about why the United States alone of the developed countries has no viable left-wing party. Students will be surprised to discover that such parties, vestigal though they are, exist at all.

MODEL SYLLABI

The model syllabi are framed on a thirteen-week term, with week 14 being exam week. You can adapt them to your own number of weeks (if different) and number of class meetings per week. The model syllabi sometimes adapt the assignment sequences they use, omitting some questions or substituting others — you should feel free to be similarly flexible in developing your own syllabi. Remember, the sequences are not designed to be lockstep processes.

We assume that you will work in class on the reading questions accompanying the assigned selections as well as on the assigned writing and sequence questions (sometimes we give you suggestions in the syllabi for how to do so). Note that work on these questions can often be performed profitably in class in small groups. (For more information on group work, see p. 14.)

We suggest that students keep a class journal in which they write responses to the reading questions before the questions are discussed in class. (Also remind students to read the headnotes accompanying the selections before they come to class.) In other words, our plan is that each reading assignment ("Read Carnegie") also constitutes a writing assignment because they should jot responses to the text's reading questions in their journals. (For more information on the class journal, see p. 12.)

You should collect and review these journals at least as often as you collect students' writing portfolios. We suggest that students be graded according to some version of the portfolio method. (For more information, see p. 17.)

Syllabus using two sequences from Unit Four

This syllabus covers nearly all of the readings in Unit Four. It uses writing assignments from sequence 1 and from the selections themselves, and borrows from sequence 3 as well. This combination allows ample time to investigate the Gospel of Wealth in its own terms, but then adds the context of working conditions to refocus the issues.

Week 1

Read: Unit Four introduction; Alger
Write: Sequence 1, question 1

If there is time in the first class meeting, have students begin to draft a response to sequence 1, question 1, and discuss their responses. Otherwise, pursue this assignment in the next meeting.

Week 2

Read: Alger (continued)
Write: Alger, writing question 2
Collect: Essay from week 1

Students should now have read enough to discuss the reading questions. Also discuss the assigned writing question and work on the drafting process. When you return the drafts of sequence 1, question 1, with your comments, begin to explain how revision works.

Week 3

Read: Carnegie
Write: Writing question 1, 2, or 3
Collect: Essay from week 2

Carnegie can be read quickly, but discussing the reading and writing questions takes time. You may wish to give one writing assignment to the whole class, form groups to take different questions, or simply allow students to choose. Note that question 3 calls for additional reading.

Week 4

Read: Councill
Write: Writing question 1 or 2
Collect: Essay from week 3

Week 5

Write: Sequence 1, question 2 (draft)
Collect: Portfolios, including class journals

This is a good time to catch up. Have an in-class writing workshop on revision; give lessons on any grammar or mechanics problems common among your students; continue discussions of the readings; discuss first drafts of the sequence writing assignment. Help students prepare their portfolios for collection at the end of the course — for example, putting their class journals in order, choosing a paper to revise, and so on. If your students can handle more reading, assign Conwell and discuss the reading and writing questions: Writing on Conwell can be part of the sequence assignment.

Week 6

Read: Bellamy
Write: Writing question 1 or 2
Collect: Essay from week 5

You may wish to have students submit a draft of the sequence essay this week — if not, then next week.

Week 7

Read: Bellamy (continued)
Collect: Essay from week 6

Use the Bellamy writing questions 3 and 4 as journal/discussion questions.

Weeks 8–9

Read: George or Lloyd
Write: Writing question 1 (George) or writing question 3 (Lloyd)

George is the most ambitious piece in the unit (Lloyd is difficult as well, but not as difficult as George). The discussion of George will need to be careful and slow. The essay question, too, calls for a complex response — drafts will take extra time.

Week 10

Read: Phelps; Gompers, Stow, and Wingate testimony
Write: Writing question 3
Collect: Essay from weeks 8–9

Week 11

Write: Sequence 1, question 2 or 3
Submit: Portfolios and class journals

The writing assignments for this week and next week are complex and synthetic. Have students draft both and then choose one to develop fully as the major paper for the course.

Week 12

Read: Workingmen's Party
Write: Sequence 3, question 2 or 5

Week 13

Collect: Essay from week 12; portfolios (week 13 or 14)

Syllabus using sequence 2 and requiring a research paper

Week 1

Read: Unit Four introduction; Alger
Write: Sequence 1, question 1

Students can draft the essay during the first class meeting if there is time and then discuss it at the second meeting.

Week 2

Read: Alger (continued)
Write: Alger, writing question 2
Collect: Essay from week 1

Discuss the Alger reading questions in class. Work on the writing assignment and discuss the writing process.

Week 3

Read: Carnegie
Write: Writing question 1

Discuss Carnegie carefully to bring out the theory that explains the success of people like Carnegie and Ragged Dick. Prepare students for the writing question.

Week 4

Read: Conwell
Write: Sequence 2, question 2
Collect: Essay from week 3

Devote part of a class to group revision of the Carnegie essay. Discuss the Conwell reading questions and draw out the definitions of self-making that the first three readings offer. Note that using sources means both generalizing (by combining common features of the sources) and acknowledging differences among sources.

Week 5

Collect: Draft of essay from week 4; portfolio, including previous essays (revised)

Use this week to catch up. Have an in-class writing workshop on revision; give lessons on any grammar or mechanics problems common among your students; continue discussions of the readings; discuss first drafts of the sequence writing assignment. Help students prepare their portfolios for collection at the end of the course — for example, putting their class journals in order, choosing a paper to revise, and so on. If students are caught up, advance the schedule to create more time for research later.

Week 6

Read: Lloyd
Write: Sequence 2, question 4

In addition to discussing Lloyd, work in class on the writing assignment, treating it as an example of how to work with sources — a controlled mini-research project. Note the way the question itself focuses the project; emphasize that the center of the project is a conflict, an argument, not a smooth and coherent narrative.

Week 7

Read: Research Kit
Collect: Essay from week 6

Continue work on the current writing assignment, which can be submitted this week or next. Students should choose a research assignment from the Research Kit or formulate one of their own this week. Several of the topics relate to the readings in this syllabus; students can also choose to use other readings in the unit. Finally, discuss the written research proposal, due next week.

Week 8

Collect: Research proposal
Schedule: Conferences and library visit

Don't let students dawdle in choosing a research topic. Try to have a short conference with each student to solidify his or her proposal. Schedule a library visit with the research librarian, who can direct students to the key resources and bibliographies for the kinds of projects they will be working on.

Week 9

Write: Preliminary bibliography

Set guidelines for the number of items to be in the bibliography (perhaps ten). In class, discuss the research process (selection, organization, documentation, and so on).

Week 10

Write: Initial draft of research paper

In addition to using class time for writing workshop activities, consider showing a film like *Matewan* and discuss the way that films, television shows, interviews, and other nontraditional materials can be used in research papers.

Week 11

Schedule: Conferences

Review the projects individually this week and allow students some class time to write.

Week 12

Oral reports

Brief oral reports are an excellent way to force out a draft, focus the topic, and create a real audience for student work. In addition, the reports demonstrate to the whole class the wide range of topics being investigated and the growing expertise of the student researchers.

Week 13

Collect: Final research papers

Depending on the time you have remaining, finish oral reports, review citation and documentation methods, and have an in-class editing workshop. Collect final papers at the end of week 13 or exam week.

UNIT FIVE

Japanese American Internment and the Problem of Cultural Identity

THEMES AND ISSUES IN UNIT FIVE

The purpose of this unit is not to prove that the internment was wrong. It has already been pronounced wrong by the United States government, which has apologized and begun to pay reparations to the victims. In this sense the internment can be treated somewhat like the issue of slavery in Unit Two. You should establish at the outset that, yes, the internment was wrong, and debating it is not our purpose here.

Rather, what we want to look at is the rich diversity of responses to injustice. We do not get simple indignation or dramatized tales of victimhood from all of these writers. It cannot even be said that the purpose of each is to convince us that the internment was wrong. That might be true of Michi Nishiura Weglyn and Jeanne Wakatsuki Houston and James D. Houston, but the other Nikkei writers have more complex purposes, we think. For instance, Minoru Yasui is reflecting on the options and consequences of civil disobedience; Hisaye Yamamoto is exploring the possibilities, awakened by the internment, for alliance among people of color; and so on.

This complexity helps you to deal with the complexity of student responses to the internment story. Contrary to what you might expect, not all students leap indignantly to the side of the Nikkei — although many do, even becoming angry that more Nikkei did not resist the internment more violently. Other students, though, will be inclined to see the reasonableness of suspicions of the Nikkei. To many students, Asian faces still look "foreign," and these feelings of Asian "foreignness" may make the internment seem more defensible to some.

To help personalize this problem, Asian students in your class — even the Korean adoptee who's been here with European American parents since she was seven months old — may be able to testify how often they are asked if they speak English, if they know karate, and so on. Asian students in your class may be able to help the others see how they are still subjected to suspicion of not belonging here. Latino students may have experienced this kind of racism, although to a lesser degree to the extent that they are not necessarily visibly identifiable as Latino; and African Americans, who certainly experience other forms of discrimination, will nevertheless be able to point out that their "nativeness" in America is usually unquestioned (note, for example, as mentioned in the unit introduction, that discriminatory immigration legislation passed at the end of the nineteenth century provided that only those of European or African descent could become U.S. citizens).

Japanese Americans may also be associated in some students' minds with contemporary Japan and may be given a less sympathetic hearing because of students' resentment of Japan's recent economic successes, which many perceive as coming at the expense of Americans. You might point out that the ancestors of most Nikkei came to the United States at the turn of the century — they've been gone from Japan for a long time. Also, they came at about the same times as most of the ancestors of today's Italian Americans. Yet few people today link Italian Americans with what goes on in contemporary Italy (and Italian Americans were not interned en masse during World War II, even though the United States was also at war with Italy).

Personal Testimony

Unit Five is a good unit to choose if you want your students to do a lot of writing about their personal experiences. One theme that the unit raises powerfully is the issue of how personal testimony can be used to make a point, even an implicit argument. All eight Nikkei writers included here write about the internment out of their own experience in one way or another, whether in autobiography, fiction, history, or essay.

What's the rhetorical problem here? When you are talking to other people face to face, personal testimony is a very powerful kind of argument. Sometimes only one example, powerfully told, convinces you. You might ask students to consider how often they have been turned off to a professor because of a negative experience recounted by one friend. With more serious subjects, it might take hearing the story of only one rape victim or genocide survivor to realize the horror of the experience. The emotions generated by personal testimony can be tremendously powerful.

Moreover, people respond to personal testimony because it conveys an ethnographic richness of detail that more objective accounts cannot bring, even if they can base their claims on the statistical survey of far more examples. You feel you learn things from personal testimony that you can learn no other way.

At the same time, personal testimony can be called into question precisely because it evokes such a powerful emotional response. You might feel that your emotions are being unfairly manipulated, that you are not being given you a chance to think through the issues. You might feel that the person testifying is not interested so much in enlightening you as in gaining sympathy and indulgence for himself or herself.

Personal testimony can also be questioned precisely because it is the experience of one person, and perhaps those immediately around him or her. You might say that this is not a large enough sample. Or if you have decided that the narrator is a manipulator, you may simply withhold credibility. Students will note that they don't listen to every negative story they hear about a professor; sometimes they "consider the source" and are not dissuaded. More seriously, sometimes people grow numb and indifferent to testimony of injustice from the United States and around the world because they want to solace themselves with the idea that the injustice is just "an isolated case."

You can invite students to examine the various ways in which these writers make use of their personal experience. What do they tell or omit? How do they present themselves as narrators? You can also ask students to consider the "fictional" or deliberately shaped qualities even of narratives such as Weglyn's and Masaoka's that are presented as "straight" history. (See also our discussion of narrative in Unit One of this manual, p. 23, and our discussion of ethos in Unit Three, p. 88.) Many of the writing questions in Unit Five, then, invite students to generate their own reflective personal testimony in connection with issues the unit raises.

Definition

The "Officicial Documents Establishing the Internment" and "Opinions on the Japanese 'Threat'" sections may be treated simply as background for the personal testimonies, to give students some historical information to help them understand where the Nikkei writers are coming from. Certainly our selection of material is sparse enough that we cannot claim to be representing anything like the full diversity of opinions on Japanese American assimilability. (A fuller range of opinions in a controversy may be found in Units Two and Three, and these units are the place to turn if you want argument to be a major part of your course.)

The "Opinions" section here, however, can be treated as a mini-argument unit. A useful way to focus it would be to look at the function of definition in setting up and pursuing an argument. You might ask students to examine how these four sources define "assimilation" and how their definitions fit into their overall argumentative strategies. For example, if the Department of War in the *Final Report* wants to justify the internment on grounds that the Nikkei are unassimilable, it defines assimilation to mean, among other things, "no education of the young about Japan." The JACL brief, in contrast, in defense of the Nikkei, emphasizes as evidence of their assimilability their success in American schools.

NOTES ON THE UNIT READINGS

Each selection in the unit is accompanied by its own headnote, reading questions, and writing questions, so it can be assigned independently of the other readings or combined with others as you see fit. We have also grouped each reading with several other selections in at least one of the three assignment sequences offered at the end of the unit (the sequences are discussed on p. 175). We urge you to assemble your course reading and writing into one or more assignment sequences, of either our design or your own.

In the following notes, we provide commentary on each of the unit's selections as well as guidelines for approaching and evaluating the writing questions.

You will notice that the readings in the "Testimony of the Interned" section are organized in roughly the chronological order of the internment. Masaoka and Weglyn discuss events immediately preceding the internment. Weglyn, Yasui, and Houston and Houston describe the internment experience itself. Sone presents the situation of people leaving the camps. Okada, Houston and Houston, and Yamamoto describe the aftermath.

OFFICIAL DOCUMENTS ESTABLISHING THE INTERNMENT

FRANKLIN DELANO ROOSEVELT, EXECUTIVE ORDER 9066 (p. 617)

The key point about this document is highlighted in the writing question, namely, that it does not mention the Japanese Americans or their internment and economic despoliation. Students will probably react with cynicism to the document's vague wording, arguing that Roosevelt must have known what DeWitt was going to do with the power the document granted him.

Writing Analytically

The document is so short that it can easily be read in an opening class, and the writing question can be given as an in-class writing assignment or a small-group discussion topic.

JOHN L. DEWITT, "INSTRUCTIONS TO ALL PERSONS OF JAPANESE ANCESTRY" (p. 619)

Like Executive Order 9066, the "Instructions" can be considered blandly deceptive, as its simple-seeming orders do not reflect the emotional and economic chaos visited on the Nikkei by the relocation process. Also like the Executive Order, this document is so short that it can easily be read in an opening class, and the writing questions can be given as in-class writing assignments or small group discussion topics.

Writing Analytically

Writing question 1 suggests a reading of the "Instructions" as manipulating the Nikkei into complying with the relocation and internment process by veiling the traumas of the process. Of course, some students may feel that the document's attempt at manipulation falls short, that its provisions are sufficiently alarming even couched in dull official language. Some students may be reminded of the Nazis telling their Jewish captives that they were going to the showers while sending them into the gas chambers. While you do not need to violently squelch this comparison if it arises, you should point out that the Nikkei, unlike the Jews, were not slated for extermination. A few, it is true, were killed by camp guards, but there was no program of mass murder.

Writing question 2 imagines situations in which the deceptively bland picture of the relocation and internment process created by the "Instructions" is corrected by eyewitness testimony in Weglyn or Houston and Houston. The alternative assignment is a good way of approaching this work, especially if you urge students to illustrate their letters with specific details such as they can glean from the other sources. The letters may be rather melodramatic; don't spend too much time worrying about that at the beginning of the course. Students might profitably return later in the semester to what they've written for this assignment, when they will be in a better position to complicate it in interesting ways.

OPINIONS ON THE JAPANESE "THREAT"

MONTAVILLE FLOWERS, FROM *THE JAPANESE CONQUEST OF AMERICAN OPINION* (p. 623)

Although Flowers's racism is so extreme as to be almost laughable to students, his arguments are hauntingly relevant not only to the internment but also to contemporary racial and ethnic concerns. For example, Flowers argues violently against "racial mixture," that is, intermarriage between Asian and Caucasian people. Most students will disagree with him — since they are usually keen to defend personal choice — and insist on people's right to marry whomever they please. Yet some students will be aware that intermarriage is likewise opposed within many racial and ethnic groups (to which these students may belong) who wish to preserve their distinctive character. Ironically, it was partly the Nikkei's lack of intermarriage that preserved the distinct racial identity that made them easy targets for the internment.

Flowers also argues against the possibility of "social assimilation," that is, the adoption of mainstream American social mores — through education, leisure activities, professions, and so on — by a group that remains racially distinct. Again, many students will disagree with him and insist that all people can and should have equal opportunities to obtain education, work, and so on. But some students will recognize that assimilation risks destroying the valuable particular culture of distinct ethnic and racial groups. Ironically, the Nisei would argue so forcefully (for example, in the JACL brief) that they were indeed socially assimilated and therefore unfairly interned that they would seem at times to be betraying the Japanese aspects of their parents' culture.

Writing Analytically

We think it's important to prevent classroom discussion of Flowers from dismissing him as an outrageous racist. Writing question 1 deflects some of the scorn students may want to heap on him and focuses on an analysis of his intended or imagined audience. Rather than simply condemning Flowers, this assignment, we hope, gets students to see how a writer like Flowers actually tries to manipulate readers into a racist position; he constructs an audience that holds racist attitudes and then invites readers to be a part of this audience. You might think of this assignment as investigating the kind of subjectivity to which students are hailed by a text of this kind.

Writing question 2 underscores another area of contemporary relevance in Flowers. The sorts of arguments he makes occur frequently in xenophobic discussions, no matter who is being vilified. We want students to begin to be able to recognize and analyze such patterns. This assignment also asks students to apply their personal experience by bringing in materials particularly from contemporary arguments about immigrants that echo Flowers's.

It is possible, of course, that this assignment will elicit defenses of immigration restrictions from some students (more likely in some parts of the country than others, perhaps). They may discover contemporary arguments against immigration that they find persuasive. We don't think you need to take the position that all restrictions on immigration are unfair or basely motivated. Simply insist that students defending anti-immigration arguments analyze their assumptions and strategies carefully in comparison and contrast with Flowers.

Writing question 3 invites students actually to adopt Flowers's voice. This is in a way a more extreme version of writing question 1 in terms of getting students to imagine how Flowers is trying to manipulate them to adopt a racist position. For students who find Flowers completely disgusting, this assignment can be used as an occasion for parody. For comic effect, they may exaggerate what they see as his offenses. If completing writing question 2 has left some students more sympathetic to immigration restrictions, however, they may not want to write this assignment in a vituperative style. Since it would be hard to be moderate in imitating Flowers, you might offer these students the option of imitating the contemporary writer whose example they used for writing question 2.

U.S. DEPARTMENT OF WAR, FROM *FINAL REPORT: JAPANESE EVACUATION FROM THE WEST COAST, 1942* (p. 628)

This and the excerpt from *Personal Justice Denied* are the two most important texts in the "Opinions" section. The *Final Report* develops the government's wartime position on the military necessity for the internment, while *Personal Justice Denied* explicitly refutes the reasoning in the report and indicts it for misinformation and racism. Thus, the two reports taken together give the clearest picture of the U.S. government's evolving views on the internment, including the edifying spectacle of the government changing its mind and admitting that it made a mistake.

Students may need help understanding the collective nature of the authorship of these two texts. Both were prepared by teams, so it is usually difficult to name the person who wrote any given passage (an exception is the memo authored by John L. DeWitt, from the appendix to chapter 3 of the *Final Report*). Nevertheless, these texts were intended by their authors to perform particular rhetorical functions, and to accomplish these goals, the authors used particular rhetorical strategies. Thus, students can perform the same kind of analysis on these texts that they perform on texts with a single author, where "intention" is easier to discuss.

Writing Analytically

Writing question 1 invites students to connect some of the *Final Report*'s arguments with their own lives. If at all possible, students should choose a contemporary example that they have participated in personally. Many students may have experience with supplemental schooling in their ethnic culture, such as in the afternoon schools common in the Chinese, Greek, and Jewish communities, to name just a few. Some Native American communities have maintained their own religious traditions and rituals into which young people are initiated. Students who do not have this kind of experience, however, might be allowed to consider their membership in a scout troop, sports team, street gang, or other such tightly knit group as analogous to participation in an ethnic community. They could be invited to ask the same questions about what, if anything, in their group activities could be considered to undermine their commitment as good citizens.

Writing question 2 investigates the rhetorical effectiveness of the *Final Report* in accomplishing its main purpose, namely, to justify the internment. The quality of the evidence and the logic of the arguments should be the focus here. Whether or not students choose the letter-writing option, they should be encouraged to respond to this assignment in their own voices, not adopting any hypothetical personae.

Taking a slightly different angle, writing question 3 focuses on another purpose of the *Final Report*, which was to vindicate the behavior of the man in charge, General John L. DeWitt. We can imagine students responding to writing question 2 with the judgment that the internship was not justified —

so that the *Report* fails to that extent — while responding to writing question 3 by saying that, nevertheless, DeWitt acted in good faith and made an honest mistake — a success for at least one part of the *Report*'s mission. Analysis should focus on the rhetorical strategies that attempt to make DeWitt look like a responsible public servant.

JAPANESE AMERICAN CITIZENS LEAGUE, FROM *THE CASE FOR THE NISEI* (p. 647)

Assign the *Final Report* if you assign this excerpt from the JACL brief, as the brief explicitly cites and refutes the *Report*. Although it seems rather long, the brief can be read quickly because much of it consists of specific examples of Japanese Americans who have excelled in what the brief's authors consider to be typically American activities. The brief's eagerness to demonstrate Nisei assimilation with these examples may arouse mixed reactions in students. Some will be indignant on the Nisei's behalf that such overwhelming evidence in favor of their Americanization and patriotism was overlooked. Others will find the catalog a pathetic attempt to curry favor with an unsympathetic authority or even a betrayal of the JACL's own cultural roots. Rather than attempting to adjudicate among these reactions, you can channel the energies they generate into the writing questions.

Writing Analytically

Writing question 1 focuses on the issue of potential cultural betrayal in the JACL brief. Neglecting the Issei (if indeed the brief is open to that charge) means neglecting that part of the Nikkei community most closely associated with Japanese culture. And it is striking that the brief offers no defense for the Nikkei community's continued interest in Japanese culture as evidenced by the afternoon schools, which most Nisei attended. Remind students that in analyzing these strategies in the brief, they are to judge their potential persuasiveness as well as their morality in terms of loyalty to the Nikkei community. There is room for a range of student responses here, and, if they wish, students should be allowed to draw on their own experience balancing dual allegiances to American mainstream culture and their own ethnic cultures.

Writing question 2 takes a more argumentative tack, asking students to extrapolate a definition of *assimilation* from the evidence presented in the brief. Make sure that students notice here (as reading question 3 attempts to point out) that the brief apparently is not calling for intermarriage or the end to the Nikkei as a distinct group. Rather, *assimilation* here means that the Nikkei are adopting American mores while continuing to live in their own community. Most likely, the analyses generated in response to this writing question will mitigate charges of betrayal that might have emerged from writing question 1. You might give half of each small group question 1 and half question 2, and then have the students report on their findings in their groups before everyone writes question 3.

Writing question 3 requires an understanding of what *assimilation* means in the brief (from writing question 2), so that the hypothetical speaker (Sone or Houston) will be able to show that she understands what she is being asked to do. Students who gain an appreciation of the complex issues of loyalty and betrayal by answering question 1 will be better able to guess whether the hypothetical speaker in question 3 will want to assist the JACL or will regard the organization as having sold out. We think most students will imagine that Sone would be willing to cooperate with the JACL, while Houston might reject their request as supportive of a notion of assimilation that gives up too much of Japanese culture. Just to complicate matters, you might point out that Sone did not intermarry — her husband is a Nisei war veteran — whereas Houston did. Students might like to share some of their letters with the whole class or in their small groups.

U.S. COMMISSION ON WARTIME RELOCATION AND INTERNMENT OF CIVILIANS, FROM *PERSONAL JUSTICE DENIED* (p. 661)

This and the excerpt from the *Final Report* are the two most important texts in the "Opinions" section. The *Final Report* develops the government's wartime position on the military necessity for the internment, while *Personal Justice Denied* explicitly refutes the reasoning in the report and indicts it for misinformation and racism. Thus, the two reports taken together give the clearest picture of the U.S. government's evolving views on the internment, including the edifying spectacle of the government changing its mind and admitting that it made a mistake.

Students may need help understanding the collective nature of the authorship of these two texts. Both were prepared by teams, so it is usually difficult to name the particular person who wrote any given passage (an exception is the memo authored by John L. DeWitt, from the appendix to chapter 3 of the *Final Report*). Nevertheless, these texts were intended by their authors to perform particular rhetorical functions; and to accomplish these goals, the authors used particular rhetorical strategies. Thus, students can perform the same kind of analysis on these texts that they perform on texts with a single author, where "intention" is easier to discuss.

You might point out to students that the second quoted passage on page 670 ("Henry went to the Control Station . . .") is from Monica Sone's *Nisei Daughter* (p. 748).

Writing Analytically

Writing question 1 calls attention to the striking fact that *Personal Justice Denied* actually uses the word *racism* to characterize some of the attitudes that led to the internment. In their work on this assignment, though, students should be encouraged to look for places in the text where a charge of racism, although not explicitly stated, may be inferred. This paper should be a fairly straightforward exercise in collecting and analyzing evidence.

Writing question 2, in contrast, asks students to speculate about more abstract and ineffable issues. In effect, they will have to extrapolate a definition of "personal justice" based on highly inferential reasoning. The "justice" part of the concept may not be so hard to grasp — it implies, among other things, that the Nikkei did not receive evenhanded treatment, that they were treated unequally and unfairly in comparison with other groups (such as Germans and Italians). The "personal" part, however, may be harder to grasp. Why the emphasis on the personal? Why not just speak of "justice denied"? We think there is a wide range of possible responses to these questions.

Writing question 3 invites an overall evaluation of the persuasiveness of *Personal Justice Denied.* This assignment calls for the most extensive knowledge of the text and the most detailed, lengthy analysis. You can make the assignment even more challenging by asking students to include the *Final Report* in their analysis, comparing and contrasting the credibility of the two reports. This kind of comparison which will require equally detailed knowledge of the *Final Report,* will probably encourage students to decide that one or the other of the texts is more persuasive. But the issue of credibility might be more complicated than that. A historian faced with conflicting sources might not always want to totally discount the one that he or she finds less credible. To add a final level of sophistication to this assignment, ask students to comment on how a historian should negotiate among conflicting sources. This writing question might work best assigned after the class has worked through the reading questions and perhaps done another writing assignment or two for both *Personal Justice Denied* and the *Final Report.*

TESTIMONY OF THE INTERNED

MIKE MASAOKA WITH BILL HOSOKAWA, FROM *THEY CALL ME MOSES MASAOKA: AN AMERICAN SAGA* (p. 676)

Should the Nikkei have resisted the internment? Masaoka's account provides helpful evidence for considering this question. Masaoka was the most important Nikkei leader at the time, and our excerpt from his autobiography describes his work for the JACL during the tense and confusing period immediately preceding the internment. It's clear from Masaoka's account that it would not have been easy for him to decide when or if to call for either armed or passive resistance amid the uncertainties of the times. Students will probably not notice the defensiveness of his account and will appreciate the difficulties of his situation, although they may still feel he should have been more aggressive in fighting for Nikkei rights at the time of the internment. The Masaoka reading pairs well with the Yasui and Okada selections, which describe alternative, more resistant responses to the internment. Also, for writing question 2, you will have to assign Weglyn.

Writing Analytically

Writing question 1 calls students' attention to the issue of Masaoka's anxiety about the judgment of history on his quality as a leader. Students are usually interested in discussing what makes a good leader, and Masaoka's situation is nicely complex. Make sure that students see the connection with the trustworthiness of Masaoka's account of the history of the time: If he has an agenda of self-defense, how might this affect his reporting of the facts?

Writing question 2 is meant to focus more on the issue of how Masaoka tells the history of the time than on the personal aspects of his persuasive project. Students playing the part of Yasui will of course want to comment on Masaoka's remarks on Yasui's case, but you should remind them also to consider the larger question of what the JACL and the entire Nikkei community should have done in response to the internment (at the end of his oral history, Yasui discusses the possibility of violent resistance). Students should approach the Weglyn review with the understanding that Weglyn shares with Masaoka the vocation of amateur historian (though Masaoka had help with his account from the academically trained scholar Bill Hosokawa) and the desire to vindicate the Nikkei — but unlike Masaoka, Weglyn does not also have an agenda of personal defense. Both Weglyn and Yasui, we might infer from the tone of their writings, would have favored a more vigorous, if not actively violent, response to the internment.

MICHI NISHIURA WEGLYN, FROM *YEARS OF INFAMY: THE UNTOLD STORY OF AMERICA'S CONCENTRATION CAMPS* (p. 689)

The Weglyn reading can be useful to assign early in the course because it supplements the basic history of the internment given in the Unit Five introduction. In our excerpts, Weglyn describes how the government decided to proceed with the internment and what the actual process of relocating and settling into the camps was like for the Nikkei.

Weglyn's history has a distinct agenda, which is to indict the injustice of the internment and to vindicate the Nikkei. You might point out to students how her title indicates this agenda. The phrase "years of infamy" alludes to President Roosevelt's remark that the day the Japanese bombed Pearl Harbor was a "day of infamy." Weglyn implies that the retaliation taken against Japanese Americans outweighed in severity whatever was done at Pearl Harbor (whether this is true, of course, is a matter of opinion). Weglyn's use of the term *concentration camps* also emphasizes the suffering the internment entailed by evoking comparison with the extermination camps into which the German Nazis, also U.S. enemies during World War

II, herded European Jews, gypsies, homosexuals, and others they considered undesirable. (You might point out that this comparison is rather exaggerated, since the Nikkei were not starved, worked like slaves, or murdered en masse in the American camps.)

Writing Analytically

Writing question 1 asks students to consider whether Weglyn's agenda hurts her credibility as a historian. Students are usually divided on this issue. Those who are still wedded to the dream of a purely objective history will protest her attempts to drum up sympathy for the Nikkei (which we feel are really not excessive or melodramatic). But others will respect her compulsion to step forward and speak up for her people at a time when few were willing to talk about the internment or to condemn its perpetrators. Lead this discussion toward the question of what history is *for:* Does society need historians? Why or why not? What have students been taught about the internment before taking your course, and what do they think they should have been taught? Could Weglyn's account be used as a school text? Why or why not?

Writing question 2 also raises the issue of credibility, from a slightly different angle: through the eyes of two other writers who generated their own accounts of the internment. Weglyn shares with Masaoka the vocation of amateur historian (though Masaoka had help with his account from the academically trained scholar Bill Hosokawa) and the desire to vindicate the Nikkei — but unlike Masaoka, Weglyn does not also have an agenda of personal defense. We imagine that Masaoka, in reviewing Weglyn, might wish for more attention to be given to the JACL, and perhaps also to himself, while still pretty much agreeing with her version of what she does cover. We imagine that Houston would be quite sympathetic to Weglyn's account, if anything wanting it to be even more graphic in exposing government venality and Nikkei suffering.

Writing question 3 asks students actually to step into the role of historical analyst. Of course, the two sources this assignment offers are both highly critical of the government's role in the internment. You might handle this assignment by having students write the first part (the history) first and share their papers in small groups before discussing the issues to be addressed in the appendix. They could then write the appendix after the in-class discussion.

JEANNE WAKATSUKI HOUSTON AND JAMES D. HOUSTON, FROM *FAREWELL TO MANZANAR* (p. 715)

Students usually enjoy reading this very personal and dramatic account of the internment, and we think it is one of the essential texts to be assigned in this unit. It provides an excellent counterpoint to the drier histories and official documents that we have also included.

One of the great pedagogical advantages of this excerpt (the first of two we have included from the book) is that the narrator, young Jeanne, tells very little about her own hardships during the internment. She doesn't complain about missing her friends, her toys, or her favorite foods or any other of the trials of internment that we might imagine would loom largest for a small child. Her focus is on her parents, primarily her father. This is an advantage because it tends to disarm students who might dismiss as self-ish any victim's account that is primarily self-focused. They are usually will-ing to give Jeanne some sympathy for her concern for her parents, and this initial point of contact helps them to take her whole account of the intern-ment trauma more seriously.

Writing Analytically

Writing question 1 highlights this focus by asking students to collect evi-dence about Jeanne's depiction of her father. Make sure that students fo-cus on the *changes* he undergoes in this portrayal, from before to after in-ternment and as the loyalty questionnaire controversy escalates. Also make sure they consider our final question in the assignment about how his ex-perience is meant to be taken as representative. You might reserve this ques-tion for class discussion after students have written a paper that simply ad-dresses the first part of the assignment.

Writing question 2 centers on the issue that concludes writing question 1, namely, the ways in which personal testimony can be used to advance abstract arguments. This is a more sophisticated assignment than the first one because it asks students not only to collect the personal evidence that illustrates loyalty and patriotism but also to move back and forth between this concrete evidence and the abstract concepts they want to use it to de-fine. Encourage students to use not only evidence from *Farewell to Manzanar* but also their own experience in considering such issues. Students who have become naturalized citizens or who have served in the armed forces may have reflections that bear on this assignment.

Writing question 3 also looks at the uses of personal testimony, consider-ing not so much how such testimony relates to the elucidation of abstract principles as how it conveys historical "reality." The comparison with Weglyn breaks down the dichotomy students like to set up between the purely ob-jective accounts of history and the subjective versions of autobiography. Houston and Houston's book is an avowedly personal work, a memoir, that also purports to tell something about the history of the internment; Weglyn's book presents itself as a history, yet it clearly is invested with a personal agenda. Should people ever have their emotions aroused by historical ac-counts? This is the ultimate question we hope this assignment will lead stu-dents to consider.

MINORU YASUI, ORAL HISTORY (p. 729)

Should the Nikkei have resisted the internment? Yasui's account provides helpful evidence for considering this question. Yasui resisted the internment by various legal means, enduring a jail term for his protest, and concludes this interview by considering whether violent resistance would have been justified (he rejects it). Yasui's account pairs well with the Masaoka and Okada readings. Masaoka, the most important Nikkei leader at the time, defends himself for not supporting Yasui's protest. In describing his work for the JACL during the tense and confusing period immediately preceding the internment, Masaoka makes it clear that it would not have been easy for him to decide when or if to call for resistance amid the uncertainties of the times. Okada tells the story of a young man who resisted even more strongly than Yasui, refusing to answer yes to the controversial questions on the loyalty questionnaire and ultimately going to jail for refusing military service.

Yasui, along with Masaoka and Okada, will interest students who feel that the Nikkei should have resisted the internment, a common student reaction. These readings also add an important dimension to our composite picture of Nikkei experience in the internment, to supplement the more passive accounts of suffering and endurance offered by Houston and Houston and Sone.

Writing Analytically

Writing question 1 addresses another theme prevalent in this unit, assimilation. Yasui's degree of assimilation, as he explains, became an issue in his trial. Students may simply collate a definition of *assimilation* according to Judge Fee. Or the option can lead them in either of two directions. If they choose to compare Fee's definition with Flowers's, they can begin to see how abstract racist arguments connect to concrete cases, with serious consequences for the victims. A contrast with the JACL brief will illuminate the restrictiveness of Fee's concept and the extent to which Yasui was indeed assimilated by JACL standards.

The issue of resistance to the internment is explored extensively in writing question 2, which invites students to compare Yasui's responses with those that particular ethnic or cultural groups today can or do make to repressive measures taken against them. You might wish to explain the concept of "civil disobedience," mentioning examples by William Apess (see Unit One), Thoreau, Gandhi, Rosa Parks, and Martin Luther King Jr.

The alternative assignment suggests that students generate a discussion between two people who both favor working within the system to protest injustice but who differ in the degree to which they are willing to actively challenge mainstream society and its laws. While students will, correctly we think, perceive Yasui to be the more challenging of the two, you should make sure they notice that he remained a loyal member of the JACL and participated actively in Masaoka's initiative to recruit Nikkei men from the camps for the army.

MONICA SONE, FROM *NISEI DAUGHTER* (p. 748)

Students who are made uncomfortable by emphasis on the injustice and suffering caused by the internment will like Sone. In sharp contrast to Weglyn and Houston and Houston, she appears to offer a very upbeat account, concluding with her own American dream-style social ascent from camp to college.

Writing Analytically

As writing question 1 suggests, we think this upbeat vision of Sone is an oversimplification. We hope this assignment will help students see that Sone does in fact provide quite a lot of negative testimony about the effects of the internment and American racism generally. The interesting question for students to consider is why Sone chooses to present this evidence in a way that downplays the injustice and suffering involved. You should encourage class discussion about whether her rhetorical approach or the more confrontational styles of Weglyn or Houston and Houston are more effective.

Writing question 2 invites students to make personal connections to Sone's story. Sone is, after all, a college student in the chapter we excerpt. The headnote gives some information about Sone's academic interests — she did graduate work in psychology — and students may want to talk in their letters about what their school offers in this area. But you should suggest that the most important issues concern how well an Asian woman will be accepted on their campus. Are there social organizations for Asian students, or are students of color welcome in campuswide organizations (as they were not at Wendell College)? Do cocurricular events, such as concerts, art shows, and so on, reflect any Asian content? Sone can be expected to care about these kinds of resources for Asian students because even though she shows herself to be eager to participate in mainstream culture, she also makes clear that she does not intend to leave her Japanese identity behind.

If any students complain that they do not know enough about their campus to respond to such concerns, you should encourage them to find out. They need specific examples and details. It might also be interesting for students to share these letters in small groups or with the whole class. You will probably find that the perceptions of all students of color (not only the Asian students) about their campus's receptivity to Sone will be different from those of white students. Other variables that will influence responses include the number of Asian students on your campus, perceptions of them as competing with other students for admission and other resources, and so on. It may be instructive for everyone to hear about these differences in perception.

Writing question 3 is a challenging assignment asking for sophisticated consideration of what it means to be bicultural. Okada's protagonist, Ichiro, is being torn apart by the agony of his dual identity. Young Jeanne, in the Houston and Houston account, is able to negotiate relations with the mainstream culture only at great cost to her self-respect. Sone, at the other end of the spectrum, asserts that she emerges from the internment experience with a comfortable bicultural identity. Not coincidentally, she is the only one of the three who also describes herself as being on good terms with her parents.

Students who are not bicultural should not be excused from the effort of imagination required to write this paper; but we might expect their conclusions to differ significantly from those of students who are bicultural. Again, students might benefit from sharing these papers in class. You might organize informal debates on whether it is or is not possible to be *comfortably* bicultural or whether it is or is not possible to generalize from the Nikkei experience to that of other bicultural people (a topic you probably cannot address unless you have enough bicultural students in your class who are willing to testify).

We hope these writing questions indicate the seriousness of the issues we see raised in Sone. While we want you to unsettle students who attempt to take refuge in a Pollyanna-like reading of her, we also think it's important not to encourage cynicism at her expense. To those who think Sone is the Asian equivalent of an Uncle Tom, telling white culture what they want to hear, you can point out that it is not for others to dictate what Sone's response to the internment, or her choice of rhetorical strategies in presenting this experience, should be. If nothing else, we hope this unit will drive home to students that a particular cultural group's responses cannot be stereotyped but that a wide range, reflecting human variation as well as cultural particularities, should be expected. Interestingly, Sone married a Nisei man — unlike Houston, Weglyn, and Yamamoto she did not "marry out" — which some students may want to take as a strong sign of her allegiance to the Japanese part of her dual identity.

Jeanne Wakatsuki Houston and James D. Houston, from *Farewell to Manzanar* (p. 757)

As we noted about our first excerpt from the Houston and Houston book, students usually enjoy reading this very personal and dramatic account of the internment, and we think it is one of the essential texts to be assigned in this unit. It provides an excellent counterpoint to the drier histories and official documents that we have also included.

As noted about the first excerpt, early in the story the narrator, young Jeanne, tells very little about her own hardships during the internment, focusing instead on her parents. Here in the second excerpt, however,

Jeanne talks much more about herself and her trials facing racism and sexism in school after she and her family are released from the camp. Especially because the analysis implied by the story suggests a gender-based aspect to the injustice Jeanne experiences, those students who react with impatience to feminist perspectives (unfortunately, there seem to be a few in every class) may start to withhold sympathy from Jeanne's story on that account. You might reclaim their attention by pointing out that even in this part of the story, Jeanne's concern for her parents is still evident, and at the end she admits some truth in her father's views on sexuality and cultural assimilation, even though he might be regarded as a male chauvinist.

Writing Analytically

Writing question 1 focuses on the issue of assimilation presented by Houston and Houston. Perhaps better than any other text in this unit, this excerpt shows just what it might cost a person of color to win acceptance in mainstream society. It is important for you to get students to see that Jeanne's pathway to acceptance is painful. Some may try to deny it, insisting they see nothing wrong in her activities as a drum majorette or carnival queen. You can say that while being a majorette or queen may not be an oppressive or immoral activity in and of itself, it is certainly oppressive to force a woman who does not really want to display her body in these ways to do so in order to gain simple social acceptance. Some students may want to make the case that these activities *are* inherently oppressive, as requiring the domination of the female body by the male gaze, even without Jeanne's quid pro quo. We think that while encouraging such discussion, you probably should not take sides.

Even if students admit that much of what Jeanne does to facilitate her own assimilation is painful to her, they may well disagree about whether she should be striving to assimilate as much as she does. There is room for honest disagreement here, which you should encourage. Fortunately, the text is nicely complex on these issues, and the complexity is enriched even further by the addition of Okada and Sone. As we note in discussing writing question 3 in Sone (p. 172 — essentially the same as writing question 1 here), Okada's protagonist, Ichiro, is agonized by his dual identity. Sone, meanwhile, asserts that she emerges from the internment experience with a comfortable bicultural identity. Note that she is the only one of the three who also describes herself as being on good terms with her parents. And Jeanne is able to negotiate relations with the mainstream culture only at great cost to her self-respect.

Jeanne's father's fears that she will marry a white man — a quintessentially assimilationist act — are presented as an instance of his unreasoning tyranny over her. He expresses these fears in a tirade that is undercut both by the way he is described in the story and by the way Jeanne and her mother react at the time. Hence this scene seems to be endorsing Jeanne's desire for the freedom to date, and perhaps marry, a white man (which, as it happens, Jeanne did do). On the other hand, the lascivious behavior of the white boys in the gym when Jeanne appears in her sarong suggests that there may be dangers for an Asian woman in contemplating interdating or intermarriage: She might not be able to know whether her partner really loved her for herself or for her "exotic" sexuality (she might be sexy, but at least not exotic, to a fellow Asian).

We want to encourage students who have their own experiences of struggling with assimilation to bring these experiences into their papers and, if possible, to share them with the class. To make the climate more comfortable for them, we suggest that you acknowledge that, contrary to popular American ideology, a person might legitimately limit certain upwardly mobile goals, including marrying out of one's ethnic group, in order to respect parents' wishes or remain in touch with the home culture. In fact, as you may know, research has suggested that some minority groups' lack of success in school results from deliberate decisions not to adopt the school culture and values to the extent that these alienate the students from their home cultures. Students who are aware of these motives operating in themselves should be encouraged to bring these experiences to the discussion.

Writing question 2 also focuses on the assimilation question but foregrounds the double burden of racist and sexist oppression that Jeanne feels she faced in the process. We suggest that you give students a choice of responding to either of the two writing questions. There is much overlap in the kinds of in-class work necessary to prepare for both, as our discussion of writing question 1 suggests. Students who are more interested in issues of cultural transmission and family relations should choose the first question. Those who are more interested in pursuing feminist analyses should choose the second.

JOHN OKADA, FROM *NO-NO BOY* (p. 766)

This excerpt from the first chapter of Okada's novel presents Ichiro Yamada's pain so graphically that many students may be put off at first. We think, however, that it is important to keep them on task, as this excerpt presents perhaps the most sophisticated discussion of biculturalism in any text in this unit.

Students may try to deflect the text's message on biculturalism by reducing the conflict to a personal problem between Ichiro and his domineering mother and vacillating father. While we agree that Okada wants us to empathize with this human drama (and writing question 3 gives students an opportunity to explore it), we would also argue that these family relations can be read as representative of problems concerning biculturalism and assimilation. After all, it is through the family that a native culture is — or is not — transmitted successfully. Mainstream culture is pounded into young people from a thousand channels — public school, mass media, and so on. Perhaps Ichiro's mother's aggressive promotion of what she considers to be proper Japanese attitudes is an index of the kind of determination that may be necessary in the home culture to influence young people who are exposed to so many powerful mainstream influences. At least you can suggest this possibility to students inclined to write off the whole story as merely personal.

Also, in the Kumasakas, Okada provides an example of a family that has apparently not tried to maintain the Japanese part of its identity as aggressively as Mrs. Yamada has. While this couple is presented sympathetically and Mr. Kumasaka, in particular, seems to provide the kind of older male role model for whom Ichiro yearns, the death of the Kumasakas' son suggests that behavior like theirs is not always rewarded in ways the American Dream ideology would have us believe.

Writing Analytically

Writing question 1 calls attention to the inflection given to biculturalism in this selection. The problem is not so much whether or not the protagonist should assimilate (a kind of dichotomy that might emerge, for example, from reading Houston and Houston), but rather whether or not the protagonist can maintain both American and Japanese identities harmoniously. Ichiro's pain highlights the difficulty of doing so.

This assignment offers varying levels of engagement. The easiest version simply asks students to describe Ichiro's dual identity. The next step is to describe and also to generalize about how representative Ichiro is of bicultural people. This step is best taken by students who have some personal experience of biculturalism either in themselves or in their families. The third step is to build up a general model by adding descriptions of the protagonist in either Sone or Houston and Houston as an example of a bicultural person. It might be interesting, if the population of your class permits, to make this a collaborative assignment and pair monocultural students with students who are self-identified as having bicultural experience.

Writing question 2 picks up on what are essentially minor details in our excerpt from Okada (although, as the entire novel shows, clearly not minor in Okada's overall conception of the story). Especially if students do not add Yamamoto to this assignment (the entire focus of her essay is solidarity among people of color), you should encourage them to use personal experience to flesh out their arguments. You might also encourage them to include contemporary materials that deal with cross-racial solidarity, such as Reverend Jesse Jackson's Rainbow Coalition work.

Writing question 3, like question 1, offers varying levels of engagement. Students may simply choose one of the two scenes from Okada mentioned in the assignment and analyze the interactions in that scene. This analysis may be primarily personal — that is, drawing on students' sense of how parents and grown children should interact, although you might also encourage students to think about how the pressures of immigration, assimilation, and biculturalism affect these relationships. The alternative assignment brings in a second text, Houston and Houston, and thus clearly makes both Okada and Houston and Houston into *examples* to be used in the service of a larger generalized argument about bicultural family relations. One way to deal with this writing question would be to have students work on the scenes from Okada in class in small groups and then work on the alternative assignment at home.

HISAYE YAMAMOTO, "A FIRE IN FONTANA" (p. 779)

This is a rather difficult essay, not because the language is obscure or the argument dense but because Yamamoto's style is studiedly offhand and indirect and may puzzle students who are expecting something more obviously polemical. For instance, it is sometimes hard for students to see that Yamamoto is using the paired examples of Bix Beiderbecke and Johnny Otis, introduced seemingly out of the blue at the start of her essay, to illuminate her sense of her own progress toward racial solidarity with African Americans. It is also often hard for students to catch the essay's many subtle allusions to cultural crossings, as in the penultimate paragraph where Yamamoto describes herself making tacos for supper while watching the Watts riots on television in her home in a white neighborhood, where she knows she probably would not be welcome, were it not for her "pale" husband (he is Italian American). Our reading questions will help students to become more alert to and appreciative of these effects.

The Yamamoto essay is important to the unit because it gives the fullest treatment of any selection to the issue of cross-racial solidarity. It is, then, the selection that does the most to facilitate generalization from the Nikkei internment experience to the experiences of discrimination and persecution other American communities of color have suffered. You should consider assigning the Yamamoto selection if your class is racially diverse. Also consider assigning it if you plan to ask students to write a research paper as a follow-up to their Unit Five work; her perspective can help students generate research ideas on themes analogous to those raised in this unit.

Writing Analytically

Writing question 1 helps students to see the "story" that Yamamoto assembles through her series of seemingly unconnected examples, anecdotes, and vignettes. It is the story of her own growing solidarity with African Americans and, consequently, her growing feelings of inadequacy about her inaction on their behalf. The assignment simply asks students to describe the story Yamamoto tells, a difficult enough task for many, given her challenging style. If you think your class would like an additional challenge, however, you can add an evaluative aspect to this assignment: Ask students to discuss in their papers whether they find themselves agreeing with Yamamoto's subtle self-indictment or whether they think she is being too hard on herself.

Writing question 2 also focuses on Yamamoto's main theme of solidarity among people of color, but it enriches the analysis with the example of

Okada. Both Okada and Yamamoto could be construed as being rather negative about the possibilities for solidarity: Yamamoto reproaches herself for not doing more to fight white racism, while Okada shows African Americans being overtly hostile to Ichiro. On the other hand, it could be seen as a hopeful sign for the possibility of solidarity that both Yamamoto and Okada are so concerned about addressing it. At any rate, you should remind students that they must use specific examples from the two sources to illustrate their arguments; encourage them, too, to use personal experience as well as any contemporary materials that address the possibility of cross-racial solidarity (movies, TV shows, rock videos, advertisements, song lyrics, sermons, political speeches, and so on). The alternative assignment here probably should be attempted only by more accomplished student writers; imitating the style of either Okada or Yamamoto will be quite a challenge.

ASSIGNMENT SEQUENCES

As noted in the introduction to this manual, we see the assignment sequences as an integral part of the approach we wish to promote in *Negotiating Difference*. The sequences put provocative voices directly in dialogue with each other — both in the readings and then, in discussion of the readings, among the students in your class. Of equal importance, the sequences stress the need to develop material carefully — rereading, rethinking, and revising — in order to produce the richest rhetorical responses in student writing.

You can use the reading questions that accompany each selection to aid students in preparing to write for the sequences. If you wish, you can discuss all the readings for a sequence in class before beginning to work on the sequence questions. You might use some of the writing questions accompanying the readings as warm-up exercises (in the class journals, perhaps). It is not necessary to proceed this way, however, as our model syllabi suggest (p. 182). As you move through the sequence, you can add the readings as they are introduced by the sequence questions, taking time in each case to work through the reading questions before tackling the sequence writing assignment.

While the writing questions in each sequence tend to build on one another with added complexity as one moves through the sequence, you should also feel free to select among these questions to tailor the sequence to your students' needs and interests (you will see some of this adaptation of sequences going on in the model syllabi). In what follows we will briefly discuss each sequence and its writing questions.

Sequence 1: What is "assimilation"? (p. 787)

Of the three sequences offered in Unit Five, this one places the most emphasis on students' personal experience, particularly experience dealing with assimilation to mainstream American culture. Thus, obviously, students who have indeed had experience with assimilation will be best equipped to write these assignments. Students whose grandparents were born in the United States and who are third- or fourth-generation monocultural will be at such a disadvantage here that if your class is made up primarily of such students, you may not want to use this sequence.

Question 1 looks like a definition question, but the main emphasis in the students' papers should be on self-description. They will not have to spend too much time extrapolating a definition of *assimilation* from either Flowers or the JACL brief, which can then guide their descriptions. In fact, establishing the working definitions might be a good thing to do in class as preparation for writing the essay. The assignment could also be a journal entry. Another suggestion: Ask half the class to work from Flowers and half from the JACL brief, since these two sources have very different ideas of assimilation. Then let students share their results in small groups.

Questions 2 and 3 also bring together sources with different reactions to assimilation. By asking students to compare sources, these questions begin to move them away from the more personal focus of question 1 (although students can still use themselves as one of the examples in question 3) and toward a more general argument on the meaning of assimilation. We would expect responses to question 2 to reflect that, although both Yasui and Ichiro have used civil disobedience to protest the internment, Yasui's brand of challenge suggests that he is much more hopeful than Ichiro about his ultimate ability to integrate with mainstream American society. We would encourage students writing question 3 to choose two textual examples that contrast, such as Yasui and Ichiro or Sone's Itoi Kazuko and Houston's Jeanne. Since writing an imaginary dialogue, such as question 2 requests, is not to every student's taste, you might offer students a choice of writing either question 2 or 3.

Question 4 builds in the dialogue option, but whichever way the paper is written, you should encourage students at this point to move clearly into a more abstract argument on assimilation in general in the United States. Still, they should use their own experience as one source of evidence to support their argument.

You may have to spend some time in class discussing why anyone would *not* want to assimilate. American ideology has promoted "melting" into the "melting pot" for so long that any other course of action will seem counterintuitive to many students. These students may be inclined to dismiss a particular person's reluctance to assimilate as merely a function of his or her personal problems. We hope that the multiple examples in the readings for this sequence will help show students that so many people have had trouble with assimilation that it would be hard to consider these problems as all merely personal.

Bicultural students in your class, including those who are recent immigrants, will have a lot to contribute to this discussion if you can invite them into it in a sufficiently nonthreatening way. It is very important that you make no prior assumptions about what these students may want to say about assimilation. While some may testify to experiencing the kinds of conflict over assimilation recounted in Okada or Houston and Houston, others may say that they have had no problem keeping as much of their "nonmainstream" culture as they care to preserve. Some may say that they are eager to Americanize themselves as quickly as possible. You should accept all contributions.

Question 5 again combines abstract arguments on assimilation with even deeper personal reflections, asking students to explore the relations between assimilation and family life. (Some of these concerns may well have emerged in the personal material elicited by earlier questions.) All the evidence should be put in the service of an overarching argument concerning why, how, or if people with a "nonmainstream" cultural heritage should attempt to preserve and transmit it. We expect that some part of these essays would address the *how*'s — that is, either the ways that the home culture can be maintained or the ways that mainstream culture can be inculcated (if the student is arguing for wholesale assimilation). Students choosing the alternative assignment will have to give most of their attention to the *how*'s, actually presenting a detailed plan of action. Remind them, however, that the plan will need some accompanying argument about why it should be adopted, which will include addressing the *why*'s of assimilating or resisting assimilation.

Sequence 2. What is "race"? (p. 788)

The emphasis in this sequence is on race as a rhetorical construct — that is, on how concepts of race have been used to bolster arguments. We, of course, make no claims about the essential qualities or boundaries of racial categories such as Caucasian, Asian, and so on. Rather, we want to get students to see how their own attitudes about race function in their thinking.

"Race" is obviously a very sensitive subject. Many students will be apprehensive about discussing it for fear that they will be subjected to tales of victimhood, accusations of blame, unpleasant confrontations with classmates they'd prefer to be on good terms with, and so on. You may be able to allay some of these fears by pointing out that the focus of the sequence is not necessarily to indict racism but rather to explore how concepts of race operate in a variety of rhetorical contexts, in arguments that seek to promote racial harmony as well as in arguments most people would be likely to condemn as racist.

You should also know that the sequence questions are designed to contextualize students' own experiences with race. The assignments encourage not an exchange of victim stories or accusations but rather more measured consideration of the possible range of responses to racial arguments. Students are usually obliged by the assignments to put their experiences in dialogue with one or more of the readings.

Still, it might be easier to teach this sequence to an all-white class. European American students are probably those who are most in need of this sequence's critical examination of race. Because they belong to the dominant race, they have been able to forget about race in their everyday thinking, to forget that they have a racial identity as well as do those they perceive as "of color," and to ignore the possibility that all these racial categories are as much rhetorical as biological.

If your class population is racially mixed — especially if the mix is 90 percent white — you need to feel fairly confident of a high level of mutual trust in the class before attempting this sequence, so as not to place an undue burden on the few students of color. Perhaps you might lead into this sequence with work earlier in the semester on other material that has allowed the class to develop some rapport on racial issues, for example from Unit Two (see the model syllabus on p. 184 that combines material from Units Two and Five). Or you might give students a choice of sequences to work on in Unit Five and pursue this sequence only if the class chooses it.

Question 1 would be a good writing assignment to give in class on the first day of work on this sequence, perhaps before any of the reading is done. Students might then share in class or in small groups what they've written as a way of building trust. The alternative assignment here could be done after all the readings for the sequence have been discussed, which, as we noted earlier, need not necessarily be the case when you begin work on a sequence. If the readings have not been done at this point, you can ask students to bear this sequence question in mind as they do the readings and to jot responses to the question for each reading in their class journals.

Question 2 also assumes that a number of readings have already been completed. If you are working through the readings more gradually, we suggest you use only Sone and Masaoka for this assignment. Make sure students realize that what they are being asked to study is *how* the authors present their incidents of racial awareness. For example, they are not being asked to evaluate whether it was an injustice for the sorority to refuse to admit Sone; rather, they should be looking at whether Sone presents this incident as an example of injustice and how she conveys her interpretation stylistically.

Question 3 turns from the implicit arguments of accounts of personal experience to the overt arguments of these expository texts. Again, the focus is not on whether these texts are immorally racist. Rather, students are being asked to explain how these texts define *race* and how they use these definitions to support recommendations for action concerning the Nikkei. Of course, we think these texts, which are rather similar in their definition of *race, are* immorally racist. Nevertheless, we wish to allow for the possibility that some students may find the arguments (especially in the *Final Report*) persuasive on their own terms. We think you have to be open to this possibility — and we also think that if you convey this openness, you will have much better luck getting students to see the racism in these arguments than you would if you began by condemning them.

Question 4 now asks students to synthesize a number of sources around the issue of cross-racial solidarity. Students may wish to argue that there are merely pragmatic grounds for, or obstacles to, such alliances, or they may wish to develop a concept of race that facilitates or bars such alliances. Okada and Yamamoto are rather negative on the possibility of such alliances, although their very concern for them could be taken as a hopeful sign. Houston and Houston have less to say, although they do show a "brown" boy, Leonard Rodriguez, helping Jeanne win the carnival queen election.

Students may also draw on any other readings for this sequence to make up their required total of three; you should remind them to use their personal experience as well if they wish. If they apply their argument to a local controversy, they may want to use local written materials. The option to frame the paper as if for publication adds another variable in terms of audience definition for students to consider. Since this assignment is already quite a bit more challenging than those that have preceded it, you may not want to offer students this option unless they are fairly accomplished writers.

Question 5 mirrors question 4 in structure, so our comments in the previous paragraph apply here. This time, though, the assignment points to the possibility of alliances between people of color and European Americans. Masaoka and Sone seem more positive about such alliances than do Houston and Houston and Yamamoto. You might offer students a choice of responding to either question 4 or question 5. It might also be interesting to arrange for at least some of the papers to be presented in class, perhaps in an informal debate — let two or three volunteers present their papers on either side of the alliance issue (yes, there can be, or no, there cannot be, alliances) for each of the two sequence questions. Of course, this will work only if the climate of trust in the class is such that students will feel able to speak against the possibility of alliances in the presence of those whom they reject as allies. It could be a nicely challenging rhetorical problem for them.

Question 6 turns students loose to speculate on the issues they have been considering throughout the sequence. There will be a wide range of responses here, from those advocating insular monoracial solidarity to those whose utopia comprises the disappearance of racial discourse altogether. Fine! Just make sure everyone supports his or her position with good arguments and references to the readings. Personal experience can also be important in these essays.

Sequence 3. *How could this happen in the United States?* (p. 789)

Of the three sequences offered in Unit Five, this one is the most focused on argument. Several of the questions invite students to bring in contemporary materials of interest to them, but there is relatively little scope here for the use of personal experience, unlike the other two sequences. For a model syllabus integrating this sequence with one from Unit Two, see page 184.

Question 1 could be used as an in-class writing assignment on the first day of class. We suggest that you do not ask students to share what they've written immediately. Begin work on *Personal Justice Denied* in the next class, and then ask students to discuss what they wrote in the first class. They may wish to read what they wrote or to talk about how they would now change what they wrote, having read *Personal Justice Denied*. We would not press too hard to make these papers into in-depth considerations of the issues, however. They might remain in the class journals. They are intended mainly to set an initial benchmark against which students can measure the development in their thinking when they come to write the last assignment in the sequence.

Question 2 asks for a rather straightforward argument paper, in which students must use textual references in the process of assessing evidence. Students will have to attend to the definitions of *racism* put forward by the Commission, Weglyn, and Masaoka. Basically, all three contend that singling out the Nikkei for internment solely because of their easily identifiable racial "difference" from the white majority (and similarity to the enemy Japanese), not because of any real threat they posed, was racist. Presumably, then, by this logic, the internment would not be racist if the threat were real — that is, if there were good reasons to believe that the Nikkei, because of their racial and cultural ties with Japan, were aiding the enemy. Be prepared for some students to think that there were such good reasons and that therefore the *Final Report* and the other sample texts are not racist.

Questions 3 and 4 both deal with the issue of potential Nikkei resistance to the internment. After working through both questions in class, you might give students the option of writing one or the other.

The focus of question 3 is on psychological barriers to resistance. Students' arguments here should concentrate on whether or not the sources do seem to indicate the presence of a crippling diffidence among the Nikkei. Calling attention to the "double impulse" that Houston and Houston analyze, you might discuss the process whereby racism becomes internalized by its victims. Students in your class who have been victims of various forms of discrimination may want to testify on this topic. To write the alternative assignment, students will have to decide if the person to whom they are addressing their letters does suffer from the "double impulse" and, if so, how they, writing as non-Nikkei, can successfully address it. Class preparation for both choices in this sequence question will be the same: Students might then select one assignment to write.

Question 4 deals with the more pragmatic aspects of resistance: What did the Nikkei do to resist? What should they have done? Between them, Masaoka and Yasui raise the possibility of a full range of responses, from peaceful compliance to civil disobedience (you should explain this concept to students) to violent opposition. The two sources also provide information on how practical it would have been to try these various responses.

If students have already written question 3 (that is, if they were not given a choice between questions 3 and 4), you might want to ensure that question 4 becomes more challenging by requiring students to select the option of comparing the Nikkei resistance with resistance mounted by another American group (e.g., Native Americans or African Americans). The alternative assignment, to construct a panel discussion, is even more challenging and not for every taste: We suggest offering it as a possible choice only if students are fairly accomplished writers.

Question 5 raises discussion in this sequence to another level of abstraction. Up to now, in asking what happened, we have been basically assuming that we could get answers to the question from the assigned readings. Now we are asking students to consider the reliability of these sources, posing the problem in terms of two sources that dramatically disagree. We also like the option here and strongly suggest that you push students to add one of the personal accounts to the mix.

We hope that question 5 will have a sobering effect on students before they write question 6. In their responses to question 6, we don't want them to simply pick one account they like and agree with it right down the line. Rather, we want them to reflect on the difficulties of responding to the assignment question and to synthesize several sources in putting together their response. You might suggest that students reread what they wrote for the first sequence question; they may want to incorporate parts of it in this paper or discuss how their thinking has changed. This question also asks students to evaluate the morality of the internment. While their own moral judgments will of course have been evident in much of what they've already written in this sequence, this is the first time we have put this issue front and center. It may well occupy the bulk of students' papers.

RESEARCH KIT

Please see our remarks on Research Kits in the introduction to this manual (p. 11).

One way to organize your class's research in this unit is to develop a project of supplementing the unit's selections. Students could work in teams to collect examples of various genres: histories, autobiographies and memoirs, fiction, poetry, visual arts, and so on. There is a great wealth of such materials, far more than we could include in *Negotiating Difference*. Students could choose, from among the texts they find, those they would recommend for inclusion in this book and write headnotes and reading and writing questions for them. We would be happy to hear their suggestions!

Note that assignment 4 in "Ideas from the Unit Readings" suggests interviewing people about the internment. Students will probably discover that most non-Nikkei knew very little about the internment, unless they happened to live in an area that was directly affected, and that they basically regarded it as a wartime necessity, not a grave injustice, at least at the time.

Also note that assignment 11 calls for an "autoethnography" from Nikkei students. You might adapt this assignment so that all students in the class can participate: Each one could prepare the kind of account that's called for concerning his or her own cultural background.

A particularly interesting "Branching Out" idea is assignment 6, which invites various comparisons between the Nikkei and Native American experiences dealing with the federal government. This might be combined with assignment 3 and with research on other resident groups on whom special restrictions have been placed as a class project in researching the government's handling of such groups.

MODEL SYLLABI

The model syllabi are framed on a thirteen-week term, with week 14 being exam week. You can adapt them to your own number of weeks (if different) and number of class meetings per week. The model syllabi sometimes adapt the assignment sequences they use, omitting some questions or substituting others — you should feel free to be similarly flexible in developing your own syllabi. Remember, the sequences are not designed to be lockstep processes.

We assume that you will work in class on the reading questions accompanying the assigned selections as well as on the assigned writing and sequence questions (sometimes we give you suggestions in the syllabi for how to do so). Note that work on these questions can often be performed profitably in class in small groups. (For more information on group work, see p. 14.)

We suggest that students keep a class journal in which they write responses to the reading questions before the questions are discussed in class. (Also remind students to read the headnotes accompanying the selections before they come to class.) In other words, our plan is that a reading assignment ("Read Yasui") also constitutes a writing assignment because students should jot responses to the text's reading questions in their journals. (For more information on the class journal, see p. 12.)

You should collect and review these journals at least as often as you collect students' writing portfolios. We suggest that students be graded according to some version of the portfolio method. (For more information, see p. 17.)

Syllabus using two sequences from Unit Five

Here we have combined sequences 1 and 2 to enrich the discussion of race in sequence 2 with the discussion of assimilation in sequence 1. This combination also allows you to use all the readings in Unit Five except the documents, *Personal Justice Denied,* and Weglyn.

Week 1

Read: Unit Five introduction; Flowers

In the first class, ask students to write about whether they are managing a dual cultural identity — Mexican American, Polish American, and so on. If so, ask them to describe how they do it — that is, what is American and what is Mexican, Polish, or whatever, in their lives. If they are not, ask them to describe what they think is most American about themselves. They can read Flowers for the next class; discuss his reading questions in class.

Week 2

Read: *The Case for the Nisei;* Yasui
Write: Sequence 1, question 1

Week 3

Read: Okada; Sone
Write: Sequence 1, question 2
Collect: Essay from week 2

Week 4

Read: Houston and Houston (p. 715)
Write: Houston and Houston, writing question 1
Collect: Essay from week 3

Week 5

Read: Houston and Houston (p. 757)
Write: Sequence 1, question 3
Collect: Essay from week 4

Week 6

Read: *Final Report*
Write: Sequence 1, question 4
Collect: Essay from week 5

Week 7

Write: Portfolios, including class journals; revision of essay from week 6

In class, help students prepare their portfolios to be submitted next week. Help students select one paper from their previous assignments to revise for a grade. Some of this work might be done in small groups with peer editing. This is a good time to give lessons on any grammar or mechanics problems that are common among your students. Also tell them to make sure their journals are up to date.

Week 8

Read: Yamamoto
Write: Sequence 2, question 1
Collect: Portfolios, including class journals and revised essay assigned
in week 6

Week 9

Read: Masaoka
Write: Sequence 2, question 2
Collect: Essay from week 8

Week 10

> Write: Sequence 2, question 3
> Collect: Essay from week 9

In preparing to write question 3, students may want to review what they wrote for sequence 1, question 1. They may want to compare and contrast Flowers's arguments concerning assimilation with those concerning race.

Week 11

> Write: Sequence 2, question 4 or 5
> Collect: Essay from week 10

Students can choose question 4 or question 5. Both questions lend themselves to in-class presentation of differing positions. See our comments on them in the discussion of the sequences (p. 178).

Week 12

> Write: Sequence 1, question 5, or sequence 2, question 6
> Collect: Essay from week 11

Both sequence questions lend themselves to in-class debate. Students can choose whether to take the issues in this course inward, to a more personal application (the sequence 1 question) or outward, toward more cultural and political applications (the sequence 2 question).

Week 13

> Write: Revised essay from week 12
> Collect: Portfolios, including class journals (week 13 or 14)

In class, help students prepare their portfolios for final submission. Students should select one paper from weeks 8–12 to revise for a grade. Some of this work might be done in small groups with peer editing. Each portfolio must contain a revision of the essay from week 12. Collect portfolios at the end of this week or exam week.

Syllabus using sequences from Units Two and Five

Here we are combining Unit Two, sequence 2, ("What power should society have over the individual?"), with Unit Five, sequence 3 ("How could this [the internment of Japanese Americans during World War II] happen in the United States?"). Both sequences deal with issues of social control versus the guarantee of civil rights, white racism and opposition to racism, and more.

To make the reading manageable, we suggest eliminating from Unit Two, sequence 2, the Rhode Island resolution, the proslavery petition, and Fitzhugh; and from the Unit Five, sequence 3, Executive Order 9066, "Instructions to All Persons," and Masaoka.

Week 1

Read: Unit Two introduction; Declaration of Independence

In class, discuss Unit Two, sequence 2, question 2 (without the option), and ask students to sketch a response to it in their class journals.

Week 2

Read: Douglass

Discuss how Douglass might be used in Unit Two, sequence 2, question 3.

Week 3

Read: Langston
Write: Unit Two, sequence 2, question 3

Week 4

Read: Bledsoe
Write: Unit Two, sequence 2, question 4 (modified to omit Fitzhugh
    and contemporary examples)
Collect: Essay from week 3

Week 5

Read: Garrison
Write: Unit Two, sequence 2, question 5; class journals
Collect: Essay from week 4

In class, help students prepare their class journals for submission next week.

Week 6

Read: Unit Five introduction; *Personal Justice Denied*
Collect: Essay from week 5; class journals

Discuss Unit Five, sequence 3, question 1. Students might sketch a response to this question in their class journals.

Week 7

Read: *Final Report*

Week 8

Read: Weglyn
Write: Unit Five, sequence 3, question 2 (modified to omit Masaoka,
    Executive Order 9066, and "Instructions to All Persons")

Week 9

Read: Houston and Houston (pp. 715, 757)
Collect: Essay from week 8

In class, ask the students to compare the ways racist arguments are supported in Bledsoe and the *Final Report* and the ways they are resisted in Weglyn and Langston or Douglass. You might also ask students to write about these comparisons in their class journals.

Week 10

Read: Yasui
Write: Unit Five, sequence 3, question 3 (modified to omit Masaoka)

In class, ask the students to compare Houston and Houston with Langston on the ways blame is assigned to people of color for encouraging white racism. You might also ask students to write about these comparisons in their class journals.

Week 11

Write: Unit Five, sequence 3, question 4 (modified to omit Masaoka)
Collect: Essay from week 10

In class, ask the students to compare Yasui and Houston and Houston with Garrison and Langston on the ways people should resist social oppression and oppressive laws. You might also ask students to write about these comparisons in their class journals.

Week 12

Write: Student-designed essay (optional; see the following discussions)
Collect: Essay from week 11

In class, ask students to consider what we can learn from these two units and sequences about the issue of civil rights versus social control in the United States. You might use this just as a synthesizing discussion and ask students to react to it in their class journals, or you might encourage them to devise their own final paper assignments responding to the discussion.

Week 13

Collect: Student-designed essay; portfolios, including class journals
      (week 13 or 14)

Work with students to select for their portfolios one paper from each sequence to revise for a grade. Some of this work might be done in small groups with peer editing. This is a good time to give lessons on any grammar or mechanics problems that are common among your students. Also tell them to make sure their journals are up to date. Collect portfolios at the end of this week or exam week.

UNIT SIX

Policy and Protest over the Vietnam War

THEMES AND ISSUES IN UNIT SIX

The war in Vietnam ended more than twenty years ago, before most of our students were born. Yet the trauma is still with us, and with them. News stories about the war still surface regularly. In 1995, for example, Robert McNamara published an autobiographical account of the war years, President Clinton normalized diplomatic relations with Vietnam, and the twenty-fifth anniversary of the Kent State killings was observed. These events were accompanied by innumerable news articles and television shows about veterans, former protesters, MIAs and their families, Vietnamese immigrants, and the effects of the war on military policy.

But even when the Vietnam War recedes farther into the past, it will remain an important moment of conflict and negotiation in American history. The war took place during a time of social and cultural ferment. The civil rights movement, student activism on a variety of social issues (including nuclear proliferation, racism, cold war militarism, the widening gap between the rich and the poor, and governmental arrogance), the explosion of youth culture, and the beginnings of the women's movement all contributed to the sense of conflict and change in the Sixties and early Seventies. Protests against the war inevitably carried the weight of other dissatisfactions with the established order, just as support for the war effort often signaled a rejection of cultural change. The war was a lightning rod for the times themselves, and the conflict over it was not only about government policies but about the way Americans envisioned the nation's political and cultural ideals. While it was impossible to include materials explicitly addressing all of these issues (a fact, by the way, that makes for a number of research projects that are exceptionally appealing), they are evoked in a number of the selections in the unit. (Of course, if you have your old Country Joe and the Fish album in the back of a closet, this is an opportunity to dust it off and play it for your students.)

Unit Six is a good choice if you want your course to focus on an issue of public policy and widespread popular debate on a matter that is still in the press and that will have affected the families of a great many of our students.

The Rhetoric of Policy and of Protest

Most of the discourse in Unit Six is aimed at a very wide audience and is explicitly intended to shape public policy about what is arguably the most important single activity a nation can engage in. While the stakes were high for the arguments in all of the units in *Negotiating Difference,* the immediacy of the issues and decisions here is unparalleled. The way in which history was understood by the State Department and by U.S. presidents, for example, affected decisions about dropping bombs. Martin Luther King's very different version of the same history galvanized antiwar protesters and sent them into the streets.

Reading the selections galvanizes students, too. While they can treat World War II and the Korean War as distant and neutral historical events, Vietnam has an immediacy that stirs strong feelings and sparks debate. In accounts of courses on the Vietnam War, a number of teachers have reported that students do not participate in the current consensus that the war was a mistake. They enter readily into debates for and against as if it were an issue of the moment. While this is to the good, we recommend (as we recommend in all the units of *Negotiating Difference*) that the debate not be conducted in general terms: Focus on the texts and the ways that the actual arguments were made at the time. Create a historical context in which to ground student debates. The selections and questions will facilitate discussion of how arguments shape history and the ways that policy is based on versions of history.

The selections reveal the main arguments for and against the war. Anticommunism was the initial and primary reason for U.S. aid to France, support of Ngo Dinh Diem, and military intervention. The need to oppose aggression from the North was invoked in the mid-1960s. Lyndon Johnson at the end of his presidency and Richard Nixon during his realized that the United States could not win the war and, scrambling to find a "peace with honor" that would allow them to get out, meanwhile claimed that Hanoi would not negotiate in good faith and that therefore the United States could not leave.

The antiwar forces began by arguing that the United States was intervening in a civil war, violating the Geneva agreement to reunite Vietnam, and supporting the tyrant Diem. War tactics like defoliation and napalm bombing of villages soon came in for criticism. Protesters attacked anticommunism as a cold war reflex and downplayed the seriousness of communism as a worldwide threat, especially in regard to Vietnam. As Vietnam veterans became active in the antiwar movement, the incoherence of the military mission became a point of protest, and stories of atrocities committed by U.S. troops became more real than the prospect of possible Communist massacres in the event of a takeover by the North.

An additional criticism through most of the war was that the government was simply untrustworthy. Official histories of the conflict were distorted, body counts of enemy dead were grossly inflated, major escalations in the war effort were kept secret, North Vietnamese offers to negotiate were misrepresented, and so on. The *Pentagon Papers* showed that efforts to keep the American public in ignorance were quite deliberate and of long standing. Nixon's reaction to the publication of the *Pentagon Papers* and the subsequent Watergate coverup only reconfirmed the government's disdain for truth and democratic values. Most Americans were reluctant to believe that the government was systematically lying to them, even in the face of clear evidence.

The opponents in these arguments took a dim view of each other personally. Supporters of the war policy stereotyped protesters as "commies," traitors, draft evaders, and ingrates. Long hair, rock music, psychedelic drugs, and openness about sex contributed to the sense that young protesters were out to destroy American society. Protesters, on their side, saw the war's supporters as unreflective promoters and beneficiaries of a military-industrial complex that tolerated racism, poverty, environmental decay, and the destruction of weaker countries for its selfish ends.

While the selections in this unit reveal some of this stereotyping and its bitterness, they suggest for the most part that the two sides could not be so readily characterized. Perhaps the most moving of these pieces for students are those at the end of the unit by veterans who reveal their ambivalence, first answering the call of patriotism and then questioning the policies of their government.

Ethos and Audience in Political Argument

In these selections, many of them by important public figures, *ethos* plays a large role in persuasion. In classical rhetoric, a speaker's ethos is the sense of himself or herself conveyed to the audience by specific personal statements as well as by his or her choices of a general style of language use, dress, gesture, and so on. The "ethical appeal" is the persuasiveness of the speaker's ethos to the audience; the more likable, trustworthy, and respectable a speaker appears to be, the better chance he or she has to persuade the audience. The speaker's position of authority also works here. Protesters of the war were often told, for example, that the president and the Pentagon knew more than they did about the situation and should be trusted, not opposed. If people today seem to be less persuaded by presidential ethos, it may be at least partly because of the events of the Vietnam era. Still, it is important to see in the selections here the way that speakers position themselves either as powerful players or with respect to that power.

Speakers in this unit include a U.S. senator, the U.S. State Department, two U.S. presidents, a vice president, a Communist leader, and a U.S. civil rights leader. The presidents and the civil rights leader (Martin Luther King Jr.) refer to their own positions and use their authority as part of their persuasive appeals. This is not arrogance, though the particular ways in which they used that self-reference are certainly open to criticism. Students usually don't need to be invited to be critical of such self-reference where it is so evident, but they do need to be shown that ethos operates in all discourse, including their own.

The public nature of the discourse in this unit highlights the presence of multiple audiences. A number of the writing assignments focus on this fascinating problem. Right from the start we see careful attention to widely divergent audiences in Ho Chi Minh's attempt to declare independence and gain U.S. approval. Senator Dodd cautions his North Vietnamese audience that the Senate may talk about negotiation, but that it doesn't mean anything, no sir. The Mobilization Committee's "Message to GIs and to the Movement" names its audiences but clearly addresses both messages to both audiences. President Nixon wants to use just the right code words for each of several audiences, while Vice President Agnew loves to appeal to his friends and anger his enemies.

As in writing assignments in other units, we ask students to imagine the reactions of the players themselves, to project not only into the period and its conflicts but also into the minds and emotions of people quite unlike themselves. In most cases, even more audience divisions can be made (for example, the widows of slain soldiers or the parents of protesters) to make the assignments and discussions even richer.

NOTES ON THE UNIT READINGS

Each selection in the unit is accompanied by its own headnote, reading questions, and writing questions, so it can be assigned independently of the other readings or combined with others as you see fit. We have also grouped each reading with several other selections in at least one of the three assignment sequences offered at the end of the unit (the sequences are discussed on p. 208). We urge you to assemble your course reading and writing into one or more assignment sequences, of either our design or your own.

In the following notes, we provide commentary on each of the unit's selections as well as guidelines for approaching and evaluating the writing questions.

A PRECURSOR TO WAR

HO CHI MINH, "DECLARATION OF INDEPENDENCE OF THE DEMOCRATIC REPUBLIC OF VIETNAM" (p. 804)

This selection focuses the unit briefly but strikingly on the situation in Vietnam before the United States became an active participant in the war. It documents the passage in the introduction where we mention Ho Chi Minh's appeals to the United States for help in gaining independence from France.

(Some students may recall that in 1776 American revolutionaries appealed to France for help in gaining independence from England.)

Students' knowledge of Ho Chi Minh is not at all predictable. Some will think of him as the enemy and therefore not to be trusted, while others will think of him as a national hero. An argument on these issues is likely to be entirely fruitless and frustrating. Our intention in using this document is to call attention both to history and to some of the terrible ironies in the U.S. involvement in Vietnam. We suggest a discussion of the reading and writing questions to focus these issues.

Writing Analytically

The writing question should start several lines of analysis that will make students reflect on the complexities of political rhetoric. Is the appeal to equality genuine? If so, how does it argue for national sovereignty, in either the Vietnamese or the American declaration? It is reasonable for students to assume that both declarations are perfectly sincere and to explore the connection between individual liberty and national sovereignty. Some students will be more suspicious. If the appeal is not genuine, what function does it have in either document? Is the appeal to equality simply a ploy by Ho to gain U.S. favor? Students who retain the evil-empire view of communism may assume so, but they will still have to wonder why Ho wanted the United States as an ally or could hope that his appeal would work.

The questions of purpose and audience also need to be raised. What are the declarations for? Who was supposed to read them? If Ho is addressing his to the United States, to whom was Jefferson addressing his? How do these considerations shape what was said? Both declarations give a partisan version of history. What is the purpose of including the history? You can use these questions to open up a preliminary discussion of the assignment or to help students develop a first draft.

The alternative assignment does not require extensive knowledge of the British colonization of America, which was very, very different from the French colonization of Vietnam. You may wish to take an "inventory" of class knowledge on the subject. The inventory is a critical-thinking exercise in which students brainstorm about a subject, saying everything they can think of about it, every phrase or half-idea ("Boston Tea Party") as well as more substantial information, all of which you write on the board. What should come out, at the very least, is that the American revolutionaries were descendents of the colonizers and that the British were not "exploiting" the colonies in anything like the way the French exploited Vietnam. Comparing the two declarations will further reveal such differences and help students with the assignment.

1965: YEAR OF ESCALATION AND PROTEST

THOMAS J. DODD, FROM A SPEECH TO THE U.S. SENATE (p. 808)

Dodd powerfully evokes the image of a global war of good against evil that dominated Americans' thinking about communism in the cold war era: "At stake may be the survival of freedom." This is an important selection, assigned in all three sequences, for it reveals a mind-set that is becoming increasingly alien both to our students and ourselves.

The fact that Dodd was wrong, in the end, about his predictions does not mean that his arguments were baseless or can be ignored or that he was not arguing in good faith. As in other issues raised in *Negotiating Difference*, we are looking not for the winners but for the ways in which ideological ground was contested. Dodd, in fact, was the "winner" for a long time: The administration followed his recommendations during most of the war.

Writing Analytically

Writing question 1 asks about a recurring rhetorical strategy in Dodd's speech — the idea of imitating Churchill's resolve never to give in during World War II. Dodd's analogy has both strengths and weaknesses that students should be fairly able to identify. The brainstorming suggestion in this question applies not only to World War II but also to the Vietnam War — that is, it will help students review some of the information in the introduction.

Writing question 2 focuses on a small but revealing part of Dodd's speech, the proposal to form a kind of NLF of the North. Because students will have to be clear about what the NLF was, at least in Dodd's view, and what Dodd was proposing, this is in part a critical-reading assignment. The question also asks students to articulate an argument using Dodd's voice, an exercise that will help them understand the prevailing attitudes of the time.

In place of these writing questions, you may wish to assign question 2 from sequence 1, which asks for a comparison between Dodd's speech and Ho Chi Minh's "Declaration of Independence."

U.S. DEPARTMENT OF STATE, FROM THE WHITE PAPER *AGGRESSION FROM THE NORTH: THE RECORD OF NORTH VIETNAM'S CAMPAIGN TO CONQUER SOUTH VIETNAM* (p. 824)

The white paper assumes as an established fact that South Vietnam broke away from the North to avoid domination by Communists, as in the case of South Korea. (The badness of communism is also assumed, and no reasons are offered for why the North went in that direction.) The real issue the white paper addresses is the nature of the resistance movement in South

Vietnam. This appears to be the document that Senator Dodd refers to in his speech (p. 817) to show that NLF resistance in South Vietnam is directed and supplied by North Vietnam. The NLF (called the Viet Cong in the paper) is openly supported by Hanoi. But can support be called aggression?

The white paper answers that question by stating that a "new kind of war" is being waged in Vietnam: an invasion disguised as an insurgency. The paper's argument, in other words, is that there is no real insurgency at all. To prove this point, the paper shows material evidence that most of the NLF's people and supplies are from North Vietnam — one country infiltrating another in order to conquer it. Forces from the South were not absent, but, the paper claims, the "hard core" of the forces, the "key leadership," "many" of the technicians, and so on come from or are trained in the North, just as "many of the weapons" and other matériel come from the North. The paper writes off the indigenous South Vietnamese members of the NLF.

Finally, the white paper reviews the history of the country since 1954, arguing that the Communists planned from the beginning to infiltrate the South and stir up trouble and that South Vietnam detected and thwarted this effort. The history the paper presents is tendentious and quite incomplete, but most of what it does include is accurate. The economic history it provides is correct, for example: The North did face economic disaster while the South was growing strong. (For an account of this history that stands up to modern scrutiny, see the King selection.)

As a statement of the case for U.S. intervention in Vietnam, the white paper shows quite clearly how strong an argument was being made in Washington and across the country for supporting the war. Despite criticism, this remained the official story for years to come. (See Nixon's speech "Vietnamization," which relies on the white paper's history.)

Reading question 4, which asks about the motives that the white paper attributes to the parties, is an important discussion point that can easily be turned into a writing assignment. It does not ask what the actual motives are, but rather what the white paper implies they are. This positioning is important for the rhetorical effect that the paper achieves or seeks to achieve, and it can lead to a useful general discussion of the ways that the motives of others are described.

Writing Analytically

Writing question 1 is a fairly straightforward analysis. The subquestions give an outline of some basic elements to consider in analyzing an argument, and you should urge students to answer all of them. The last subquestion asks for speculation about attitudes and motives. For some students, this will be the most interesting part of the paper. Others may find it difficult, especially if you assign this selection early in the semester before you've discussed other positions on the war. If you are using the portfolio method, this part of the paper can actually be left until later in the semester. Allowing students to revise after further study reinforces the idea that writing is a process and a way of learning.

Writing question 2 asks about audience and rhetorical aims. This can be assigned as a continuation of question 1 or as an alternative to it. The white paper was published in the *New York Times* and was quoted widely as the official story on the war, as indeed it was. The appeal of authority here is strong (see the discussion of "ethos" p. 189), and you may wish to add a note about it to the assignment. Identifying the "American ideals" in the selection is important for understanding the appeal to principle that can be found in all of the arguments in this unit. You might focus preliminary discussion of this question on identifying those ideals and understanding what a "premise" is.

You may wish to have students read the Stone reply to the white paper and then write from the questions following that selection. Note also that the last three questions in sequence 1 use the white paper in combination with other readings.

I. F. Stone, "A Reply to the 'White Paper'" (p. 834)

Students may find it difficult to articulate exactly what Stone is arguing in this piece beyond dismantling the white paper's argument. Is he saying that North Vietnam does not support the NLF? Clearly not — his first sentence acknowledges that support. Is he arguing that the war between North and South is a civil war? He does argue that the insurgency in the South should be seen as genuine, and this is an important point. But his main thrust seems to be that the U.S. government is arguing falsely — and, he implies, that the distortion is deliberate.

The flaws in the white paper's argument do not prove that North Vietnam is not an aggressor. However, the white paper cannot establish that the North is an aggressor on the basis of the argument it makes and the evidence it supplies. Thus, Stone's strongest accusation is that the government is, at best, disingenuous and, at worst, lying outright — rationalizing its actions with false history and distorted evidence.

Stone shows dramatically that evidence is not self-explanatory, a point that you should emphasize in class discussion. Evidence requires interpretation — or, to put it more accurately, data require interpretation. Once the data are interpreted, they become evidence. The process by which Stone subjects the white paper's data to scrutiny is worth close attention and will serve as a warm-up for the first writing question.

Writing Analytically

Writing question 1 focuses on argument and refutation. The goal is not to evaluate the arguments (though students can certainly include that in an essay) but to see how an apparently seamless argument can be answered. Direct students, either before they begin to write or in your response to their drafts, to discuss the way that Stone's opening concession acts as part of his rebuttal. Also urge students to note where rebuttal is directed at evidence, where at logical arguments, and where at conclusions.

Writing question 2 can stand alone or can easily be appended to question 1. It addresses the issue of ethos, discussed earlier.

DAVID DELLINGER, A. J. MUSTE ET AL., "DECLARATION OF CONSCIENCE AGAINST THE WAR IN VIETNAM" (p. 840)

Discussion of the first reading question — "What reasons do the signers give for opposing the war?" — should reveal a very different approach from Stone's (or Potter's or King's). There are only four reasons, all of which could easily be refuted by supporters of the war. Ask students to supply the refutations as an additional journal entry or class discussion point. What assumptions, you can then ask, make the signers believe that their reasons are good ones? In fact, the reasons are not arguments at all, but conclusions. This sort of document telegraphically asserts beliefs and principles. It says, in effect, "It's too late for argument; it's time to take action." Still, such documents have persuasive force.

Implicit in the declaration is the rejection of the idea that communism needs to be opposed in Vietnam. It echoes the U.S. Declaration of Independence and, whether deliberately or not, Ho Chi Minh's declaration of Vietnamese independence, putting the right to national self-determination ahead of the form of government the nation chooses. Again, it is worth pointing out that this principle was anathema to the cold warriors in power at the time. Thus, it was not their arguments that they hoped would persuade the government to change course in Vietnam, but rather the pressure of popular resistance. Even this is perhaps too much to assert. It may be that this declaration was purely an act of conscience.

Writing Analytically

Writing question 1 addresses a concern students frequently cite: their reluctance to do something illegal deliberately. As with other questions of this type, students should air their responses in class discussion. This discussion will very likely broach the issue raised in question 2, which can then be assigned as a follow-up. It's also a good way to redirect attention away from student responses and back toward the text and the issue at hand.

Writing question 3 calls for analysis of the text. A preliminary discussion of the question should consider the issues raised at the beginning of this entry if they have not already come up. The phrase in the question about assessing "the strength of its arguments" may seem like a trick question given our comments (that is, the best answer is that there are no arguments in the declaration), but it seems to us the best way to open the issue. Students might also speculate about the effect of announcing one's intention to commit civil disobedience, which might be called a form of argument.

It is worth pointing out that the government persistently refused to rise to the bait. Officials just ignored statements like this one as they ignored draft card burnings, saying that Selective Service offices would simply issue new cards to those who had "lost" theirs.

BARBARA BEIDLER, "AFTERTHOUGHTS ON A NAPALM-DROP ON JUNGLE VILLAGES NEAR HAIPHONG"; HUY CAN, "TRUTH BLAZES EVEN IN LITTLE CHILDREN'S HEARTS" (p. 842)

Beidler's moving poem — all the more moving because it was composed by a twelve-year-old — vividly demonstrates the rhetorical force of imaginative writing. That its rhetorical force was felt is witnessed by the fact that the government, absurdly and frighteningly, attempted to suppress it.

Beidler's issue in the poem is, in larger terms, the conduct of the war itself, the strategies used to fight an insurgency within South Vietnam. This is part of the focus of sequence 3 in this unit.

Huy Can's poem is far less striking than Beidler's, but it has its points and obviously makes a good companion piece. The poem plays on Beidler's "gold" image, converting it into "Golden fire of dollars." Notice also that in its strong final stanza, the poem refers to the U.S. Defense Department's effort to censor Beidler's poem.

Writing Analytically

Writing question 1 can be a topic for a journal entry and class discussion to make way for the more important (for our immediate purposes) question 2. Discuss writing question 2 before students set about writing their essays in response to it. Like other questions with several subquestions, this one presents the opportunity to discuss the nature of college writing assignments by trying to figure out *what the professor wants*. Analyzing the assignment is a typical strategy in writing centers and should be brought into every writing classroom. Ask students to analyze the question itself: Which of the subquestions should they answer? Can they imagine an outline for an essay that would satisfy the assignment? What is their strategy for writing such an essay?

If you found your Country Joe and the Fish album as we suggested earlier, you might consider using some of its lyrics as part of this assignment or at least as part of the preliminary discussion.

PAUL POTTER, FROM "THE INCREDIBLE WAR" (p. 845)

Potter's disillusionment is powerful and his resentment deep. There is an appealing highmindedness in his use of terms like *morality* and *freedom* and *decency*. He does not sound like a "commie" or a traitor, but like someone who would prefer to see the ideals of the United States embodied in the country's policies and actions. Supporters of the war brushed off sentiments like these as idealism and naiveté. The real world bruises, knocks off the corners of ideals. Potter wants to keep those ideals from crumbling into dust under the hammer of expediency.

Potter speaks of the cultural disruption in Vietnam, a subject that Frances FitzGerald explores thoroughly in her book *Fire in the Lake.* Like the French, the U.S. strategists in Vietnam had no interest in the nation's history or cultural heritage. Potter also puts the war protest movement in the context of social reform movements in the United States — a reflection of the SDS agenda. He addresses the anticommunism argument directly, attacking the effects of cold war overreaction and facing the fact that a Communist government would inevitably succeed an American withdrawal. This issue is raised in sequence 1, question 4.

Potter's discussion of the "system" reflects growing disaffection with a large set of policies and attitudes about wealth and power that had been criticized by SDS in its 1962 Port Huron statement. (This document would make a good supplement to this unit if you wish to pursue the issue of the larger social reform efforts of the period.) This is the subject of reading question 4 and writing question 1.

Writing Analytically

Students can successfully answer writing question 1 from Potter's speech alone (though their answer can be supplemented by King's speech). The assignment calls for critical reading to define the terms *system* and *movement,* followed by an analysis of Potter's assumptions, as revealed by the meaning of the terms. Some students will regard Potter as naive and unrealistic. That's not a problem, as long as they understand his purpose in contextualizing the war as he does.

Students should anchor writing questions 2 and 3 in the answer to question 1 — that is, in an understanding of the difference between a particular policy and a philosophy (for question 2) or the difference between a cause and a reform agenda (for question 3). These questions allow students to speculate about whether anything has changed fundamentally since the time that Potter spoke. Potter was a student leader (though a graduate student at the time of his presidency of SDS), and many students today are fascinated by the prominent role of students in the antiwar effort. These questions call for speculation and personal views: Your standards for judging them should be adjusted accordingly.

Writing question 4 assumes that students have done a good deal of other reading in the unit. If they have, this comparison and contrast assignment can lead to a deeper understanding of the strategies of counterargument and the management of ethos.

THE WAR AT HOME

MARTIN LUTHER KING JR., "DECLARATION OF INDEPEN-DENCE FROM THE WAR IN VIETNAM" (p. 850)

This is a masterful speech that contrasts interestingly with Potter's in its approach to antiwar argumentation, especially as many of the points in the two speeches are the same.

King's stature as a public figure allows him — perhaps requires him — to manage ethos directly, as he does at the beginning of the speech. King's reputation with students seems to be intact, so few will wonder at his assumption that his audience knows a great deal about him. King's antiwar stance has received little attention, though, in the years since his death, so that few people now think of him as an antiwar leader. Yet his arguments here are bold and cogent, perhaps even surprising.

King addresses the links between the war and civil rights early on, citing the war's threat to poverty program funding, the "cruel irony" of an integrated army wreaking havoc in Vietnam only to be segregated back at home, and the model of violence condoned as a way to solve problems. More of his effort, though, is spent on reviewing the recent history of Vietnam and the U.S. role there. King even defends communism as a legitimate and reasonable choice for the Vietnamese after years of French colonial rule. He unremittingly denounces the United States for blocking the legitimate aspirations of the Vietnamese people. Finally, he imagines the Vietnamese view of the United States, painting a devastating portrait of a betrayer insanely presenting itself as a savior. Finally, in his call for a "radical revolution of values," King addresses what Potter calls the "system." King's call is for true social justice.

Reading question 1 asks for King's seven reasons for speaking out on the war. They are not all that easy to find: (1) the threat to the poverty program, (2) the irony of sending black men to fight for "freedom" for other people, (3) the use of violence to solve problems, (4) American integrity, (5) the meaning of his Nobel Peace Prize, (6) his ministry, and (7) the people of Vietnam.

Writing Analytically

Writing question 1 reminds us of Dodd's speech on anticommunism, which preceded King's speech by a mere two years. Dodd opposed even the suggestion of negotiation, but King goes much further in his proposal, urging a scheduled withdrawal and inclusion of the NLF in negotiations. The challenge of this assignment is to represent both sides of this argument, which is deeply embedded in the spirit of the period. You can suggest that students have some fun with the form of the essay — drawing up an indictment, imagining the courtroom arguments, or writing editorials or news broadcasts about the case.

Writing question 2 focuses on the practical proposal that King makes. The proposal is bold but easy to criticize. Nixon, for example, rejects a scheduled withdrawal in his speech on the grounds that the Communists would simply wait until U.S. troops left and then take over. Nor is it difficult to challenge the other recommendations in his proposal. As in the reaction to Potter's speech, it is possible to argue that King is idealistic and naive, that his goals are noble but unattainable, and that his proposal means, in effect, simply giving up. And as in writing question 1, students must be able to articulate clearly the issues on both sides.

Treat questions 1 and 2 as alternatives, allowing students to choose which they would like to write on.

Writing question 3 calls for a structural analysis of the speech. There is no need to use rhetorical terminology for this assignment, though it provides an opportunity to introduce arrangement formally if you wish. The goal, of course, is to help students see how arrangement (or organization) can affect persuasion.

LYNDON B. JOHNSON, FROM "PEACE IN VIETNAM AND SOUTHEAST ASIA" (p. 860)

This speech reveals the dilemma of the war from the Johnson administration's perspective. It seemed (accurately) that the war could not be won outright. What, then, could be done to achieve the equivalent of victory and end the war? If your class reads King's speech and works on writing question 2, evaluating King's proposal for pulling out of Vietnam, it will be clear that what King envisions is an orderly transfer of power in South Vietnam from the current government to the NLF and the North Vietnamese. This was the inevitable consequence of a U.S. withdrawal and was indeed what finally occurred. But Johnson was not prepared in 1968 to accept the inevitable.

This speech, therefore, seems to be an attempt to entice North Vietnam to make peace in exchange for the promise of U.S. economic aid. This offer, though, is not highlighted in the speech, a point that could be discussed in answering writing question 1. Most of the speech is devoted to a justification for having kept U.S. troops in Vietnam for so long. Johnson's reasons (which the class should discuss in connection with reading question 2) are rather different from those put forward by Dodd and the white paper. Johnson mentions South Vietnamese self-determination but does not describe the horrors of communism. Perhaps this is a rhetorical decision on Johnson's part because he is appealing to the North Vietnamese for negotiations — students should consider this issue in answering writing question 1. Johnson also refers to America's security. Earlier this was part of the argument based on the threat of worldwide communist domination, but Johnson soft-pedals that threat too, leaving the concern for America's security coded, if not exactly unexplained. Mostly, though, Johnson just seems tired of the war, like everybody else.

Writing Analytically

Writing question 1 calls for a wide-ranging analysis aimed at trying to understand the complexities of this official public statement from the nation's highest office. The audience orientation of the question creates a number of possibilities for managing the assignment. Individual students should be capable of imagining the responses of all four audiences. But you may wish to set up four teams, each of which can brainstorm and present the views of one of the audiences. Or teams of four representing the different perspectives can present panel discussions evaluating the speech. You should stress that there is no single view that represents each audience. Those opposed to the war, for example, were divided on whether the speech was full of clues that Johnson was ready to accept a real compromise with the Communists or whether the speech was just more of the same old policy.

Writing question 2 goes back to the issue of negotiation raised by Dodd. The United States would not be negotiating from a position of strength. The only card the United States had was that it could prolong the horrors of the war. From the point of view of Dodd's speech, this was precisely the sort of situation that would encourage the Communists. Writing this essay will remind students of the very different discourse being used a mere three years earlier.

NATIONAL MOBILIZATION COMMITTEE TO END THE WAR IN VIETNAM, "A MESSAGE TO GIs AND TO THE MOVEMENT" (p. 868)

This selection gives a wonderful twist to the theme of multiple audiences. Writing question 1 describes the audience challenge, and you should discuss it in class even if you don't assign it for writing.

The pamphlet's rhetoric echoes the systemic analysis in Potter's speech, and you should bring the two pieces together. The claim that the military establishment — in this case the Pentagon and its suppliers — has a stake in keeping the war going arises in just about every shooting conflict. There is not enough information in the selections in this unit to weigh the claim, but even so, students can argue its plausibility and evaluate its use in persuasion.

Another issue raised in passing here is the draft laws that allow deferments for college men. Even when automatic deferments were dropped and the lottery system went into effect, it was still easier for those in college to get counseling and find ways to avoid the draft. Class and caste distinctions were not a major theme in the antiwar movement as a whole, but those in the movement who had broader social reform agendas brought it up when they could.

Writing Analytically

Before students tackle writing question 1, you can have them role-play the two audiences and brainstorm the responses. The assignment works better if each student answers the entire question, but it is possible to divide it into group tasks. You may wish to elaborate the question when you give the assignment, specifying that students should reflect on the style, on the depiction of the other group in each part of the message, and on the range of possible reactions by each group.

Writing question 2 should not be construed as a simple comparison between the "Message" and King's speech: Their purposes are too different for that. The idea is to abstract the arguments and assumptions in the "Message" to see how it makes a case against the war, using King's much more comprehensive set of arguments as a kind of reference source of possible arguments. This question asks for a distinction between logical and emotional appeals; take the opportunity in discussing the assignment to present and define these terms.

RICHARD M. NIXON, FROM "VIETNAMIZATION" (p. 871)

When Nixon died in 1994, the press and many public figures (including President Clinton) took a rather positive view of him, downplaying talk about Watergate and Nixon's general nastiness. Students are likely to reflect this mood. Many see political dirty tricks as par for the course, not something to pillory a president for. This is, perhaps, a good attitude to have when reading the Vietnamization speech. Nixon delivered the speech well before Watergate, during his first year as president, in fact — a time when many people hoped that he could provide relief from a war associated with the Democrats. Early in the year, antiwar activity slowed, presumably to give Nixon a chance to engage his secret plan for peace, though by November antiwar protests were once again in full swing. In this speech, Nixon was trying to take advantage of an opportune moment when his public image was still that of peacemaker.

Writing Analytically

Part of the positive reaction to Nixon's speech came from its acknowledgment of the country's domestic distress, the war at home. While those who opposed the war were disappointed in the speech, hearing a policy essentially unchanged from Johnson's, there was a broad perception that Nixon was being conciliatory. Writing question 1 explores this issue in a multiple-audience question.

Like Johnson, Nixon will not consider handing Vietnam over to the Communists. And so, like Johnson, Nixon does not say anything about what the actual populace of South Vietnam might favor. He argues that the United States must honor its commitments or the world will face chaos. However, to extricate the United States, he proposes to shift the responsibility for events in Vietnam to the Vietnamese. This principle of Vietnamization can be found in Johnson's speech a year and a half before. But unlike Johnson, Nixon appears to be determined to actually implement it. His way of presenting the proposed policy is the topic of writing question 2.

Nixon's concern to position himself in history is evident in the speech, undisguised by his wooden prose. If you wish to follow up on the theme of ethos, consider comparing Nixon's self-presentation with King's and Johnson's and assign writing question 3.

Draw students' attention to Nixon's version of history (addressed in sequence 1, question 3). Nixon relies on the official history provided by the white paper, and then deletes details that might look bad for the United States: He mentions neither the period of French colonization nor the inconvenient Geneva accords.

SPIRO T. AGNEW, PARASITES, PROTESTERS, AND THE PRESS (p. 881)

As we note on page 191, ad hominem attacks in the rhetorical war between the hawks and doves were common, the counterpart of the physical attacks described in part by Kovic. While most of the arguing presented in this unit is pretty polite and moderate, Agnew stands for the immoderate element in the discourse.

Agnew was much admired. With the help of his speechwriter William Safire, he was the articulate spokesman of angry ordinary citizens who despised the protesters. Many harsh words were exchanged on both sides. They can be read in letters to the editor and in editorials, and they can be heard in documentaries about the war, if students wish to follow up. But Agnew was unusual not only because he was a thesaurus hound, framing his vitriolic opinions in elegant, amusing, and startling ways, but also because he was the vice president, for heaven's sake. Nixon's fury at the antiwar movement was barely disguised and Agnew's was not disguised at all. Agnew got mad and Nixon got even. In any case, the administration position was that protesters were scum.

Writing Analytically

As writing question 1 suggests, vicious, unmoderated attacks on liberals and the press are once again in fashion, so students will be amused but probably not shocked by Agnew. Not to worry. If you are assigning Agnew as part of sequence 3, as we recommend, the next readings are the selections by Kerry and O'Brien, which put Agnew in context and respond to his main charge — that the protesters are stupid, selfish, and unpatriotic.

Agnew argues a number of points quite well and raises some interesting questions. Should a high official like the vice president always take a conciliatory tone and express only moderate views? When does civil disobedience become an excuse for mere lawlessness? How much of the demonstrations was just carnival? Should universities be bases for political activism? Students can examine these points and use them as the foundation for answering writing question 2. That assignment also asks about the effect of Agnew's style, which is a curious issue indeed. Why should his lexical extravagance have been so appealing (at least to those who agreed with him)?

Question 3 focuses on the issue of "positive polarization." This is no easy matter and can be the topic of a class debate if students find the question interesting. Ideological debate in the United States is very subdued. In the two-party system, the majority of votes will generally be in the middle, discouraging clear differentiation on ideological grounds. Agnew suggests that mucking about in the middle may not be best — and he may be right. Here again, you can put off this question until students have read Kerry and O'Brien, and possibly also Kovic. You might well move past Agnew quickly, discussing the reading and writing questions and holding off until later to assign a writing question, such as sequence 3, question 4.

JOHN F. KERRY, TESTIMONY BEFORE THE U.S. SENATE FOREIGN RELATIONS COMMITTEE (p. 890)

As we write this, Kerry looks like a shoo-in for reelection to the Senate, so here, at last, is someone from the unit who will still be an important public figure, and someone your students may recognize.

Kerry, as a Vietnam veteran and an articulate speaker, is a powerful witness against the war. His compelling testimony and the other selections by veterans will certainly be your students' favorite pieces in this unit. Kerry explains how the atrocities of the war, which were arguably little different from the atrocities committed by every army in every war, should be viewed as part of the incoherence of the war mission and a reflection of the flawed political motives for the war.

Reading through the unit or through sequence 2 or 3 will prepare students to understand the issues Kerry raises as well as his tone of anger and frustration. His long attack on Agnew and his defense of the antiwar protesters call for comparison not only with Agnew but also with Potter and the "Message to GIs." His account of the Vietnamese attitude toward the war, his insistence that it is a civil war, and his analysis of cold war anticommunism should recall the white paper, Stone's reply, and King's speech. In addition, Kerry prepares students to read of the horrors recounted by the veterans in the next section. His statistics about the medical care of returning veterans will be illustrated in stomach-turning ways in Kovic's story, for example.

It is easy, in reading this selection, to be overwhelmed by the information about the war. Careful rereading is essential. The reading questions point to elements in the testimony that may be overlooked — we trust that students will talk and write about Kerry's graphic descriptions of Vietnam.

Writing Analytically

Writing question 1 is an important exercise in critical reading. If you prefer to assign a different writing question on Kerry here or in sequence 2 or 3, at least make question 1 a journal entry and point of class discussion. On the one hand, Kerry says that the soldiers commit crimes. On the other, he defends Calley. How does he separate those who commit crimes from those who are responsible for them? The final part of the assignment asks students to try to see what Kerry means by his question "How do you ask a man to be the last man to die for a mistake?" Behind this is the question of how any of the veterans deal with their actions in the war once they lose faith in it or return to a country where the war is an embarrassment and its veterans a shameful reminder.

Writing question 2 asks for a synthesis of several readings and can spark students toward a larger research project. The assignment is an exercise in using several sources — summarizing, paraphrasing, and citing are essential — and in generalizing about substantial issues that are not fully explained in the sources themselves. Students typically shy away from such material in their research projects because they fear they will have to do additional research into all the side issues, in this case the civil rights movement, the cold war, and so on. The goal of this assignment, though, is to show that reading carefully and asking the right questions can enable a novice writer to respond to serious issues without becoming an expert. Students should demonstrate that Potter, King, and Kerry are indeed referring to the same set of social problems; they should attempt to characterize those problems and the significance attached to them; and they should try to explain why the three speakers see them as part of the moral world that includes the war.

VETERANS REMEMBER

TIM O'BRIEN, "ON THE RAINY RIVER" (p. 898)

It takes a while to make students see that O'Brien has simply reversed the usual understanding of courage during wartime. He is ashamed that he did not flee to Canada, that he lacked the courage to refuse the draft. Like the picture that is either two faces or a vase, once you see it you wonder why everybody else is still confused.

O'Brien's testimony carries conviction because he is a veteran, after all. Like Kerry and Kovic, he is a powerful defender of antiwar protesters because he fought in the war first. One wonders what story he could have told had he in fact gone over to Canada. Could he have made a case that he acted courageously? These questions are good ones to raise in class, since they delineate O'Brien's dilemma in the story and the dilemma of all those who opposed the war and then faced the draft. Ask your students to try to make the case for a draft evader's courage. Some students will be completely unsympathetic, while others will frighten themselves trying to imagine what they would do in O'Brien's place. Class discussion will be lively.

Writing Analytically

Writing question 1 allows students to process the issue of courage. Students will want to evaluate O'Brien's decision: Remind them to answer the question completely before they do so.

Writing question 2 is very similar to question 1 but puts the issue of defining cowardice and courage in the context of Agnew's vilification of protesters and Kerry's attack on Agnew. It asks, that is, where our definitions of these terms come from. While students could answer the question with reference only to Agnew and O'Brien, it is best to include Kerry and Kovic, so you may wish to hold off on this question until students have read all of those selections. Note that O'Brien and Kovic are articulating their positions well after the war. Their arguments could not have affected any potential draft resisters or changed the way that critics of the protesters spoke about them. Rather, like many of the arguments in *Negotiating Difference*, they are intended to make a claim on history and its interpretation — a very important piece of territory, especially for those who may still be fighting these battles.

HAROLD "LIGHT BULB" BRYANT, ORAL HISTORY (p. 911)

Bryant tells a gripping story and does not appear to be arguing at all, so the conclusion of his tale has several surprises. One is that he says that he would leave the country before allowing his son to fight in a war like the one in Vietnam. The second is the statement that the United States could have won in Vietnam had the military been given a free hand. Neither statement gets any further elaboration. Bryant is very much like the young Tim O'Brien, with half-formed opinions and a sense of shock that world events could impinge on his own life. Much of the power of all the veterans' stories comes from the lurching disorientation of being called suddenly to make decisions or take actions of a magnitude truly disproportionate to their self-image.

Writing Analytically

Writing question 1 gives students the opportunity to discuss their own assumptions, desires, fears, and confusion about military service. It is especially important to give students the chance to process their reactions to the selections at the end of this unit, either in journals or in personal essays such as the assignment given here. The first assignment in each of the three sequences in this unit asks for personal reflection on sensitive issues surrounding the Vietnam War. You may wish to substitute one of them for writing question 1 in this selection.

Bryant represents rather than explains the experience of the soldier — the African American soldier at that. He notices acts of discrimination, of course, but does not analyze them for us. He does not have a civil rights agenda. Writing question 2 asks for a careful look at the way Bryant frames events, the assumptions he might be making about his own position, and so on. The idea here is not to turn Bryant's story into an argument but to give students practice in interrogating this kind of text. To write this essay well, students will have to modify their claims and support them carefully. They will also have to abandon temporarily the expectation that the selections will have a consistent theme and argument and clearly-stated purpose.

LESLIE MCCLUSKY, ORAL HISTORY (p. 923)

McClusky is more thoughtful and self-reflective than Bryant, and her story is more linear than his, but it is similarly full of sensory detail. Also like Bryant, McClusky is doing her duty in Vietnam and does not have a women's rights agenda: She is not a battlefield feminist. She is focused entirely on how she is managing, on what is happening to her, and she produces a striking case study in how participation in a war shapes one's attitudes. Fortunately, McClusky moves through her nightmare with her mind at work: "How, I wondered, could I ever come to believe I hated a baby? I had lost all perspective."

Coming home, she says, is worse than going over. McClusky gives a better picture than Kerry of what it was like for the ordinary soldier to return and be ignored. She casually drops the information that for fourteen years she never told anyone that she had been in Vietnam! Veterans of other wars speak of the special bond they have with fellow veterans, even those who had been their enemies. But many Vietnam veterans echo McClusky in asserting that Vietnam was so transformative that they cannot relate at all to anyone who was not there.

As with Bryant, McClusky does not make an argument to be analyzed but gives us a story that fleshes out the arguments of others. She draws even fewer political conclusions than Bryant — none, in fact.

Writing Analytically

The writing question sets out some preliminary work that could be expanded into a research project on women in Vietnam or the widespread problems of returning veterans (see the Research Kit for suggestions).

RON KOVIC, FROM *BORN ON THE FOURTH OF JULY* (p. 931)

This piece will have a powerful emotional impact on students (as it does on all its readers). If your students are not keeping reading journals in which they can react freely, it will be a good idea to give a journal assignment for this reading. There will be time enough later to ask whether the conduct of a war or the experiences of people who must endure war are legitimate considerations in making policy decisions. At first, students will have to deal with the horrifying story Kovic tells, the story of someone their own age.

Kovic says that he was unaware of any antiwar protests until 1965, when he was already in Vietnam. He does not discuss the reasons for the war or arguments against it. He is simply doing his duty as a patriotic American. Later, too, he says that he lost his belief in the war but also does not give any political reasons. (Breaks in the text, like those on p. 938, do not conceal any political or historical meditations.) Kovic is driven unabashedly by his feelings, and chiefly by his sense of the pointlessness of what happened to himself. When he does intimate that he informed himself about the politics of the war, he does not mention any specifics.

The trip to Washington provides a fair snapshot of the kind of activity that Agnew denounced as carnival, followed by a glimpse of the physical conflict in the war at home. The final scene, in which Kovic disrupts the Republican National Convention, is presented as triumphant. But, as students should be reminded, Nixon and Agnew were reelected anyway, and the war dragged on until 1975.

Writing Analytically

Writing question 1 takes off from Kovic's recollections of his youth and his comment on page 942 that his generation was shaped by images of official patriotic violence. No deep analysis is assigned, but our goal is to stimulate a discussion, in the essays or in class, about the ways that images transmit values and, in some cases, substitute for thought.

Writing question 2 asks about Kovic's credibility as an antiwar activist (compared, for example, with Kerry's). Kovic is, at the very least, relentlessly honest in refusing to provide well-argued reasons for the positions he takes. Like many other protesters, he is convinced and emotional, but his sort of protest can be challenged by the question of whether his personal experience has any policy implications.

Writing question 3 gives students an opportunity to imagine Kovic's point of view and to connect with Kerry's argument about the betrayal of American soldiers and veterans by the government.

ASSIGNMENT SEQUENCES

As noted in the introduction to this manual, we see the assignment sequences as an integral part of the approach we wish to promote in *Negotiating Difference*. The sequences put provocative voices directly in dialogue with each other — both in the readings and then, in discussions of the readings, among the students in your class. Of equal importance, the sequences stress the need to develop material carefully — rereading, rethinking, and revising — in order to produce the richest rhetorical responses in student writing.

You can use the reading questions that accompany each selection to aid students in preparing to write for the sequences. While the writing questions in each sequence tend to build on one another with added complexity as one moves through the sequence, you should also feel free to select among these questions to tailor the sequence to your students' needs and interests (you will see some of this adaptation of sequences going on in the model syllabi that we include beginning on p. 212). In what follows we will briefly discuss each sequence and its writing questions.

Sequence 1. Why were we in Vietnam? Why did we stay? (p. 947)

This sequence focuses on the history and policy questions in the unit. It is a fairly short sequence of readings and allows for considerable discussion of the rationale for engaging in the war (chiefly anticommunism) and the inability to disengage later. These pieces include several head-on arguments for analysis.

Question 1 can be assigned on the first day of work on this sequence. The first draft can be done in class or as a journal entry. Students' range of experience is great. Some will have powerful stories about parents or other relatives. Others may be a bit embarrassed at their ignorance of the war. The point of the essay is to get not a history of the war or a record of students' confusion but a collective sense of how the students and their families have experienced the war. The essays should be shared through reading or discussion — anonymously, if students prefer. The final part of the question assumes that students will be revising their essay for submission in a portfolio and can add a final reflection before doing so.

Question 2 asks students to contrast the perspective of Ho Chi Minh, who portrays his country as a victim of colonialism and betrayal with the right to independence, with that of Thomas Dodd, who portrays Ho and his government as the foes of freedom. Dodd's argument is extended and Ho's is telegraphic, so the pieces are unevenly matched, but several basic ideas can be brought out nonetheless. Ho does not mention communism, and Dodd elaborately hedges the notion of self-determination. If we were to ask why Ho's appeal to deeply felt American values did not override all other considerations in gaining American support, Dodd certainly provides the answer.

Students tend to read past historical accounts, but the way history is told has a powerful effect on the way the present is understood. Question 3 forces students to focus on differences between historical accounts and to understand them as deliberate choices rather than minor disagreements about which facts to include. One of the hardest tasks for students in this question is simply to be clear about who said what. Taking care about this fundamental task of dealing with academic discourse is an important part of this exercise. Beyond that, students should consider why the different versions of history are told and what rhetorical purpose the history serves. Note that the main selections to use to answer this question are the first four named. Nixon's contribution can be found in two short paragraphs on page 873.

The basic policy issue of anticommunism, its various manifestations through the war, and the counterarguments raised against it are the focus of question 4, along with the claim that the United States was protecting a sovereign nation, South Vietnam, from outside aggression. These two reasons for U.S. engagement in Vietnam are supported by a variety of subordinate claims and appeals to the high ideals of freedom, self-determination, democracy, and so forth. The assignment calls for a straightforward analysis and evaluation of arguments. One part of the argument concerns the ways that history is understood, so the answers to questions 2 and 3 come to bear here. Ideological argument can become quite heated. There is no reason to try to prevent students from airing their own views about communism, but it is important to insist that the analytical part of the question remain foremost.

Question 5 can be an alternative to question 4 or a purely historical mini-research paper. The basic question is What happened to anticommunism? While it doesn't entirely disappear, it clearly loses its power as an argument for pursuing the war effort.

Sequence 2. *What was the U.S. military mission in Vietnam?* (p. 948)

The focus here is on the way that the actual conduct of the war came to be a factor in arguments over whether to continue U.S. involvement. The selections show the original rationale, the very early recognition that U.S. tactics like napalm bombing were horrifying, the wavering of Johnson and Nixon on how to proceed with a distasteful war, and, finally, veterans' accounts of what it was like to fight without a sense of mission and to feel betrayed by a government that maintained an incoherent policy and lied about the progress of the war.

Question 1 can be assigned on the first day of work on this sequence. The first draft can be done in class or as a journal entry. Students will have a wide range of experiences and views about the military in general. Few students have very much knowledge about Vietnam specifically, though. You may wish to assign the appropriate pages from Kovic (934–38) to give students a sense of what the question means by "images of war and patriotism." The essays should be shared through reading or discussion — anonymously, if students prefer. The final part of the question assumes that students will be revising their essay for submission in a portfolio and can add a final reflection before doing so.

Students can answer question 2 after reading Dodd and Johnson. Another piece to add to the list for this question is the white paper. The question is not about military strategy, of course, but you can encourage students to speculate about strategy — the purpose, say, of bombing North Vietnam or of dropping napalm on villages where Viet Cong may have been sheltered. This essay should help students get a sense of the U.S. mission before they read the accounts of its failure.

Question 3 takes the other side of the issue — what it felt like to be in Vietnam attempting to carry out the mission purportedly stated by Washington. Kerry makes the connection between the soldiers' experience and the problem of the mission, but that is not the focus of this question. The question as stated asks for the emotional effect that these selections have on first-time readers. Students must have an opportunity to express their personal reactions. Many will be disgusted or frightened, and some may cry or lose sleep after reading this material. The alternative offered at the end of the question will allow those who cannot express their emotions to deal with the selections in a more distanced way.

Finally, question 4 draws the other essays together to ask the long-delayed question about whether war policy should be linked to the conduct of a war. While students will be defending their own theses in this essay, it is important to remind them to use the selections to establish what the arguments were, to refer to the selections carefully, to avoid attributing arguments without clear justification, and to distinguish their own positions from those of their sources. Students may need help articulating the issues and organizing the essay as well.

Sequence 3. How was the war fought at home? (p. 950)

This is the longest of the sequences, but the writing assignments give some choices about which selections to use in particular essays. The sequence focuses on the antiwar movement and reactions to it. The selection by Dodd is included to set the stage and give students a sense of the basic rationale for the U.S. presence in Vietnam in the first place.

Question 1 asks students to describe their impressions of the protest movement, the images they associate with it. Some have little or no sense of the period, though most students can be stirred up by an open brainstorming session or inventory if need be. In the inventory exercise, students simply name everything they can think of on the topic — people's names, events, places, ideas, songs, TV shows — which you write on the board. The last part of the question assumes that students will be revising their essay for submission in a portfolio and can add a final reflection before doing so.

Question 2 can be answered in stages, like a developing research paper, as students read and discuss the appropriate selections. A series of summaries will do at first. Summaries are a good way of processing the readings and are not as easy to write as students may think at first. After summarizing most of the pieces, students should sort the arguments into categories. The final version of the essay should be organized thematically, with careful references to those who make each kind of argument.

Question 3, which is essentially the same as writing question 2 for the John Kerry selection, asks for a synthesis of several readings and can spark students toward a larger research project. The assignment is an exercise in using several sources — summarizing, paraphrasing, and citing are essential — and in generalizing about substantial issues that are not fully explained in the sources themselves. Students typically shy away from such material in their research projects because they fear they will have to do additional research into all the side issues, in this case the student movement, the civil rights movement, the cold war, and so on. The goal of this assignment, though, is to show that reading carefully and asking the right questions can enable a novice writer to respond to serious issues without becoming an expert. Students should demonstrate that Potter, King, and Kerry are indeed referring to the same set of social problems; they should attempt to characterize those problems and the significance attached to them; and they should try to explain why the three speakers see them as part of the moral world that includes the war.

Question 4 asks for an analysis of the main issues that sparked the protests (topics 1 and 2) and the arguments over the protests themselves (topic 3). The first two topics are dealt with at greater length in sequences 1 and 2, but they are germane to the question of sequence 3. This assignment calls for careful rereading of the selections. Dodd, for example, decries his fellow senators' calls for negotiation as tantamount to treason: What would he say about antiwar demonstrations? The categorizing of arguments that students did in question 2 will stand them in good stead here. They will once again need to organize thematically and refer to the sources accurately. This question can be treated as a controlled research paper, for which students can practice all of the reading, note-taking, and documentation tasks of a research project. Moreover, this question is a good one to initiate further research projects (see the model syllabus for a course with a research paper, on p. 216).

RESEARCH KIT

Please see our remarks on the Research Kits in the introduction to this manual (p. 11).

Students are drawn to many of the research topics for this unit, in particular the youth culture of the period and the stories of veterans. The suggestions under "Ideas from Unit Readings" stay close to issues that immediately relate to the Vietnam War, many of which we could not represent in the unit. Assignment 4, for example, asks about the *Pentagon Papers*. Please note (and reassure students) that the assignment does not call for a reading or analysis of them. Assignment 9 follows up on the McClusky oral history with research into the stories of women during the war. This assignment and others, like numbers 5, 7, and 8, can be enhanced by personal interviews with veterans, both of the war and of the protests. See comments on interviewing, p. 12.

Two other attractive topics in the "Ideas" section are in assignments 12, on Hollywood films, and 14, on music. Students initially will see these as opportunities to watch lots of movies and listen to old albums. (We suggest that you do not lend your Country Joe and the Fish album to students.) But these topics are difficult to write about. Students will need help to make sense of the material and learn how to write about nontext sources. Don't be put off, though — very good papers can come out of the work. Encourage students to consider assignment 15, on other arts, if you have library and museum resources nearby to support it. Assignment 16, on literature, is rather difficult, since it requires a considerable amount of reading and careful attention to avoid becoming a set of book reports.

Suggestions under "Branching Out" look at other events and issues of the period and connect the Vietnam War and its opposition to other wars and resistance efforts. As elsewhere in *Negotiating Difference*, the "contact zone" in Unit Six is a space that cuts across group identities and other contact zones, some of which are identified in these research suggestions. Students can easily be led off into the field of, say, the early women's movement and leave the connection to the Vietnam War behind. You will have to decide how closely you want to bind them to the unit theme if they go branching out.

The suggestions in the Research Kit do not repeat directions to be fair and accurate in presenting and assessing arguments or to analyze the ethos and audience or other rhetorical features of the documents or other materials students unearth. Remember to give students a set of guidelines on these matters when you set the research task.

One last note: The topics here lend themselves to fascinating oral reports. As we suggest in the second model syllabus (p. 216), it's a good idea to have students present their discoveries and interpretations in oral reports in class toward the end of the semester. Another benefit of oral reports is that they force students to focus and organize their material and think about how to present it coherently to a real audience. To make the most of this effect, schedule oral reports before the final paper is due so that they can serve as aids for revising.

MODEL SYLLABI

The model syllabi are framed on a thirteen-week term, with week 14 being exam week. You can adapt them to your own number of weeks (if different) and number of class meetings per week. The model syllabi sometimes adapt the assignment sequences they use, omitting some questions or substituting others — you should feel free to be similarly flexible in developing your own syllabi. Remember, the sequences are not designed to be lockstep processes.

We assume that you will work in class on the reading questions accompanying the assigned selections as well as on the assigned writing and sequence questions (sometimes we give you suggestions in the syllabi for how to do so). Note that work on these questions can often be performed profitably in class in small groups. (For more information on group work, see p. 14.)

We suggest that students keep a class journal in which they write responses to the reading questions before the questions are discussed in class. (Also remind students to read the headnotes accompanying the selections before they come to class.) In other words, our plan is that each reading assignment ("Read Dodd") also constitutes a writing assignment because students should jot responses to the text's reading questions in their journals. (For more information on the class journal, see p. 12.)

You should collect and review these journals at least as often as you collect students' writing portfolios. We suggest that students be graded according to some version of the portfolio method. (For more information, see p. 17.)

Syllabus using two sequences from Unit Six

This syllabus uses most of the readings in the unit and combines writing assignments from sequence 1, which focuses on the history of the war and questions of United States policy in Vietnam, with assignments from sequence 3, which concentrates on the protest movement. Several writing questions from individual selections are also assigned. This combination of readings and assignments maximizes the context for considering questions about the uses of history, the creation of policy, and the ramifications of policy decisions for individuals.

Week 1

Read: Unit Six introduction; Ho Chi Minh
Write: Sequence 3, question 1, or Ho Chi Minh, question 1

Students can begin the writing assignment on the first day of class. It will give them a sense of what the readings will be about and allow you to talk about drafting and journal writing. The last part of the sequence question asks if students have changed their attitudes and assumes that this essay will be revised, perhaps several times, on the way to being turned in with the portfolio. If you assign the sequence question for in-class writing, leave time for some sharing and discussion, which can be continued at the next class meeting. Assign students to read Ho Chi Minh and begin their journals. If you wish to begin with a more formal assignment, use the writing question that follows the reading.

Week 2

> Read: Dodd
> Write: Sequence 1, question 2
> Collect: Draft of essay from week 1

The discussion of Dodd should take up the reading questions and include an analysis of the writing assignment, which plunges students into the task of identifying arguments in the first two readings.

Week 3

> Read: White paper; Stone
> Write: Stone, writing question 1
> Collect: Draft of essay from week 2

Assess your students' progress on the writing assignments. If they are having difficulty, slow down and work on developing the first papers. Move the assignments back and catch up in week 7. If you are moving ahead, discuss the white paper first. Use its writing questions as additional reading questions for journal writing and discussion.

Week 4

> Read: Dellinger, Muste, et al.; Beidler; Huy Can
> Write: One writing question from the selections
> Collect: Class journals

All of the writing questions for these pieces can be answered briefly. Dellinger, Muste, et al., writing question 1, and Beidler/Huy Can, writing question 2, are particularly good choices.

Week 5

> Read: Potter
> Write: Potter, any writing question
> Collect: Draft of essay from week 3

Week 6

> Read: King
> Write: Sequence 1, question 4
> Collect: Draft of essay from week 5

In class, help students prepare their portfolios for collection at the end of the course — for example, putting their class journals in order, choosing a paper to revise, and so on.

Week 7

Collect: Draft of essay from week 6; portfolios, including class journals

Use this week to catch up. Continue discussions of the readings; have an in-class writing workshop on revision to help students prepare their portfolios; give lessons on any grammar or mechanics problems common among your students.

Week 8

Read: Nixon; Agnew
Write: Sequence 1, question 3

Discuss the writing assignment, including conventions for referring to the different selections.

Week 9

Read: Kerry
Write: Sequence 3, question 3 (see week 10)

The last few sequence questions (sequence 1, question 3; sequence 3, question 3) require longer and more developed essays, one of which should be the major paper in the final portfolio. Sequence 3, question 4 (week 12) can also serve this purpose.

Week 10

Read: O'Brien
Write: O'Brien, writing question 2
Collect: Draft of essay from week 8

You may wish to give students a choice between the writing assignments for weeks 9 and 10.

Week 11

Read: Bryant; McClusky
Collect: Class journals; draft of essay from weeks 9 and 10.
Schedule: Conferences

Catch up this week. Schedule conferences to discuss drafts of the longer essays.

Week 12

Read: Kovic
Write: Sequence 3, question 4, topic 3

Week 13

Collect: Portfolios, including class journals (week 13 or 14)

Before you collect the portfolios, students may want to share their essays, perhaps in small groups. In class, help students to prepare their portfolios for final submission at the end of this week or exam week.

Syllabus using sequence 3 and requiring a research paper

Week 1

Read: Unit Six introduction; Dodd
Write: Sequence 3, question 1, or Dodd, writing question 1 or 2

Students can begin the writing assignment on the first day of class. It will give them a sense of what the readings will be about and allow you to talk about drafting and journal writing. The last part of the sequence question asks if students have changed their attitudes and assumes that this essay will be revised on the way to being turned in with the portfolio. If you assign the sequence question for in-class writing, leave time for some sharing and discussion, which can be continued at the next class meeting. Assign students to read Dodd and begin their journals. If you wish to begin with a more formal assignment, assign one of the writing questions that follow the reading.

Week 2

Read: Dellinger, Muste, et al.; Beidler; Huy Can; Potter
Write: Potter, writing question 1
Collect: Draft of essay from week 1

Several of the other writing questions for these selections make excellent journal starters and discussion points in class.

Week 3

Read: King
Write: One of the writing questions from King
Collect: Draft of essay from week 2

Week 4

Read: Kerry
Write: Sequence 3, question 2 or 3

The assignments now begin to use several readings and become mini-research projects. Start to discuss ways of using sources, being fair and accurate, delineating arguments and positions, and so on.

Week 5

> Read: Johnson; National Mobilization Committee
> Collect: Portfolios, including class journals and writing assignments
>   for weeks 3 and 4

This is a good time to catch up. Have an in-class writing workshop on revision; give lessons on any grammar or mechanics problems common among your students; continue discussions of the readings; discuss first drafts of the sequence writing assignment. Help students prepare their portfolios for collection at the end of the course — for example, putting their class journals in order, choosing a paper to revise, and so on. If students are caught up, advance the schedule to create more time for research later.

Week 6

> Read: O'Brien; Kovic
> Write: Sequence 3, question 4

This is the last writing assignment before the research paper. Students will need to read the Nixon and Agnew pieces, assigned for next week, to complete this week's writing assignment, but they can start it now. Discuss it in class as a model for a research project: A general issue is set forth; several possible lines of inquiry are defined; and part of the research has been done. What is the strategy for pursuing the work? How can an initial draft help shape the direction of further work? Later, consider how the new material in the next readings affects or reshapes the concept in the initial draft.

Week 7

> Read: Nixon; Agnew
> Read: Research Kit

Continue work on the current writing assignment. Students should choose a research assignment from the Research Kit or formulate one of their own this week. Several of the topics relate to the readings in this syllabus; students can also choose to use other readings in the unit. Finally, discuss the written research proposal, due week 8 or 9.

Week 8

> Collect: Research proposal
> Schedule: Conferences and library visit

Don't let students dawdle in choosing a research topic. Try to have a short conference with each student to solidify his or her proposal. Schedule a library visit with the research librarian, who can direct students to the key resources and bibliographies for the kinds of projects they will be working on.

Week 9

Write: Preliminary bibliography
Collect: Portfolios, including essay from week 6; five essays, at least
two revised

Set guidelines for the number of items to be in the bibliography (perhaps ten). In class, discuss the research process (selection, organization, documentation, and so on).

Week 10

Write: Initial draft of research paper

In addition to using class time for writing workshop activities, consider showing a film like *The Deer Hunter* or the PBS documentary (a list of Vietnam films and documentaries is in the Research Kit bibliography) and discuss the way that films, television shows, interviews, and other nontraditional materials can be used in research papers.

Week 11

Schedule: Conferences

Review the research projects individually this week and allow students some class time to write.

Week 12

Oral reports

Brief oral reports are an excellent way to force out a draft, focus the topic, and create a real audience for student work. In addition, the reports demonstrate to the whole class the wide range of topics being investigated and the growing expertise of the student researchers.

Week 13

Collect: Final research papers

Depending on the time you have remaining, finish oral reports, review citation and documentation methods, and have an in-class editing workshop. Collect final papers at the end of week 13 or exam week.